THE SOCIAL CONSTRUCTION OF
INDIAN FORESTS

The Social Construction of Indian Forests

Edited by

ROGER JEFFERY

Centre for South Asian Studies, Edinburgh

MANOHAR

1998

First published in 1998 by

Roger Jeffery
Centre for South Asian Studies
c/o Department of Sanskrit
University of Edinburgh
7 Buccleuch Place
Edinburgh EH8 9LW

Ajay Kumar Jain
Manohar Publishers & Distributors
2/6 Ansari Road
Daryaganj
New Delhi 110002

ISBN 1 900 795 07 8 (UK)
ISBN 81-7304-220-9 (India)

Typeset in 10/12 pt Times

Cover design by Anna Carothers
Typesetting by Katharine Charsley
Proof-reading by Laura Jeffery

Printed at
Rajkamal Electric Press
B35/9 G.T. Karnal Road, Indl. Area
Delhi-110033

Contents

Transliteration

For Hindi and Sanskrit words, we have marked the Hindi long 'a' as 'ā,' (as in 'father') the long 'i' as 'ī,' (as in 'machine') and the long 'u' as 'ū' (as in 'rule') to distinguish them from the short versions, and 'k͟h' (as in the Scottish 'loch') to distinguish from 'kh', an aspirated 'k'. An 'e' is pronounced like the 'é' in French. Where possible we have distinguished the two forms of 'r' and 'r̤' but we have not distinguished between different Hindi 't' and 'd' sounds. In most other respects we have followed the transliteration schema in R. S. McGregor (1993) *The Oxford Hindi-English Dictionary* Delhi: Oxford University Press. For Bengali and south Indian languages we have followed as closely as possible the appropriate transliteration conventions.

1

Introduction

Roger Jeffery

The forest lies on the village's horizon and is, in a certain sense, integrated into village life. ... Yet, this fusion of village and forest is so beautiful in the eyes of the Indian authors, and fundamentally so unrealistic, that they exclude it, at times, from the realm of the possible in our present age of iron, declaring that it can only be found in a distant past, in the wonderful age of the *rishis*, of those inspired seers who received the Vedic revelation. (Malamoud 1996: 85, 86)

Creating a category of the physical environment that pre-exists any social framing is highly problematic, in two senses.[1] Our notions of the natural world are not given to us by the world about us: in some important senses we act upon that world, we construct it through our categories of thought, categories that are social in origin.

This insight is becoming a common-place, as the titles of recent books testify (Eder 1996; Bruun and Kalland 1995). Not only is there a considerable literature on differences in the way that cultural variations manifest themselves in different constructions of the natural, but within societies, differences have been traced between men's and women's views (Shiva 1988; Kelkar and Nathan 1991; Agarwal 1992; Jackson 1994).[2] Many authors have drawn on Mary Douglas' classic insights over the relationships between ideas of pollution and danger and our understandings of how our environments may be 'at risk' (Douglas 1970). Others have pointed out that, as social conditions change, so our constructions of the 'natural' may also change; thus, Escobar argues that in the invention of 'sustainable

---

[1] This chapter draws on work being carried out in the research project 'Organising Sustainability: NGOs and Joint Forest Management Agreements in India', funded by the ESRC. Neither the other grant holders nor the ESRC are responsible for the views expressed here.

[2] Less has been written on class or other sources of differences in views.

development', 'nature is reinvented as environment' by post-modern capitalism through a discursive process 'so that capital, not nature and culture, may be sustained' (Escobar 1996: 49).

But this viewpoint has not gone unchallenged. In an influential piece of writing, Ted Benton suggests that sociology (and, by implication, anthropology) has some hard problems to face in coming to terms with the environment. As with much Western academic thought, these social sciences are predicated on concepts often expressed as binary opposites: in this case, most obviously, between nature and culture. Historically, sociology insisted on this distinction, in order to argue that social life was not determined by physical bodies or psychological processes. Social processes cannot be understood solely as a result of human biology, nor as just the sum total of individual behaviour. How could there be such major variations in social processes if solely biological or psychological levels of explanation were enough to explain social behaviour? According to Benton, this central insight cannot be abandoned, but, unchecked, it poses major problems. In particular, it leads many social scientists to argue that they do not need to discuss 'nature' directly, but only to try to understand the influences which affect people's understandings of nature. Social scientists then frequently argue as if the reality of natural processes is irrelevant.

Benton suggests that there is a danger of then assuming that '*all* views of nature are symbolic constructs of some culture or other' (Benton 1994). By implication, he argues that if the Bhils of Gujarat differ from eminent biologists in Harvard University about the nature of their environment and the threats to it, or over the most desirable form that a particular forest should take, then the views of the eminent biologists should prevail. Benton mounts a powerful case that we cannot wish away the current threats to global survival on the grounds that they are 'merely' views held by certain powerful social groups. In his view, we are mistaken if we think that 'It is all the same . . . whether we do, in fact, face ecological catastrophe, or whether environmentalists have conjured this threat out of their fevered imaginations' (1994: 46).

The social construction of forests in India can, then, be seen as a small case study in this on-going debate about the role of social processes in environmental change. On the one hand, the chapters in this volume attest to the importance of social factors in how forests are understood. The meanings of forests are not determined by their physical characteristics. The density of the tree cover, the species represented, the geological substrate or the micro-climates within forested areas, for example, do not dictate how people interact with the forest. In addition to these physical constraints, people imbue the forest with meanings which affect where cattle are allowed to graze, which trees are cut for firewood, which land is cleared for agriculture or what fruits, leaves and roots are collected as medicines or food. This much is, I think, unchallenged. Where the debate is fiercest is in trying to understand the reasons for the meanings which different groups attach to the forest environment, and the significance of the meanings in planning forest policies.

As with the nature-culture dualism, the debate over the social meanings of forests is bedevilled by contrast comparisons. It is relatively easy to characterise a modern, scientific, industrial capitalist approach to forests: for the multinational corporation, forests are a source of raw materials to be farmed in order to maximise profits. Companies have a preference for single species plantations of trees, set out in straight lines to maximise the numbers that can be grown in any plot, and designed to allow efficient harvesting on a regular cycle. Within this ideal, alternative uses of the land—for enhancing biodiversity, providing leisure facilities, or supporting a local subsistence economy, for example—have no place.

The alternative ideal type is equally easily sketched: for forest-dependent small-scale hunter-gatherers or subsistence farmers, forests provide collective resources which are most valuable when they are multi-purpose. A variety of trees, with varying densities, maximises the number of people for whom the forest provides a livelihood or insurance against crop failure (through roots and fruits to supplement diets as well as products that can be sold for cash incomes), and sources of grazing for milk and plough animals.

These ideal types establish different cultural patterns: the multinational corporation has no cultural links to the forest on which it depends, representing an industrial urban exploitative approach to nature; whereas the hunter-gatherer and subsistence farmer have holistic cultural forms that give value to the trees and the animals in the forest as well as to the human beings who inhabit the forest or its surroundings.

It is then a small step to characterise the modern industrial approach to the forest as the cause of many of today's environmental problems—global warming, the loss of bio-diversity, soil erosion and micro-climatic deterioration resulting from deforestation and mono-crop forestry—and to see in the hunter-gatherer and subsistence farmer the solution to these same problems.

Such simple contrasts are challenged by several of the papers in this volume. Rich Freeman, for example, argues that 'the modern environmentalist's interest in floristic composition or biodiversity does not inform the institution and maintenance of sacred groves. Cultural practice is not directed according to some hidden ecological imperative. Rather, the manifest cultural concept of dedication to a deity's use is the defining feature underlying a set of otherwise contingent and variable physical forms the groves or gardens may take'. He goes on to argue that 'what we actually find is that many examples of what we might regard as human disturbance, resource exploitation, and encroachment are happily accommodated within the cultural framework of the grove as the deities' preserve'.

Freeman also points out that even in the sacred groves, people have acted in myriad ways upon the world: what we perceive as natural (rather than manufactured) is even in this case usually the result of complex interactions between human beings and their surroundings.[3] More generally, the attempt to make sense of the uncertainty surrounding the category 'nature' has attracted much attention in the 1980s and 1990s, as environmentalist movements have gathered force, and debates about sustainability, global warming, pollution and the ozone layer have preoccupied international conferences and local community groups alike.[4]

Within these debates, Indian forests have received more than usual attention—far more, indeed, than their physical size would warrant. The Government of India's target for forest cover is a substantial 33 per cent, but in global terms India's forests are insignificant compared with the much larger areas in Indonesia or Malaysia, let alone those in Brazil.

One image has captured the imaginations of people across the world: that of Indian women hugging trees to prevent them being cut down, as part of the Chipko movement that started in the Himalayas in 1972. Two writers have most prominently debated the meanings of

---

[3] For innovative work on reconceptualising environmental theories, see, e.g. James Fairhead and Melissa Leach 1996.

[4] Benton 1994, discusses some of these debates from a sociological perspective.

these actions: Vandana Shiva (Shiva 1988; 1991) and Ramachandra Guha (Guha 1989). For Shiva, Chipko was in part a display of the fundamental (or essential) links between women and the environment; for Guha, women may or may not be at the forefront of environmental movements, depending on their roles in the division of labour in villages and households that depend heavily on forest products. While the two of them (and others, like Bina Agarwal 1992, who have contributed to the debate) differ in many respects, they share at least one concern in common. Both sides wish to establish that the legitimate meanings attached to the forest go beyond those to be found in silvicultural textbooks and the working plans of the Forest Department. Forests in general, a specific forest in particular, or forest products of one kind or another, are central to the world-views of many people who have close or distant attachments to those plots of land where trees grow, or used to grow. It is increasingly accepted that these meanings should be taken seriously in policy debates and actions based upon them. What is much less well accepted is what those meanings are, and how they might be analysed and discussed. This volume offers a further contribution to those debates.

Mahuā, a sweet creamy flower which can be used to make a powerful alcoholic drink, provides a good example. The origins of *mahuā* are explained by Bondo and Gadaba people as follows. A raja is feasting his subjects:

> After they had finished eating they sat around with full bellies and could think of nothing to say. Mahaprabhu came there and said, "What is the matter? Why are you so dull?" They replied, "There is no fire in us." Mahaprabhu then showed them how to make rice-beer and how to distil spirit from the mahua flowers, and from that day there has been laughter and dancing in the world (Elwin 1949, reprint 1991: 338).

Mahuā has meant many things to many people. To many *ādivāsīs*, it has meant food in the monsoon months when grain is scarce, oil in the days when kerosene was unknown or unaffordable, firewood, fencing and timber and of course liquor. But if *mahuā* brought laughter into the life of *ādivāsīs*, it brought wealth into the hands of traders, for drinking *mahuā* liquor was not confined to *ādivāsīs* alone. Under the dispensation of colonial laws (tree-taxes, cesses, etc.), *mahuā* became simultaneously a powerful source of income for the Parsis and other liquor-farmers, and its illicit distillation a symbol of popular persistence in the face of state encroachments on customary usage. In

Bastar district in Madhya Pradesh, the trade in *mahuā* and other non-timber forest products has allowed small, itinerant traders to make the transition to merchants who own fleets of trucks, and whose presence dominates the market and daily life in forest villages. And for the post-colonial state of Madhya Pradesh, in the midst of conflicting national discourses of alcoholism, *ādivāsī* rights and revenue opportunities, *mahuā* is also a substantial revenue-earner, for the State and for *adivasis* alike.[5]

Antje Linkenbach (this volume) presents another example of the multiple meanings of the forest to local residents. In Tehri Garhwal, the forest is a contested domain, and forest-dependent people are engaged in ongoing struggles for control—a control which could as likely lead to the destruction of forest resources as to conservation and pragmatic use. Struggles of this kind are normal. Forest policy is generally a battle over which of the possible meanings of the forest is to have priority, and how they will be accommodated with other competing meanings (clearance for agriculture, planting of exotic trees for timber production and revenue over different time periods, for example) that could be applied to the same plots of land and would benefit different constellations of interests in different ways.

Many of the contributors to the debates over how the Indian forest should be conceptualised have concluded that *ādivāsī* meanings deserve to be given priority. In part this reflects the under-dog status that attracts outside support; evidence abounds of the ways in which *ādivāsī* rights and interests have been systematically under-mined since colonial times. Furthermore, many authors have found ecologically sensitive perspectives on human-forest relationships in *ādivāsī* attitudes towards the use of forest products and the maintenance of bio-diversity.

But more detailed studies have thrown up problems with the simple acceptance of these points. To begin with, who are the *ādivāsīs*, the original inhabitants? Unlike the native Americans or the aboriginal people of Australasia, the original inhabitants of the Indian subcontinent have usually rapidly integrated invading populations into existing social structures, and show few physical or cultural signs of distinction. Attempts to provide a consistent way of differentiating 'tribes' from 'castes' all founder on this problem. Furthermore, some of the groups now Scheduled Tribes were part of the mainstream of

---

[5] This example is taken from Jeffery and Sundar forthcoming.

Indian society within the past three centuries, and others now considered part of that mainstream were once regarded as 'Tribals'.

On the second point, the issue of whether or not forest-dependent people have a basic ecological viewpoint has been clearly stated as follows: 'traditional societies' have shared features, including a 'knowledge system with an ecological understanding of nature', a technological system for minimising 'resource waste', and criteria for discriminating between 'resource destructive and resource enhancing technologies' (Shiva 1991: 39-41). 'Traditional societies' have holistic approaches to the local environment, seeing links between human, social and forest health which are ignored by outsiders, and investing particular trees, species or places with a religious significance which often turns out, on closer inspection, to reinforce ecological concerns. The evidence in support of these claims is often regarded as the maintenance of 'traditional societies' into the modern world: they exist, therefore they must have been sustainable.

The problem with these accounts is that they represent 'inventions of tradition', selective presentations of historical and social data in order to advance particular political projects. Of course, these arguments for the existence of 'ecologically correct' native peoples do have some validity. These perspectives on the proper uses of the forest can indeed have protective influences on the ways that people relate to the forest. But these are not the only visions available. What we are doing in this volume is an attempt to explore some of these alternative visions which underlie many of the ways in which local people in India make sense of their environments. One starting point is provided by the classical Hindu texts, which have at least as good a claim to be regarded as 'native' views on the forest as do *ādivāsī* myths and legends. But other textual traditions are also available. Alexander Dubiansky's paper in this volume discusses the role of Tamil poetry at different periods in developing the set of images associated with Murugan, whose symbol has been appropriated by the Dravida Munnetra Kazagham in its political project.

Furthermore, we should not forget the writings and oral traditions of Muslim, Christian, Sikh and Jain writers, often from the medieval period, in providing a variety of images and metaphors for forests and their uses for society at large. The Mughal gardens (particularly those of Lahore and Kashmir) and the hunting scenes so lovingly portrayed by miniaturist painters provide other versions of the landscape whose meanings are available for use in constructing alternative visions of the contemporary forest in India.

These are some of the issues addressed in the papers included in this volume. Most of the papers were first presented at the panel on 'Forests' at the European Modern South Asian Studies Conference in Toulouse in August-September 1994. This panel was originally proposed by Charles Malamoud, whose interest in the subject was first manifest in his classic article (Malamoud 1976; 1996) which is referred to by several of the authors (see, especially, France Bhattacharya and Linkenbach, this volume). Malamoud used Vedic texts to illuminate the ways in which the relationship between the village (*grāma*) and the forest (*aranya*) highlight fundamental themes of Vedic ideology. He points out that *aranya* is derived from words meaning strange, the 'other' to the village, and that synonyms for *aranya* mean empty, or interstitial places. The translation of *aranya* as 'forest' is only warranted by the use of an additional term, *vana* ('territory covered by trees') which Malamoud suggests is a particular case of *aranya* (Malamoud 1996: 76). After discussing the ways in which forest and village are linked in various sacrifices, Malamoud describes how the forest and the village intertwine within people's lives. The forest is the place where brigands and other outsiders live, but it is also inhabited by those who are in search of the Absolute, the renouncers (*saṃnyāsins*), an option for any twice-born man who has completed the obligations of the householder (Malamoud 1996: 81-85). But, as the opening quote to this chapter suggests, Malamoud concludes that we have here an early example of the invention of tradition, with the Vedic writers forced to base their views on the appropriate relationships between village and forest on a mythical golden age when the *rishis* were alive.

Aranya and *vana* are not the only local terms which have been translated as forest; a third is *jangal*. This word has at least three sets of associated meanings. As Francis Zimmermann has pointed out, *jangala* originally meant drylands, bearing sparse trees and shrubs, lands which were regarded as suitable for Aryan settlement (Zimmermann 1987: 61). The derived English word 'jungle' is usually a synonym for dense tropical 'forest', and in modern India and Pakistan is sometimes used to describe places where outlaws and uncivilised people live. Yet to many villagers in the northern Indian plains, *jangal* is another term for their fields, and the marginal areas of common property adjoining them. None of these meanings are necessarily 'natural': it is at least plausible, as Michael Dove has argued, that the *jangala* (probably particularly characteristic of the present-day Punjab) was the result of modifications introduced by the livestock and fire of the pastoral Aryan peoples (Dove 1995).

As Freeman (this volume) points out, the Vedic sources are sometimes used to argue that India's culture was imbued with a set of beliefs and practices that naturally held human demands on the environment in check. Populations and their forest environment, it is claimed, existed in a kind of ecologically sustainable homeostasis, and the religious values and institutions of Hinduism or its folk-variants somehow encoded and transmitted this ecological wisdom across the generations (Gadgil and Malhotra 1989). Yet the flexibility and multiplicity of the terms and the textual and oral sources, and their embeddedness in changing life-forms, means that it is hard to sustain a single reading of 'India's culture' along these lines. The literary sources discussed by Bhattacharya and Dubiansky (this volume) and in Elizarenkova (1994) make it clear that other ideas about the forest and people's places within it have been developed and are available for general use in India today. Thus Elizarenkova points out that in the *Rgveda*, while *vanaspati* (meaning a sacred tree) is frequently found, other words for trees (such as *vrkshā* and *vanīn*) have no such ritual significance, and are more often associated with cutting down trees or burning.

The 'sacred groves' (*devarakadus*) of Coorg (in Karnataka) and of parts of Kerala provide one example of how an Indian cultural resource has been exaggerated in the interests of a critique of colonial and post-colonial forest policies. The groves have been called 'one of the finest instances of traditional conservation practices' (Gadgil and Chandran 1992: 183). But the descriptions of these groves, even by those who celebrate their significance, show that the historical sources concerning such groves cannot be straightforwardly read off in this way. In most of the country, only a small part of the land was allocated to sacred groves, with the surrounding land usually under systems of shifting cultivation. While such plots could preserve bio-diversity, they could not in themselves maintain an environmental balance, nor did they prevent the over-cutting of trees outside the sacred groves. The religious ideals attached to these groves are also not fixed and determinate but flexible and ambiguous. Thus Gadgil and Chandran point out how 'the wild woodland spirits and deities of the pre-Brahmanic societies' are being overlaid with 'the gods of the

Hindu pantheon' (Gadgil and Chandran 1992: 187). M. A. Kalam (this volume) develops this critique with a detailed consideration of how the *devarakadus* of Coorg have been adapted to the interests of local people in ways which can hardly be described as informed by an ecological awareness. Crucially, in his view, we should not assume that these changes are merely the result of the nefarious effects of colonialism and capitalism, or of the dominance of mainstream Hinduism, though these processes have undoubtedly had an effect. We should also note those aspects of change which could be said to be inherent in the meanings attached to the groves by local people. In considering sacred groves, we must remember that traditional patterns of resource use were changing, and we must avoid selectively citing only those aspects of the *devarakadus* that appear to support claims to an ecological consciousness.

The colonial period saw the establishment of ways of perceiving and managing forests that can be discerned in the pre-colonial period, but which were much more influential under the British. Pre-British rulers had claimed ownership rights over forests, and had intervened to fashion them to their own interests, whether to limit the depredations of forest-based outlaws and challengers of their authority or to maintain them as hunting preserves (see Rangarajan 1994a, for examples of these strategies in nineteenth century Madhya Pradesh). Under the British, however, these claims were pushed much more strongly, and 'scientific forestry' came to dominate colonial understandings of forests (Sivaramakrishnan 1995). The British also controlled the resources (in terms of the organisational abilities of the colonial bureaucracy and of new capitalist firms as well as the technical capacity to rework the environment through road and railways) for turning ownership claims into facts. British rule in South Asia has rightly been criticised for forest policies that led to the widespread replacement of diverse forests by mono-species plantations, the loss of livelihood rights by forest-dependent people, and a considerable reduction in forest cover.

The three-fold distinction between prohibited (reserved), partially prohibited (protected) and open (village or *nistāri*) forests, enshrined in the Forest Act of 1878, has been well documented (Gadgil and Guha 1992: 134; see also Sarah Jewitt, this volume). In general, the colonial Government moved slowly, and not without provoking fierce resistance on occasion, to limit rights, turn them into privileges or concessions, charge for the concessions and withdraw the privileges if they were 'abused'. But this was only part of the process. A multitude of legal forms of land ownership were established or allowed by the British: for example, distinctions between land in the Princely States and that in British India (which could be further divided into land owned by the government, *khālsā* land settled under the *mālguzārī* system, and land settled as *zamindārī* land). In the *zamindārī* areas, village forests close to the village were treated differently from wasteland further from villages and owned by *zamindārs* but not cultivated. Because all of these types of land could be mixed together in a patchwork, rights could vary dramatically even within a few miles.

Despite the cumbersome apparatus of forest reservation, working plans, management regimes and punitive laws to exclude local people from access to forest resources of one kind or another, teak and sāl forests alike have been over-exploited. Many forest areas are forest in name and legal ownership only. Deforestation has often involved excessive extraction by logging companies. Some had contracts to cut a certain amount of wood and illegally exceeded their allocations; others operated by night to cut trees in plots which were not planned to be cut. Sometimes the depredations of commercial interests were exacerbated by the activities of local villagers, outraged by the illegal losses and joining in to get some benefits for themselves, or forced by the loss of other sources of livelihood to cut wood for sale or to clear land for agriculture. Thus the Kharias in Simlipal tiger reserve define a healthy forest as one with an abundance of honey available. This implies 'a high canopy, having grown through a three-four storey structure of a forest; a dense undergrowth; a rich diversity of flowering plants providing an important source of nectar' (Savyasaachi 1994). Rising commercial demand, however, has also induced a change in their attitudes towards forest produce, leading to collusion in the over-exploitation of certain species—the Kharias find themselves collecting honey before it is time, and collecting it from shorter trees, as all the sāl is being cut down. Both these have accelerated the deterioration of the forest, as understood by forest officials and by the Kharias alike.

The multiplicity of rules, rights and concessions which outlasted colonial rule remain important today for two reasons. First, customary rights, many of them unrecorded, surface at times of dispute (see Chakravarty-Kaul 1996 for a particularly good account of this phenomenon). As Stig Toft Madsen (this volume) points out, rights of access still play a central role in the management of the Bharatpur park despite the oft-repeated claim that they were all extinguished by the British. Grazing at certain times of the year, or collecting certain kinds of forest produce from a particular forest may be allowed, but the same behaviour by different people or at different times of the year, or in relation to other produce may generate bitter disputes. Instead of talking in general of 'forest-dependent people', then, we need to keep in mind the sources of variation among such people. As Madsen also points out, the meaning of 'local communities' has expanded to include different sets of locals with evolving interests in the local environment of the Bharatpur park: who is to decide whether those with more recent interests in a forest (because they have migrated to the area after losing their previous land to dams or other forms of modern development) or those from further away (pastoralists, for example) should be included in new plans for these environments or not?

Second, the government still structures people's access differently, even if not along the old rules. One example of this is the new set of programmes known as Joint Forest Management (JFM) or Joint Forest Planning and Management (JFPM) (see Jewitt, and David Potter, this volume; also Poffenberger and McGean 1996). Starting with a policy document in 1988, followed by a general letter of the Government of India in 1990, and then through a series of notifications of rules and regulations by the individual States, India has seen an explosion of attempts to introduce participatory elements into its forest programmes. The Government of India is also being urged to apply similar participatory principles into other natural resource management programmes (Singh and Ballabh 1996; Kothari et al. 1996). Each State has drawn up different rules, but in all of them, in principle, the new programmes involve forest-dependent villagers agreeing with the Forest Department (possibly through intermediaries in Non-Governmental Organisations) that they will protect areas of degraded forest, normally on Reserved Forest lands. In return for protection activities, the village committees gain legitimate access to various non-timber forest products (grass for fodder, leaves, fruits, edible roots or medicinal products, as well as dead wood for firewood). In addition, if commercially-valuable trees are planted or regenerate, the village committees are entitled to shares of the proceeds of the sale of these trees when they are mature enough to be felled.

Our own research on the introduction of these programmes has highlighted a number of these problems (see Sundar et al. 1996). For example, JFM agreements do not arrive in an uncharted sea. They are superimposed (often by people unaware of the existing patterns of rights) on complex patterns. In general, pre-existing village rights and obligations are ignored; patterns of use of non-timber forest products by men and women in different castes and classes are also often not brought to the attention of those creating these agreements. The roles of Non-Governmental Organisations (NGOs) are often unclear, yet without them, many agreements seem doomed to fail, because Forest Department staff are rarely committed to making participatory approaches work in practice.

Some conflicts have been caused by an inflexibility over the unit to be considered: in most States one 'village' must form one side of the agreement even when villages are multi-hamlet, or when two or more villages are involved in the use of a particular forest plot. Thus in Sambalpur, a multi-hamlet village was expected to form one village protection committee, yet only one hamlet was concerned with the plots to be protected. On the other hand, in Gujarat, Andhra Pradesh and Madhya Pradesh, separate agreements were negotiated rather than forest plots being considered as the unit for planning purposes. Villages in our sample often found their conflict with the Forest Department was replaced by enhanced levels of conflict with other villages over access to these plots.

The new procedures also find it hard to deal adequately with existing forest protection committees—usually ones that have been self-generated, and are based on existing village social institutions. These usually break several of the rules set down in JFM regulations. They are rarely concerned with issues of gender, ethnic or class equity, but are controlled by dominant local elites. They often protect village forest plots, not Forest Department land. The plots they protect often have high quality cover. The Forest Department itself, with its rules and regulations, and the benefits it offers to villages entering JFM agreements, are one of the biggest threats to the maintenance of these institutions.

Variability in NGOs is also considerable. The Aga Khan Rural Support Programme and the Vikram Sarabhai Trust, in Gujarat, at one extreme, have a corps of highly trained staff and a long-term record of commitment. At the other extreme there are one- or two-person units attempting to do everything—influence policy at the State level as well as be the secretariat for individual JFM agreements, and much more in between. Potter (this volume) suggests that in Karnataka FEVORD-K (the alliance of NGOs he discusses) may have been least influential when they tried their hardest to influence directly JFPM policy choices by the KFD during 1991-93; together with many other organisations and groups they may have been a bit more influential in helping to set the agenda for JFPM during the 1980s without perhaps fully appreciating that they were doing so; and Potter suggests that the Karnataka Forest Department has been sceptical of attempts to force them into supporting some of these NGOs, and the NGOs have also been critical of the Karnataka Forest Department for being unwilling to find ways of working with them. But if the JFPM policy is followed through, FEVORD-K is likely to become increasingly influential as time goes on because such a policy cannot effectively be implemented at village level throughout Karnataka without them.

Commitment to the principles of participation within the Forest Department is crucial but very variable. It may be more of a problem in the donor-assisted programmes, because many villagers, NGOs and Forest Department staff believe that the current emphasis on participation will last only as long as donor money is coming in. But everywhere there are problems because not all members of the Forest department are committed to the programme. These problems follow in part from the fact that the legal framework governing forestry is so rigid. Therefore, JFM agreements often offer no legal or other form of security. JFM agreements and micro-planning documents usually depend upon informal understandings between villagers and individual Forest Department staff. When those staff are transferred, the new staff may not feel themselves committed to these informal understandings. Villagers are understandably cynical about the longer-term promises of the benefits that are offered by the Forest Department. More importantly, NGO work (for example by the AKRSP in Gujarat) has demonstrated that some of the objectives of the whole JFM programme—particularly those concerned with gender and other forms of social equity—require long-term work to ensure they are achieved. Without more widespread support from committed staff in the Forest Departments, it is hard to see how women will be brought into the centre of forest protection activity, and become able to affect key management decisions (like the choice of species to plant, or the criteria for the distribution of benefits) rather than be increasingly marginalised.

'Success' is hard to measure since different stakeholders have not agreed criteria for what counts as success. Some donor agencies (the World Bank and some bilateral donors, for example) are very clear that the projects they are funding are part of the rolling back of the State and the releasing of entrepreneurial initiatives. The World Bank in MP wanted to change transit and felling rules in order to open up the market for farm forestry; bilateral donors may see the extension of participation as part of their mission to promote good governance. Presumably the Government of India and the individual State Governments see JFM as part of environmental policies, rather than a way of tying India more closely into globalising capitalism, but even there we do not yet have clear statements of how JFM fits into their wider goals. Forest Departments are not unitary organisations either, and different participants have different ideas of what JFM is all about. Two extreme views can be discerned: to see JFM as a peripheral part of their work, restricted to marginal, degraded land; or to see it as a model for all future forest management except for very inaccessible land. If the former, how much land, and how many villages should be part of JFM agreements? If the latter, what changes will need to be made to encompass urban and commercial interests?

In all cases, there is confusion over criteria for the success of JFM, and these differences reflect different constructions of the Indian forests and their roles in different political projects. Thus different stakeholders may consider JFM to be a success according to one or more of the following criteria: if trees—any trees—are growing where there were none before; if a forest similar to that within living memory is recreated; if biodiversity is maintained or extended; if the subsistence needs of villagers are met; if livelihood needs (including cash incomes) of villagers are enhanced.

At least in part, these differences can be traced to different visions of the forest: of what it is now, how it came to be that way, and what it should be like in the future. What is crucial is to find ways of negotiating these differences on the basis of clear understandings of the images held by each side. In this process, assumptions about the 'intrinsic eco-friendliness of the *ādivāsī*' must be put on one side. For even if we grant that many forest-dependent communities had such characteristics in the past (and as we have seen, things were much more complex than this simple model suggests) the numbers of such unstratified communities in the present are few, and under threat. To base a government policy on programmes that only seem to work well with such isolated, poor, egalitarian communities is to doom it to failure. We need more realistic accounts of who forest-dependent people are, where they are coming from, and what they want from the forest. This volume is a small contribution to providing some of these accounts.

2

Mountain Forests in Tamil Culture

Alexander M. Dubiansky

It is well known that, in ancient India, forests (*aranya, vana*) were considered to be inauspicious, dangerous places populated by giant *rākshasas* (demons), wild beasts and snakes. Generally they symbolised wilderness, foreign or distant lands, uncultivated territories. But the wilderness could be conquered by either physical or spiritual force and forested places appeared that were thought of as organised, cultivated, and sacred. The first case is represented, for instance, by the foundation of Indraprastha, the Pandavas' capital in the *Mahabharata*, or the city of Gudjorat in the *Chondimongol* by Mukundaram Chokroborti.

The second case is, of course, an *āshrama*—a forest hermitage for ascetics and sages, an island of peace, harmony and spirituality. This aspect of forests is well enough demonstrated by the existence of such terms as *aranyaka* and *vanaprastha*, that reflect one of the most important layers of ancient Indian culture.

These preliminary remarks are needed to set off the theme of forests in ancient Tamil culture represented by Tamil poetry, which is sometimes called Sangam poetry, written in approximately the first to third centuries AD. There is no doubt that the notions that I have just mentioned were known in the south but to all intents and purposes they were not reflected by the early poetry. Its treatment of forests seems to be original and specific.

Forests enter the Tamil poetry mostly within the theme of love, or *aham*, as it is called by Tamil poetical theory. The most striking feature of this poetry is a system of five themes called *tinai*. We can define *tinai* as a poetical theme which from the point of view of its contents consists of three elements: a poetical situation, its natural environment (landscape) and a specified time (a season and sometimes a part of day). Four *tinais* describe various types of separation of lovers (or a marital pair), one of which—*kuriñci*—is concerned with clandestine premarital unions. Two themes are closely connected with forests—*kuriñci* and *mullai*—and in both, the situation

17

is one in which a wife is patiently waiting for her husband. The poetical landscape of *kuriñci* is also called *kuriñci*, the region of mountain forests. The landscape of *mullai* is one of hills covered by forests and pasture-lands. Perhaps there is some botanical difference between these two kind of forests but it is not essential for the poet. More important is the fact that the two landscapes are associated with different seasons: *kuriñci* with the cold season, and season of cold dew (October—February), and *mullai* with the beginning of the rains (August). Between them lies the hot season, which belongs to the *tinai* called *pālai*, in which the situational element involves the separation of lovers. The *pālai*-land is often described as a sort of a hot desert, a barren, fear-inspiring land, where sparkling heat envelopes like a coat a long waterless road (Narrinai 99, 1-3). It is clearly opposed to both *kuriñci* and *mullai*. This opposition is very important and opens up a set of culturally meaningful oppositions, such as cool-hot, close-distant, secure-dangerous, and, in the end, life-death.

The key factor in formatting the *pālai*-landscape is climatic conditions. This is expressed in the second chapter of the poem of *Cilappadikaram* (Lay of the Anklet). This poem describes how the Sun-king swerved from the path of righteousness and the lands of *mullai* and *kuriñci* lost their essential good qualities and took up the form of *pālai*, which makes people tremble with distress (Cilappadikaram II, II, 62-66).

The main words for forest in ancient Tamil poetry are *kātu* and *kān (kānam, kānakam)*. *Kātu* is a forest in the sense of wilderness, a place which is difficult to live in, or to pass. A long-standing opposition in Tamil culture is *nātu-kātu*, where *nātu* means cultivated, civilised regions, whereas *kātu* means uncultivated, disorganised lands. Some poets who glorified the deeds of powerful Tamil kings describe lands of their enemies after a king's devastating raids as *kātu*; that is, *nātu* had become *kātu*. We can recollect also the term *chutu kātu*, which means a place for cremating bodies. The frequent expression in Tamil love-poetry *kātu irantōr* can be translated as 'those who have traversed deserted lands'.

Nevertheless in *kuriñci* and *mullai* poetry *kātu* also means forest with trees, beautiful flowers wild animals and birds. The same applies to the word *kānam*, which, however, seems to lack the hidden meaning of difficulty and danger.

Let us look more closely at forests as depicted in the poetry. We shall take up the *kuriñci-tinai*. The situational element of this *tinai* is the premarital union of lovers. The hero, a young hunter, falls in love with one of the girls (also from a hunters' tribe) who are scaring away parrots from a field of millet. It is not necessary to go into the details here. Suffice it to say that the romance of the young pair under the guidance of the girl's friend moves to its desirable end—to the marriage (which is, by the way, hardly mentioned in the poetry).

The natural background for the meeting of lovers is the mountain landscape—high peaks, dangerous clefts and caves, rivulets and small lakes and forests with blossoming trees and plants, with wild animals: tigers, elephants, bears, monkeys, peacocks and parrots. Poets describe the details of the landscape colourfully and vividly, though very laconically—with one or two strokes of brush, so to say. For example:

Listen my friend and prosper!
Our man is from mountains, where
A waterfall slithers down the slopes
Like a snake; and drops quickly
To make rocks bang together:
And it hits the flowered and swaying limbs
Of the long-trunked *vēnkai* tree
Growing among the stones,
To make these limbs barren.
The love we mingled with him
Is good
As long as he never goes away.

(*Kuruntokai* 134, translated by M. Shansugan Pillai)

Pen-pictures of mountain-forests made by Tamil poets are absolutely realistic and fully correspond to botanical descriptions of plants. But at the same time they have inner symbolical meaning which can be understood if we take into consideration the significance of the situational element of the theme. In ancient Tamil culture sexual relations between men and women were considered sacred and looked upon as a kind of a divine marriage. That is why the situational element of the *kuriñci* has its prototype in the mythology of Murugan.

Murugan, who later became Scanda, is the Tamil god of war and love. He is connected with solar energy and he is the chief of the region of *kuriñci*. His spouse Valli is a personification of an edible plant *valli* (*Convolvus batatas*), which grows in mountain forests. The coition of Murugan and Valli symbolises the union of two basic principles of nature, male and female, which is the source of its fertility and richness.

It can be demonstrated that the two lovers in *kuriñci* poetry are replicas of the mythological figures just mentioned, and that their relations are also connected with fertility and procreation. But the actual union of lovers is practically not described. It exists only in the thoughts, dreams, and recollections of the hero and heroine. Nevertheless the idea of the union finds beautiful and picturesque embodiment in the natural environment of the situation.

One of the most characteristic details of mountain forests is *vēnkai* (*Pterocarpus bilobus*)—a big tree with golden-red fragrant flowers and a black trunk. In Tamil culture it has permanent associations with Murugan. Tamil kings and warriors who impersonated the god on battlefields wore garlands made of *vēnkai's* flowers. In *kuriñci* poetry the hero often appears with them. Murugan himself in an episode from the *Kandapuranam* turned into a *vēnkai* tree.

So, when the heroine exclaims in one of the poems, 'Is there anything sweeter than the time when we, clad in skirts made of green leaves, were rocking in a swing tied to the black trunk of a *vēnkai* tree?' (Narrinai 368, 1-4), her erotic intentions (though expressed in an indirect way) are absolutely clear.

Another forest-tree that has symbolical associations with Murugan—and accordingly with the girl's lover—is sandal. Its wood is reddish in colour, fragrant and very strong. When the girl or her friend mentions sandal she always hints at the hero. Sandal is often meaningfully used in comparisons. For instance, 'His love is like beehives among limbs of a high sandal tree, where sweet honey is mixed with the cool pollen of lotuses, which was elevated by the wind' (Narrinai I, 3-4). The erotic overtones of this fragment are also indisputable.

Not only flora but also fauna and some other details of the landscape can serve as an expression of the ideas connected with the hero; or speaking more generally with the male principle of nature.

In the same manner the female principle is expressed. First of all let us name *valli*—a liana-like plant with edible tubers, which is a symbol of fertility and female sexual energy. In one of the variants of the Murugan myth there is an episode when Valli, who, as I have already mentioned, is a mythological figure impersonating the plant, climbs onto a *vēnkai* tree, plucks some leaves, makes a skirt for herself and then embraces the trunk, pressing it with her breasts

(Shulman 1980: 280-281). A clear reminiscence of this episode exists in one of the poems: 'A girl from a hunters' tribe wants to pluck new golden flowers on high limbs of *vēnkai* which grows on the slopes of mountains where *valli* twines around the trees' (Akanānūru 52, 1-3).

The next plant we shall touch on is the mango tree. In the north Indian poetical canon, the mango is associated with Kama, the god of love and obviously with the male principle. In Tamil culture associations with the female principle are stressed. One of the most typical details of a woman's verbal portrait is the colour of her body, which is like the colour of fresh sprouts of mango (*māntalir*), that is dark-blue. Generally a woman possesses the mango-beauty (*māmaikavin*), as it is put in the poems, In some versions of the story of Kannaki, the heroine of the *Cilappadikaram*, she is born from a mango tree. The fact that in some Munda tribes there is a ritual of marriage of a young boy with a mango-tree seems to be relevant in this connection.

So, again a simple pen-picture is produced, such as, for instance, 'the stream of water with flowers of *vēnkai* which have fallen into it is washing the roots of mango-trees' (Paripatal VII, 14-15) is full of inner, obviously erotic, meaning and hints at the union of lovers

There is one more important idea which is also expressed through some details of the landscape of mountain forests—the idea of ripeness. Millet is ripening in the forest fields; honey in the beehives on the trees is ripe; flowers of *vēnkai* and mango are fully open; mountain streams and lakes are full of water. All these details symbolically express the idea of ripeness of the girl, her readiness for marriage. Sometimes such details speak of the state of readiness of both partners. When the girl's friend says that the *vēnkai* has opened its bright flowers and the moon has reached fullness (Akanānūru 52, 16-17) she means that the time of marriage has come.

Now it is an apt moment to say a few words about *kuriñci*, a flower which gave its name to the region of mountain forests and to the poetical theme or *tinai*. *Kuriñci* (*Strobilanthes*) is a typical plant of the region. It produces nectar and has dark-blue petals. Strangely enough it is mentioned in the *aham* poetry very rarely (only four times) though it can be a good symbol for a woman like any other blue flower (like the lily *kuvalai*, for example). But its significance lies much deeper. The matter is that *kuriñci* blossoms once in twelve years, which is exactly the age of sexual maturity of a girl in traditional Tamil culture. This coincidence makes *kuriñci* an ideal expression of the cardinal idea of the poetical situation and the most apt symbol of a girl coming of age.

From what I have already discussed, the role of the natural environment in the poetry seems to be clear. Pen-pictures of mountain forests are not only absolutely realistic but also at the same time form a sympathetic background of the situational element of the poetical theme and are able to express the ideas important to it, such as the readiness of the partners for union (in the first place, the girl's readiness), their actual premarital union and the idea of fertility and procreation, connected with the poetical theme.

This does not mean that the pictures of a forest have no aesthetic meaning for the poets and their audience or that all the details of the landscape are necessarily loaded with symbolic meaning, but nevertheless the general symbolical role of the landscape is undeniable. It is possible to create a table which shows several levels of symbolical expression of the idea of the union of two principles of nature—male and female—in ancient Tamil love poetry and the correspondence of different elements of the poetical theme of *kuriñci*.

Table 2.1: Symbolic correspondences in Tamil poetry

Level	Male Principle	Female Principle
Anthropomorphic	hero	heroine
Mythological	Murugan	Valli
Vegetative	*vēnkai*, sandal	*kuriñci, valli*, mango, *kuralai*, millet
Zoological	tiger, bee	peacock, parrot
Details of the Landscape	mountains, streams	mountain lakes (*cunai*)
Astronomical	sun	moon
Colour	red	dark-blue (*nīlam*)

The principle of stringing together the three elements of the poetical theme, which we define as mythopoetical, can be discerned in the poetry belonging to all themes. If we take, for example, the *mullai-tinai* with its hill forests as a background for the situation of a devoted wife, waiting patiently for her husband, we see that its dominant idea—female chastity—is also expressed symbolically by numerous details of the landscape. Only in this case different plants and flowers appear in the avant scene. The most important among them is *mullai* or jasmine (*Jasminium trichotomum*) which is the permanent symbol of the idea. But I shall not go into the details of *mullai-tinai* and in the way of concluding, I shall return to mountain forests.

Conclusion

The concept of *kuriñci* mountains as the domain of Murugan and the source of fertility and plenty has become common-place in Tamil literature and culture. It has even entered the field of modern politics. The schematic picture of two black mountain peaks with the red sun in between them has become the well-known symbol of the Tamil National movement. 'Murugan is the God of DMK' once said Annadurai, the leader of the Dravida Munnetra Kazagham (Clothey 1977: 116), thus stressing the role of religious concepts (in this case the figure of the God of the *kuriñci* region) in the contemporary struggle for political power.

3

Forest and Forest Dwellers in Modern Bengali Fiction

France Bhattacharya

In an important article published in 1976, entitled 'Village et Forêt dans l'idéologie de l'Inde brâhmanique', Charles Malamoud showed the ever-present dichotomy between the village and the forest in Indian Brahmanical tradition. The Sanskrit word for forest is *aranya*, which is also used in Bengali. Malamoud suggested that *Aranya*, being outside the village, is at the same time an 'en-deça' and an 'au-delà' of the *dharmic* norm. Tentatively, we can translate 'en-deça' by 'below' and 'au-delà' by 'beyond'. The *aranya* is 'en deça' because robbers and others who commit crimes against the *dharma* live there freely. It is 'au-delà' because the deserted space that is the *aranya* is 'the image of the Absolute, or at least the place where settle those who are in search of the Absolute, those whom the Indian tradition as a whole presents like the antithesis of the *grhastha*, the renouncers (*samnyāsin*)' (Malamoud 1976: 12, my translation). Malamoud mentions Madeleine Biardeau's writings, pointing out that the initial opposition between *grhastha* and *samnyāsin*, which can also be seen as that between ritualistic sacrifice and renunciation, was modified in later Hinduism to throw open the possibility of liberation, or salvation, to all mankind. Yet the *samnyāsin* did not lose his eminent position nor the forest, abode of the renouncer, its positive value.

Keeping in mind the analysis mentioned above and the values attached to the forest, I will present, through a few works of fiction, the 'modern' Bengali view on the forest and its inhabitants. The first examples, taken from two novels by Bankim Chandra Chatterji (1838-1894) illustrate in relation to the village the two sides of the forest: the 'en deça' and the 'au-delà.'

In one of his very first novels, *Kapalkundala*, published in 1866, Chatterji uses the forest as a gruesome decor for an ill-fated love story set in seventeenth century Bengal (1866: 137-88). The writer describes it as a sparsely wooded area, bordered by a line of sand-dunes, on the sea-shore of the Bay of Bengal. The place deserves the name of *aranya*, given to it by the novelist, not because of the density of its trees, but because not a single village is located there.

> When Nabakumar had climbed on the shore, as far as his eyes went, he could see no sign of human habitation. There was nothing but the forest. But this forest was not planted with tall and beautiful trees, and it was not at all dense. At places only, small shrubs formed circular clusters (Chatterji 1866: 139).[1]

Thus, for the author, *aranya* is synonymous with *vijan*: a deserted place. According to the novel, the deltaic region of the Sundarbans, inhabited by wild animals including the famous royal Bengal tiger, was also, at that time, the dwelling place of an unsocialised Tantric renouncer, bent on achieving supernatural powers through the performance of human sacrifice:

> (W)hen Nabakumar woke up, it was night. He was surprised not to have been already eaten up by a tiger. He threw glances here and there wondering whether the wild beast was going to appear and pounce on him. Suddenly, at a distance in front of him, he caught sight of a light. Afraid that it might be an illusion, he looked carefully. . . . Only a human being could have lit this light, since it was not the season for forest fires. Nabakumar got up and started running in the direction of the light. . . . Trees, shrubs and dunes were hampering his walk at each step. He trampled on the vegetation and climbed the dunes. Coming nearer to the light, he saw that it was radiating from a fire burning on the top of a high dune. A man's figure, seated on the highest point, was standing out against the sky. He decided to come near the man and quickened his steps. At last, he reached near the top of the dune. Suddenly, he was afraid. Nevertheless he continued to climb with steady steps. When he came face to face with the seated man, he shuddered: should he stop or should he turn back? He could not make up his mind (Chatterji 1866: 141-42).

The man that Nabakumar is about to meet keeps with him a young orphan girl whom he has brought up and intends to use as a companion in his rituals. An adept of left-hand Tantric practices, he wishes to offer in sacrifice to a cruel goddess that young Brahman,

---

[1] The translations have all been done by me, from the original Bengali.

Nabakumar, the hero of the story, whom his companions have abandoned on this deserted shore. The forest, as we see, is a place where violence prevails, where asceticism is practised in the purely selfish hope of gaining supernatural powers and where the cruelty of nature is matched by that of man. A dark world, it is the opposite of the epic '*tapovan*', the abode of *dharmic* ascetic practices. The Brahman captive thus has no other means of saving his life and the purity of his Brahmanhood than escaping with the help of the girl Kapalkundala whom he marries. He goes back with her to the village and its regulated way of life. But the young girl, brought up by the Tantrika in the wilderness, does not understand why she should conform to the behaviour expected of a married woman according to the village code of conduct. She misses the freedom of the open forest though she loathes the ways of the renouncer. At the end, death unites for ever the Brahman youth and the sylvan girl.

The opposition village/forest is rendered all the more obvious by the conduct of Kapalkundala who, though as pure in heart as a *satī*, fails to give her husband and the village world the total submission expected from a married woman. She utters a sentence that would never be said by a Hindu devoted wife: 'If I had known that marriage is slavery for a woman, I would never have married' (Chatterji 1866: 175). Repeatedly, Chatterji contrasts her 'natural' morality with the culture-induced norms that regulate the married woman's life. However he does not decide in favour of the first against the second but, by the death of Kapalkundala, shows simply the incompatibility of the two worlds.

In another novel, *Anandamath*, published in 1882, Chatterji projects the forest this time as an 'au-delà' of the village. The decor recalls the sylvan environment of the *tapovan* where lived, according to the epics, in a way that Malamoud shows as an attempt to integrate the forest and the village (Malamoud 1976:17), the men who have reached the *vanaprastha* stage in life. Sanskrit literature, and particularly Kalidasa in *Sakuntala*, described such a forest, charming to the eye and to the ear. Chatterji seems to follow that classic model:

A small river was flowing through the woods with a sweet murmur. The water was very clear but black as a rain-loaded cloud. Various essences of trees were dispensing their shade on its banks. All kinds of birds made their home in their magnificent dark green foliage from which a concert of singing could be heard (Chatterji 1882: 731, my translation).

The novel presents a kingdom whose king does not rule in the proper way and has forgotten the dictates of the royal *dharma*. As an implicit consequence, a severe famine brings disaster to the land. The year is 1769, and the English have placed on the throne of Bengal a weak and treacherous man who does not care for his people. From where will salvation come? Chatterji imagines that it will come from the forest and its renouncers. These men have temporarily left the life of householders in their villages to initiate the *dharmic* reconquest of their country from the *aranya*, where they have found refuge. The novelist gives the forest the task of rejuvenating the village world through the selfless endeavours of a few dedicated men. The 'passage through the forest' in the case of these new Vaisnavas, as in that of the Pandavas in the *Mahabharata*, does not mean total detachment from the world, in the hope of attaining individual salvation, but, on the contrary, active involvement in a spirit of service, *nishkama karma*, as the author calls it:

> Don't you see that we are *samnyasin*, renouncers? We have renounced the world to cultivate these qualities. When our mission is accomplished, when our spiritual practice is perfect, we shall return to the world. We too have wives and daughters (Chatterji 1882: 727).

Yet another dimension is given to the forest by the author of *Anandamath*. In a striking prologue, the novelist describes a huge, dark and impenetrable forest in which a gust of wind suddenly agitates the trees and a voice is heard asking for total devotion, *bhakti*, in exchange for the realisation of man's desire. In the following chapters the novel makes it clear that the desire in question is the welfare of the country and the well-being of its inhabitants. In the opening page, however, the forest described is not located in any particular place: it is a metaphor for the primeval ocean at the beginning of a new evolutionary cycle, and the voice asking for *bhakti* is implicitly attributed to Vishnu-Narayana, the supreme god of the epic and pauranic cosmogony. This is how Chatterji, in the opening lines, describes the forest:

> It was a very vast forest. There were various essences of trees, but sāl were in profusion. Lines of trees were stretching up to the horizon; their top and their foliage could not be distinguished from one another. No interstice, no hole allowed the light to penetrate. It was an ocean of foliage, endless, and the wind ruffled it, wave

after wave. Underneath, there was nothing but darkness. Even in the middle of the day, the light was feeble and the forest remained fearsome: man never entered it. No noise could be heard except the rustle of leaves and the cries of birds and beasts (Chatterji 1882: 715).

In this brief prologue, the image of the *aranya* attains its greatest development, encompassing both the 'au-delà' and the 'en-deça', and going even beyond this pole of opposites to embrace the totality of the cosmic manifestation.[2]

In these two novels, *Kapalkundala* and *Anandamath*, as in the ancient literature mentioned by Charles Malamoud in his article, no mention is made of the original inhabitants of the forest. This is not true in the case of the whole corpus of Sanskrit religious texts. In the epics, the presence of non-Aryan people is alluded to at several places. The Aranyakanda of the *Ramayana*, for instance, mentions, along with the ascetic dwellers, their enemies, the *rākshasa*, in whom some scholars, in the last century, saw the symbolic representation of the first 'savage' inhabitants of the land! Rama meets other dwellers of the forest, mentioned as such, like the woman ascetic called Sabari (*sarga* 74-75) about whom not much is said but whose name indicates that she belonged to the Sabara tribe living in the mountains. Nearer to the cities of the Aryas resided the Nisadas whose king Guha is said to be a friend of Rama (Ayodhyakanda *sarga*: 49-52). In the *Mahabharata*, Ekalavya, a prince of the same Nisadas, aspires to be a disciple of Drona in archery though his low birth disqualifies him for that (I, 132). He becomes the best of archers in spite of all, but accepts without protest the terrible punishment imposed by Drona that prevents him to put his acquired knowledge to any use. The epic makes of him an example both of absolute dedication to a task and of total devotion to the guru.

Leaving epics for history, the emperor Ashoka mentions, in one of his edicts, the 'forest tribes' present in his empire. They should be reformed and subdued, orders the monarch (Basham 1971: 54).

---

[2] The 'en deça' side of the forest is not altogether absent from the novel. In a striking scene, one of the heroines comes face to face with a group of famished peasants who have become bandits and who, reduced by misery to a subhuman condition, are about to devour her and her baby daughter in the depth of the forest. The novelist seems to have in mind the model of the epic *rākshasas* while describing these poor men (Chatterji 1882: 719).

Throughout the centuries, the attitude of the Indian rulers does not seem to have changed: the *ādivāsīs* are allowed to live in the marginal space (i.e. the forest) as long as they keep a low profile and accept the life conditions created for them by the dominant village people.

The next three modern Bengali novels I will consider give a place of varying importance to the original inhabitants of the forest while, at the same time, they describe the *aranya* under different aspects.

In 1975, Mahashveta Devi, an active defender of the rights of the tribals, published a remarkable novel entitled *Aranyer Adhikar* (Propriety Rights Over the Forest). It tells the story of the revolt of the Mundas in 1899, headed by Birsa, against their exploitation by the landlords, the usurers, the missionaries and the British administration. The tribals wanted to recover their ancestral rights over the forest area of Chotanagpur. With great passion and empathy, the novelist shows the mechanism by which the *ādivāsīs* are deprived of their customary rights by the British Government with its unjust laws, its police and its courts, as well as by the non-tribal usurers, by the landlords and petty Rajas of the area. The novel starts on the morning of 9 June 1900 when Birsa dies at the age of 25 in the Ranchi jail where he had remained a prisoner for several months awaiting trial. Then, the story goes back to the birth of the gifted boy in an extremely poor Munda family. Birsa is sent to the school of the German Lutheran Mission. He gets baptised and studies there for some time. He is expected to become a Christian preacher, but the boy is not satisfied with what he is taught. He becomes the disciple of a Vaisnava, puts on the sacred thread and allows himself to become quite Hinduised. Later on, restless once more, he decides to go back to his ancestral faith and vows that henceforth Simbonga will be his God. One day, in the depth of the woods, Birsa hears the voice of the *aranya*: that ancient mother of the Mundas. The forest complains that she suffers greatly at the hands of the non-tribal Dikus and that she feels defiled. She invests Birsa with the mission of purifying her. Is she not to the tribals Mother Earth herself?[3]

The forest is thus much more than the simple setting of the story. It is an actor in the drama that is about to start at that point in Birsa's life. After his encounter with the primeval *aranya*, Birsa declares himself to be Bhagavan, the Father of the Earth, Dharti-Abba. Henceforth he decides to devote himself to a movement that operates

---

[3] The novelist acknowledges her debt to Suresh Singh (1966).

on several planes: religious, political, social, economic and political. He becomes the prophet of a religion meant to raise the Mundas' level of consciousness, to give them confidence in their destiny and to make them proud of their origin. A Messianic leader, Birsa draws to himself hundreds of his tribesmen. He declares war on the colonial Government and on the non-tribals. His declared aim is to give back their rights to his people and to make them free from all forms of exploitation. In spite of the courage of the Mundas, the unequal battle ends in disaster. Birsa and many of his companions are made prisoners. The story ends on that fateful day when Birsa dies of choleric dysentery in jail. Mahashveta hints at the possibility of his having been poisoned. The children of the primeval forest remain to this day a destitute and much oppressed people.

The novelist describes the Munda ethos and world-view with a great deal of enthusiasm and sympathy. The tribal society is contrasted favourably with the Hindu way of life. It is said to be more free and egalitarian. The women share with the men the responsibilities of raising a family, and their status is said to be equal to that of their menfolk. As a non-tribal Hindu, Mahashveta tries to atone for the sins of her Diku ancestors: on the one hand she idealises the tribals and, on the other, she creates the character of a Bengali Christian, Birsa's friend at the Mission school, who helps him in jail. The letters that friend writes to a historical person, an English lawyer, Jacob, are supposed to let the Birsa story be known in India and abroad.

Mahashveta is one of those who give to the fight launched by Birsa the distinction of being one of the first battles of the Indian Independence movement. For her, Birsa is a victim of British imperialism, of colonial exploitation and of unabashed capitalism. A Christ-like figure in his white flowing *dhoti*, the Munda hero is not presented as a revivalist, eager to keep alive or to give a new life to obsolete elements of tribal culture, nor a magician pretending to cure the sick and render bullets inoperative, nor a Prophet announcing an unlikely cataclysmic deluge, but a rationalist using his Messianic powers to prompt his followers into meaningful actions. Another biographer of Birsa, Surendra Prasad Sinha, insists, on the contrary, on the religious dimension of the young Munda's mission (1961: 51).[4]

---

[4] Though Mahashveta does not mention this book, she shares with its author a very warm approach to the man Birsa but not his emphasis on the

He does not hesitate to show him as a healer in the traditional way and a soothsayer. For example, during an epidemic of smallpox, Birsa, according to Sinha, cured some people with his peculiar utterances and the touch of his sacred thread. Mahashveta prefers to underline the way he teaches his people simple rules of hygiene. A confirmed modernist and a progressivist, the Bengali novelist underplays the influence of Christianity and Hinduism that marked, according to other biographers, Birsa's conduct and preaching. For her, Birsa was a revolutionary and a patriot, not a prophet.

Mahashveta gives the forest its due importance in shaping the Mundas' mind, and she acknowledges the fundamental bond linking the tribals to the *aranya.* This is the way she puts it:

> As soon as he (Birsa) entered the forest, he usually found peace. This time, however, it did not work that way. "It all belongs to me, hey! no rule can prevent me from entering." He entered into the forest, *jangal,* repeating these words again and again. His mother Karmi's cry: "You will go to jail, Birsa!" did not reach his ears. He was thinking: "Dhani Munda said that everything belongs to me. I shall give nothing to anyone. Forest, why don't you say that nobody has the right to take away forcibly your grace? They have invaded all nooks and corners of the forest after piercing its belly. The forest is the mother of all Mundas." Birsa understood that the Mother-forest was crying. She was violated, bound by the shackles of regulations and surrendered to the hands of the Dikus (non-tribals). The Mother-forest was saying: "Save me, Birsa, I want to be pure, stainless."

> Birsa was rubbing his face against the ground, his body against the trees. Like a bold child he made to the forest an impossible promise: "I shall do it, mother, yes, I will give you back your purity. You are my mother, for sure; you are the mother of all Mundas. You are the one who gives us the roofs and the walls of our houses, and you allay our hunger by offering us your fruits, your roots and your tubers, as well as the flesh of porcupines, deers and birds." While saying these words, he was bending his head sidewise like a swift and attentive bird when the voice of the forest was emerging from within his own blood (Devi 1977: 89).

Messianic dimension of the Munda hero. The biographer seems to take for granted the miracles attributed to Birsa by his followers.

Mahashveta is right in presenting the forest as a symbol of tribal independence, but it should be noted that, at the time of Birsa, the Mundas were primarily agriculturists fighting for the right to cultivate their own land. They were also, but only in a minor way, pastoral people wanting free access to their traditional pastures in the forest.

Undoubtedly, the writer is more interested in human relationship, both of conflict and understanding, than in the beauty of nature. So the descriptive passages in the novel are few and repetitive. On the other hand, the tribal society is shown as a strongly integrated unit with its customs, rules and hierarchy. The dialogues include large portions in Mundari, translated afterwards into Bengali. The Mundas are a poor and dispossessed people, but they are still a people. The other two novels, set at a later time, present a very different picture.

Bibhuti Bhushan Banerji in his *Aranyak*, published in 1938, shows a further step in the process of the marginalisation of the original inhabitants of the northern Indian forest. His story is set in the 1930s, more than twenty years after the events narrated by Mahashveta Devi. The narrator is a young Calcutta graduate who, in desperate need of a job, is offered the task of supervising the clearing of a vast stretch of forest in Bihar in order to get it cultivated by tenants. The young man tells the tale of the six solitary years he spent in the woods: how, at first, he pined for the lights and comforts of civilisation, the company of his friends and the noises of the city, but how, little by little, he became enchanted by the beauty of the virgin land he was asked to destroy. As always in the writings of this author, the description of nature, ever changing with the various seasons, takes an unusually important place in the general economy of the novel. While Mahashveta idealises the tribals and their way of life, Banerji prefers to idealise the sylvan setting. For him, men do not contribute anything worthwhile to the beauty of the wild. The people whom the narrator meets are mostly Bihari Hindus belonging to middle or low-ranking castes: they are impoverished peasants attracted by the offer of land against the payment of a reasonable rent. As soon as they come, these tillers of the soil build afresh a village society with its rules, its hierarchy and its values. More often than not, their sense of propriety is marked by deep-rooted prejudice and male domination.

At the beginning of the novel, the forest, big as it is, is already surrounded by human settlements, and the narrator is supposed to bring in more peasants. This is how he sees his role as time passes:

Three years had passed. During these three years, I had changed a lot. The sylvan landscape of Labatuliya and Ajmabad had drawn around my eyes a line of enchanted *kohl*. In a way, I had forgotten the city. A fascination born of solitude, that of a star-spangled generous sky, had taken such hold on me that when I had to spend a few days at Patna, I felt very impatient to leave these macadamised roads and to come back to Labatuliya Baihar where, under the blue sky looking like an inverted bowl, pastures after pastures, woods after woods were spread, where there were no roads, no brick houses, no horn-sounding cars, and where, in deep slumber, the only noises one could hear were the barking of jackals calling watches, the hurried steps of herds of *nilgai* [deer] and the deep bellowing of wild buffaloes.

In their letters, my employers started to urge me to distribute by lots all the land to tenants for farming. I knew that it was my main task but I could not resign myself to do it because the settling of peasants meant spoiling this place where Nature was the lone inhabitant. The people who would take this land on rent would not want to keep these trees and plants as they were. They would quickly "clean" the soil by cutting and uprooting the whole of its natural vegetation. Then they would sow seeds and build their lodgings. This solitary sylvan space that is so beautiful, this forest, these springs, this range of hills would be transformed and covered with a string of villages, and the crowd of newcomers would make the Goddess of the Woods flee. Men's arrival would destroy all the charm of this enchanting forest: it would deliver a fatal blow to beauty (Banerji 1938: 81-82).

The *ādivāsis* appear rather late in the narration. They are represented by a few members of an ancient Santal royal family, dispossessed and reduced to extreme poverty. Their only riches are a few cows, some hens and the memories of their past splendour when they ruled the country all around. Apparently, they have lost much of their tribal culture, and yet have not gained any access to modern education. The narrator, though full of sympathy for these excluded people, poorer than the poorest, calls them 'uncivilised', *barbar*, and show that they have accepted their deprivation and stand on the verge of total extinction. A quotation will illustrate the way he views the uneasy relationship between these aborigines and the rest of the Indians. It is the narrator's first encounter with Dobru Panna, the

Santali raja who is the descendant of those who ruled from the Himalayan foothills to the southern borders of Chotanagpur, and from the
river Kusi in the west to Monghyr in the east:

> I could see the nomadic Aryas, coming from the other side of the
> mountains, entering ancient India in successive waves. The land
> was ruled at that time by primitive non-Aryan people. All that
> India achieved later, all along her history, is the history of Aryan
> culture. The history of non-Aryan people was never written or, if it
> ever was, it was in these mountain caves, hidden in the darkness of
> that huge forest, and in the skeletons reduced now to powder. The
> victorious Aryas have never attempted to discover these lost
> pages. Even today, the unfortunate defeated primitive people are
> as neglected, as despised, as forsaken as ever. The Aryas, proud of
> their culture, have never cast even a glance in their direction. In
> the past they have never tried to understand their culture, and they
> still do not try.

> Banwari and myself, we were the representatives of this victorious
> race whereas old Dobru Panna, young Jagru and Bhanumati were
> those of the trampled upon, defeated people. On that day, our two
> people were face to face. Cultural pride, the pride of the
> handsome, sharp-nosed Aryas, made me see in Dobru Panna, scion
> of an ancient aristocratic line, an old Santali, in Princess
> Bhanumati, a Munda coolie girl, and in their palace that they
> showed with such pride and happiness, a cave without light nor
> air, the meeting-place of snakes and ghosts. That great historical
> tragedy was happening, that evening, in front of my eyes: the
> protagonists were, on one side, Dobru Panna, that poor,
> vanquished and forgotten non-Aryan king, the non-Arya princess
> Bhanumati, young prince Jagru Panna, and, on the other side, my
> accountant Banwari, my guide Buddu Singh and myself (Banerji
> 1938: 113).

A romantic to the core, the narrator, after this 'historic' encounter,
toys a few moments with the idea of settling down among these
Santali people by marrying the pretty Bhanumati, grand-daughter of
the old king, and of enjoying for ever, in her company, the beauty of
nature. Nevertheless, in the last pages of the novel, he is back in Calcutta amidst 'civilisation', years after the entire forest has been cleared
by the peasant settlers. He has married according to the rules of his

society and seems to have settled in a conventional *grhastha* life. Yet, he cannot forget the Santali maiden and all the other poor, but free, inhabitants of the forest.

For Banerji, the *aranya* is essentially an object of aesthetic enjoyment, a regret, a nostalgia and, in final analysis, a remorse. It is an 'au-delà' in the sense that it represents purity, beauty and freedom from unnecessary conventions that raise artificial barriers between men. At the same time, it is certainly not a space where men can live a life of unfettered liberty because that would disrupt the natural harmony of the primeval land.

The forest dwellers, for the novelist, whether they be tribals or ordinary Bihari peasant folk, are all victims of the exploitation perpe-trated by usurers and oppressive landlords. Banerji does not blame the alien government of the time for the degradation of a natural milieu through an insensitive legislation, as does Mahashveta. The quotation above shows that he would rather blame History, always merciless to the weak. It appears that he has taken for granted the theory of the existence of an Aryan race, superior to all others, that European scholars had put forward in the nineteenth century. As a Brahman, Banerji feels that he definitely belongs to the superior people but, as a sensitive man, he feels uneasy about it. Considering the course of events, he does not hope for any better days for the forest and its original dwellers. He has no solution to offer. In this precise sense, one hesitates to call *Aranyak* the first ecological novel in Bengali, but, surely, it is a most beautiful statement of the love of a modern man for the past beauty of his land.

The third and last novel under study, *Aranyer Din Ratri* (Days and Nights in the Forest) written by Sunil Gangopadhyay and published in 1968, was made into a film the next year by Satyajit Ray. Those who have seen the film know that the forest there, though called *aranya* in the title, is a far cry from the vast expanse of primeval woods described in the two previous books. It is reduced in size, and its trees, though not too sparse, are neatly aligned as in a plantation:

> It was a forest that did not really look like one. As far as the eye went, one could see lines of trees with thick foliage that, at places, dispensed a dense shade. But this *jangal* in which there were no wild animals, deserved as much the name of a garden, *bagan*, as that of a forest, *aranya* (Gangopadhyay 1968: 18).

Indeed, most of the time the novelist uses the word *jangal* to name it though the title refers to *aranya*, conveying in Bengali the idea of a densely wooded area where humans enter with a certain amount of fear. More than the real forest, *aranya* designates the mythical concept of the woods, and, along with it, much of the etymological sense mentioned by Charles Malamoud as 'l'autre du village' (1976: 5).

In the novel, the forest is shown as an open space where young frustrated men from the city come to experience a feeling of near total freedom. The third person narrator contrasts the metropolis, Calcutta, with the forest, or what remains of it. His heroes are four young middle-class men who, recently disappointed in love or unsuccessful in their jobs, are looking for a change. At the beginning of the novel, they are in a train going towards Bihar which is, for a Calcutta Bengali, something like the Wild West. They decide to get down at a small railway station on the advice of a travel acquaintance. They hope to find in the forest a place where they can give free expression to their 'primitive instincts'. In a gesture that mark symbolically their separation from civilisation they spit, from the top of the railway overbridge, on the glossy photo of a well-dressed couple printed as publicity in a Calcutta newspaper. Once in the forest area, they behave as if they owned the place: they forcibly occupy the bungalow reserved for the forest rangers, roam stark naked in the woods and drink country liquor till they lose their senses. 'What does culture mean when you are in the "jungle?"' philosophises one character (Gangopadhyay 1968: 58). 'We the civilised, we want to live free in the forest, letting ourselves go,' declares another (Gangopadhyay 1968: 15).

They share with the narrator of the previous novel a strong feeling of superiority and an unabashed cultural pride. The novelist has not given them much political consciousness nor aesthetic sensitivity. In the region live a few Santals who, apparently, have kept little of their tribal identity. They still speak their language among themselves, but have learnt enough Hindi, and even Bengali, to communicate their desire to leave the area to go to Calcutta in search of livelihood. They are as poor as ever, if not poorer, and find in alcohol their only solace. For the young city men, they are an object of slight curiosity and condescending pity. However, the tribal women folk in topless saris are attractive to them, and one of the Calcutta men has a brief affair with a consenting Santali, hoping to be taken to the big city. Interestingly, the third person narrator insists on the pleasure the woman gets from that encounter since she is used to being beaten and insulted (Gangopadhyay 1968: 93). The young man's libido and pride, hurt by the indifference of his Calcutta girlfriend, is eager to take revenge and assert his male superiority on any member of the other sex. He does not mind the smell of sweat, salt, rotten water and garlic the woman exudes, according to the novelist. Later, the man learns to his cost that the tribals, destitute as they may be, still value a certain code of honour and that they do not allow themselves to be completely taken for granted. Yet, from the point of view of the heroes, these men are 'primitives' who can be bullied and beaten. They can also be used freely, whenever needed, and rejected afterwards or, worse even, ignored.[5] For the boisterous Calcutta boys, somewhat as for the Tantrika of Chatterji's *Kapal-kundala*, the forest is a place, outside the 'village' and its *dharma*, where the search for unauthorised domination can be freely pursued.

On another plane, the three later novels show, in their different ways, the continuous process of degradation of the forest and its first inhabitants. The authors offer no ready solutions, neither to the ecological nor to the human problems. Mahashveta Devi has the merit of describing in passionate terms the systematic exploitation of the tribals and the process by which their spoliation was engineered from the very beginning. She sees their only hope of salvation in the advent of a true socialist Revolution—no less an ideological construction than the mythical concept of the *aranya*!

---

[5] The young men treat the illiterate and poor low-caste people of the area with no less condescension but somehow they have to accept the fact that these men, compared to the tribals, share with them a greater part of their Indianness. The tribals remain very much on the border line. One of the boys, Sanjay, a labour officer, is more sensitive than the others to the overall poverty of the people, but his interest is focused on the *chowkidar* (watchman) of the forest bungalow, not on the Santals.

4

Sacred Groves in Coorg, Karnataka

M. A. Kalam

Introduction

The 'sacred groves' (*devarakadus*) of south India have long been held up as examples of indigenous conservation and preservation. Close study suggests, however, that although the rhetoric of conservation is well established, in practice, none of the agencies supposedly concerned with protecting these plots of land have been able to prevent a steady decline in their number and extent. Similarly, the quality of biodiversity and the density of forest cover have deteriorated badly. Only those *devarakadus* that are distant from human habitations, and not easily accessible by road, are in fine fettle. Encroachments took place gradually during British colonial rule but also subsequently. In this process, the shrines at the heart of many *devarakadus* have been Sanskritised, with the attempt to eradicate animal or other blood sacrifices, often leading to damage to the local flora. In this paper I use two case studies of *devarakadus* in Coorg District to show how these changes have emerged.[1]

The present Kodagu (Coorg) district of Karnataka state was under the Lingayat Rajas until 1834 when the last Raja was deposed and the province of Coorg was annexed by the British. The British held sway over Coorg till India's Independence, with a Commissioner in Mercara and a Chief Commissioner in Bangalore. From 1947 to 1956 Coorg was a 'Part C' state along with Ajmer, Bilaspur, Tripura, etc. In 1956 Coorg merged with the then Mysore state as a district, on the recommendations of the State Reorganisation Commission.

The Forest Department in Coorg

The Forest Department (initially known as the Forest Conservancy Department) had Coorg as a range under an Assistant Conservator of Forests from 1865 to 1876; the Conservator of Forests of Mysore was

[1] I am grateful for the assistance of Jacques Pouchepadass and the French Institute, Pondicherry, during the research reported here.

in charge of Coorg forests too. From 1876 the forests of Coorg were brought under a Forest Division, and since 1878 Coorg has had an independent Conservator of Forests.

Reservation of the eastern forest tracts began in 1870 and by 1875-76 an area of 308 square miles of reserved forest was demarcated and surveyed; in addition, all the deciduous forests of Kodagu were demarcated. In 1877-78 the area was reduced to 295 square miles as a result of realignment of the boundaries. Demarcation of the Ghat Forests was taken up the next year, and in 1886-87 these were declared as protected forests, an area of 309 square miles.

Protected forests were of three types, viz., *devarakadus* (sacred forests), *urudves* (village forests) and *paisaris* (lands outside Reserves not included in revenue-paying or revenue free lands) (Stebbing 1926: 27).

The 873 *devarakadus* were spread over 10,865 acres. They were counted, registered, their boundaries were marked and the area of each grove was estimated during 1873, and the cultivation of coffee, which was hitherto allowed in them, was stopped. In 1899 the Chief Commissioner of Coorg, Lieutenant-Colonel Donald Robertson, wrote to the Secretary to the Government of India, Revenue and Agriculture Department (Forests), explaining the significance of the *devarakadus*:

> *Devarakadus* (Gods' or Demons' woods) are ordinary small hills covered with forest growth which owes its preservation to the superstitions of the people. Some of these groves are so sacred that the ryots take off their shoes before entering them and a few indeed inspire such awe that on no account will the Coorgs pass through their limits. The rules of 20th September 1888 are enforced without difficulty and no forest produce is removed without the express sanction of the Commissioner, excepting leaves, creepers, and fallen branches if required for services of the temple.

Rules were drawn up for the management of the Protected forests; those pertaining to the *devarakadus* are as under, and are enunciated in The Coorg Forest Manual 1899:

> XI. All *devarakadus* shall be recognised as sacred and shall be so maintained throughout the whole area which is entered in the register as belonging to *devarakadu*.
>
> XII. All felling, lopping, clearing, pruning or burning of trees within the limits of *devarakadus* is prohibited.

XIII. No timber, wood, branches, grass or any other produce shall be removed from the *devarakadus* on any pretext whatsoever, except on special permits which may be granted by the Commissioner.

> Provided that the villagers shall continue to enjoy such prescriptive rights as they may now possess with respect to gathering leaves and creepers, and to taking fallen branches which may be needed for use in the temple.

> Provided further that public officers may, with the permission of the Commissioner, remove such stone and gravel as may be required for public purpose.

XIV. No cultivation of any kind shall be allowed in any *devarakadu*.

In 1905 the *devarakadus* were handed over to the Revenue Department, along with the *urudves*. Around this time the extent of the *devarakadus* had increased to 15,506 acres from 10,865 acres in 1899. The *devarakadus* remained under the control of the Revenue Department for 80 years, and were considered as *paisary* land; in 1985 a notification was issued to transfer the *devarakadus* back to the Forest Department, and the *devarakadus* were declared as Reserved Forests.

But in spite of several letters and requests from the Forest Department the *devarakadus* have not been handed over to the Forest Department by the Revenue Department. Currently the *devarakadus* are under dual control. The Forest Department considers the *devarakadus* as Reserved Forest but simultaneously the Revenue Department considers these as *paisary* land. However, after the issue of the 1985 Notification the Forest Department started surveying the *devarakadus* in Kodagu District. According to the list available with them, the break-up of *devarakadus* in the three Talukas of the district, as on 28 August 1991, is as shown in Table 1.

While the *devarakadus* were under the control of the Revenue Department (for 80 years) as *paisary* land, their extent shrunk from 15,506 acres in 1905, when they were handed over to the Revenue Department, to 6299.61 acres in 1985, when the Notification was issued to return the *devarakadus* to the Forest Department. But even this area is not fully under the *devarakadus* as a further 352.38 acres has been encroached. Now, overall, it is only 5947.23 acres that is available as *devarakadus*; more than 9,500 acres has been lost during the last 80 years. After the 1985 Notification, 204 *devarakadus* have been surveyed out of 1,214. As can readily be seen these are the larger ones; the 204 *devarakadus* which have been surveyed and demarcated as Reserved Forest comprise 2397.465 acres of the total of 5947.23 acres which are spread over 1,214 *devarakadus*. The remaining 1,010 unsurveyed *devarakadus* have an extent of just about 3550 acres.

Table 1: Extent, in acres, of *devarakadus* in Kodagu district

Taluk	Devarakadus	Encroachments	Balance
Virajpet	2154.16	176.00	1978.16
Madikeri	1319.54	96.33	1223.21
Somwarpet	2825.91	80.05	2745.86
Total	6299.61	352.38	5947.23

Note: The total number of *devarakadus* in the district was 1214. See text for more details.

Table 2: Extent of the 204 surveyed *devarakadus* in Kadagu district

Taluk	Number of Devarakadus	Total Area:	
		Hectares	Acres
Virajpet	54	152.440	376.687
Madikeri	10	573.918	1418.180[2]
Somwarpet	140	243.863	602.598
Total	204	970.221	2397.465

The above is an account of the transformation of the *devarakadus* in the Kodagu District of Karnataka, and the way political, economic and other aspects have had an impact, and spurred on this process of transformation.

Classification of *Devarakadus*

There are at the most general level two kinds of *devarakadus*—those where encroachments of various kinds and degrees have taken place, and those where there is almost no encroachment. The former are the *devarakadus* which are close to human habitations, through which

---

[2] While the total extent of *devarakadus* in Madikeri taluk (surveyed and unsurveyed) is 1319.54 acres according to Table 1, in Table 2 it seems that the 10 surveyed *devarakadus* are spread over 1418.18 acres; I could not get an explanation for this discrepancy.

roads pass, or are on the sides of main thoroughfares. The latter *devarakadus* are those which are far from human settlements and more often than not access and entry into these *devarakadus* is not very easy or practicable for some reason or the other. It is around the latter kind of *devarakadus* that aspects of awe, mystery, wrath of the deities/gods/goddesses, legends of punishments, etc., are woven, and survive to this day. Similar beliefs, stories and legends that may have existed as regards the *devarakadus* close to human settlements are neither very frequent nor believed in by many today. Those who have been party to encroachments or have turned a blind eye to such happenings tend to justify the events. The general refrain being that it was possible in the olden days to adhere to the norm of protecting the *devarakadus* but with changes occurring in all aspects of life, immigration into the district being quite high, particularly of labour, and with increase in population, it has become difficult to hold on to age-old practices. This is not to suggest that there is no section that does not believe in preservation and protection of the *devarakadus*. Of course some do believe that the *devarakadus* are not to be encroached upon in any form and the pristine glory of the *devarakadus* is to be restored, but the saner group does not seem to have the clout to prevail upon the others.

Of the various *devarakadus* that I visited more than half belong to Iyappa; the rest are the abodes of Bhadrakali, Bhagavathi, Sarthavu, etc. Daily worship takes place in only very few of the *devarakadus*; these are the ones where full-fledged temples have been built. The largest and more popular of these are Bhagamandeswara at Bhagamandala and Mahalingeswara at Palur. While Bhagavathi at Cherangala is also worshipped daily, the practice has been given up for Bhadrakali at Kedakal. Except the Bhagamandeswara temple, all the other temples are within the precincts of the *devarakadus*; at Bhagamandala the temple for the deity Bhagamandeswara is not situated inside the Sangam *devarakadu* (so named due to the confluence of the Cauvery and the Kanike) but is about 400 metres from the *devarakadu*. In the rest of the *devarakadus* only annual festivals are held; these annual festivals go on for two to thirty days. Along with Iyappa, Bhadrakali and Bhagavathi, the other deities that co-exist in the *devarakadus* are Chavandi (Chamundi, Chamund-eswari), Kar Chavandi and *nagin kal* (which have a stone platform or square for cobras).

Changing Sacred Associations

Shrines and temples are being constructed for Iyappa, Bhadrakali and Bhagavathi, and overt attempts are being made to convert these deities into vegetarian ones by making only *halmathu hannu* (milk and fruit) offerings; these shrines/temples are constructed close to the road side within the precincts of the *devarakadus* to make them visible and to attract devotees. Great care is taken to locate these as far away as possible from the older and original spots where Chavandi or *nagin kal* exist. Though blood (i.e., animal) sacrifice is permitted during the annual festivals, there is a distinct proclivity to avoid these on all other occasions and to project the vegetarianised deities as the main and important ones; quite often the original spots where Chavandi and Naga dwell are relegated to the background both in the literal as well as the metaphorical sense by saying that only the tribals and the lower castes perform *pujās* there, and offer animal sacrifices. On the occasion of the annual festivals the animals sacrificed are predominantly fowls, but also some pigs and sheep.

The Kodavas (Coorgs) are the dominant community both economically and numerically, and are predominantly non-vegetarian. In the religious sphere, however, they are being increasingly influenced by a pattern that can be seen all over the state of Karnataka, whereby vegetarianising the deity is considered to be a virtuous thing to do. Hitherto all the religious practices of the Kodavas revolved around animal sacrifices, and in their lineage rituals it is true even today. But in joint religious practices, that is inter-caste or inter-community situations, they have begun to conform to the ritual practices wherein importance is placed on *hal mathu hannu* offerings. This is a distinct departure from the erstwhile situation. Besides, it is pertinent to note in this context that, as recent as about ten years ago, the Kodavas had nothing to do with the Dussehra festival or with Ganapati. But today even in small towns and villages this trend is observed.

In order to obtain a clearer picture of the *devarakadus*, as regards the religious activities that are undertaken in these, I will discuss in detail two *devarakadus*, belonging to different deities.

Bhadrakali *devarakadu* at Kedakal

Bhadrakali *devarakadu* is situated about 9 kilometres from Madikeri on the Madikeri-Mysore road. This *devarakadu* has been surveyed and the boundary demarcated with numbered 'RF' (Reserved Forest) stones. The western portion of the *devarakadu* is about 34 acres and the eastern portion has about 4 acres; the road passes though the *devarakadu* and separates it into two portions. The larger portion is surrounded on three sides by private coffee plantations and the road runs along the fourth side. After about 70 metres of an ascending, cleared pathway from the roadside, is the Bhadrakali *devasthan*, temple. It comprises a shrine for the goddess Bhadrakali with a high wall all around the shrine, which forms the temple square. On the south-western side, the wall has given way and a large gap exists in the corner, big enough for people to enter the *devasthan* if they wish to do so. On the left of the entrance a thatched shelter is put up with low benches which enables devotees to hold meetings and have gatherings without entering the *devasthan*.

Behind the *devasthan*, further west, about 25 metres away, is a *katte*, square stone platform, about a metre in height, and about 3 metres on the sides; in the middle of this square is a stone idol. This square seems to be quite old and appears to be the original abode of goddess Bhadrakali. The *devasthan* has definitely been built at a much later date. As visitors approach the pathway leading to the *devasthan* from the road, they find on the left a *hundi*, cash collection box, and a stone idol on a smaller *katte*.

An *astamangala prasana* was conducted at this *devarakadu* from 27 to 30 May 1992. I visited the *devarakadu* for a second time on the 28 May 1992; my earlier visit there was on 12 March 1992. While the *astamangala* was on, I collected the following information.

According to the astrological predictions of the *pujārīs* the *devasthan* was at least 500 years old. But people remember meetings being held and activities connected with the temple since 1936. Legend has it that tiles for the temple square were donated by an Englishman about 80 years back, who, while in Coorg, saw an old man in the vicinity of the *devasthan* trying to communicate something to him. Later in England too he saw the same old person who appeared to be urging something to be done. On his return to Coorg he consulted local people who decoded the substance of the message to him. He donated tiles for the deity and the earlier paddy straw thatched roof over the temple square was replaced with these tiles. The name of this person was Ballianter (probably a Scottish name).

Another version of the story is that the deity (Bhadrakali) appeared in the dream of the Englishman and told him to replace the thatched roof with tiles. The Englishman neglected the deity's wish and did not pay any attention to it; as a result he fell violently ill and it was pointed out to him by his neighbours that he was suffering as a result of not fulfilling the deity's wish. So he learnt his lesson and replaced the thatched roof with tiles. Subsequently he was cured and went back to England soon after India's Independence, after selling his property to the family of F. M. Khan, a Congress functionary in Karnataka. The name of the estate owned by this family is, of course, Ballianter.

The part of the temple square wall that has fallen was due to vandals breaking into the *devasthan* in August 1991 with stolen copper wire. After breaking open the door on the northern side they gained entry and started a fire to melt the wire. A part of the *devasthan* caught fire and the south western portion of the wall was gutted.

The *astamangala* was being held to remedy the wrongs that have been done; the neglect of the *devarakadu* and the deity and the subsequent misfortunes suffered by some of the people living in the area, the vandals breaking in, the fire and the burning down of a part of the temple square. The complete history of the deity from time immemorial was being obtained, all aspects connected with the deity and the *devarakadu*, what had happened in the past, what the people should do currently and the course of action to be followed in future; all these details were being obtained through the *astamangala prasana* being conducted by Sri Krishna Bhat Visharda and his *sisya* (disciple) from Bili Nale, Subramanya, an important pilgrimage centre in the Dakshin Kannada District of Karnataka.

According to the oracle that was being consulted, the deity has been in the *devarakadu* for more than 500 years. Now a new construction has to come up. All new materials have to be used for the construction. The deity has to be shifted to the back portion temporarily. The shape and size of the structure to be constructed will be revealed. People have neglected the temple, there has been no unity among the people, so the deity presently is not in the temple but somewhere around in the vicinity of the temple itself; she has been angered, but the anger has been within her tolerable limits. Hence though she does not reside in the temple proper she has, nevertheless, not left the temple for good. She can be cajoled and brought back if, even at this late stage, she is propitiated in the right way and all that was revealed during the *astamangala* is fulfilled to her satisfaction.

In March 1992 the deity gave thought to six people to initiate the work. These six went around, met other people in the area and consulted them. The general consensus was that temple astrologers had to be brought in to lay bare the reasons for the impasse. In the past, six *takkas* (village headmen) and 18 *okkas* (lineages) used to manage the affairs of the temple/deity. Gradually it so happened that many of those who were supposed to be part of the 'managing committee' of the temple/deity began shirking their responsibilities. At present only one *takka* (Pullera S. Kallappa) and only three *okkas* (Yenkana, Mukkatira and Pullera) were involved with the management and upkeep of the deity/temple. It is this kind of attitude of the people that brought about the neglect of the temple and the consequent anger of the deity. The astrologers say that the weekly worship that was on in the temple should not have been stopped after the August 1991 fire. The *pujārī* who used to come from Suntikoppa should have continued the weekly *pujā*.

Before the Forest Department put up the boundary stones, encroachments did take place in the *devarakadu*. Local people were involved; but the others did not resist or evict those who indulged in this practice, nor did they do anything when portions of the *devarakadu* were encroached upon by those who had coffee plantations adjacent to the *devarakadu*, and appropriated the *devarakadu* land for commercial purposes. The deity strongly disapproved this attitude. All through, the deity has taken care of the people's needs and welfare; she is a goddess of fertility as can be evidenced from the offerings of miniature *harike* (wish fulfilling) cradles made out of silver and wood. The deity has bestowed children on childless couples and has also given bountiful staple and cash crops.

Now the deity is demanding the resumption of *pujās* along with *bhajans* and *gāyans*, and the antelope dance which has been forgotten for ages. Also the annual *pujā* during March has not been adhered to; it was not performed during March 1992. Besides, for the last 70 years the annual *pujā* has not been performed for the full seven days but has been truncated almost every year.

In the smaller portion of the *devarakadu* there is a Chavandikal (stone) where during the annual *pujā* in March animal sacrifices are made—goat, chicken and pig are all desired by Chavandi. The main deity, Bhadrakali, is now vegetarian and accepts only *hal mathu hannu* (milk and fruits). The road side *hundi* and the idol on the stone square is just to signify the presence of the main deity inside, and on occasions when the temple is closed or when devotees do not feel like going over to the main temple they can perform puja next to the roadside and make their cash offerings there itself.

The stone square with the idol inside the *devarakadu* on the western side, behind the temple, is the spot where Bhadrakali resided when she first came to this *devarakadu*. Later, after the construction of the shrine for her she moved inside the *devasthan*. Now the old stone square is frequented by the Kuruba tribals. They offer their *pujās* there before they set off for the extraction of honey. Bhadrakali turned into a vegetarian deity only after she moved into the *devasthan*. In the erstwhile spot she used to accept animal sacrifice, but this practice has been discontinued at the old stone square. Now the Kurubas as well as others make the animal sacrifices only to Chavandi, conveniently away from the main deity, Bhadrakali, on the other side of the road. Now *pujā* is performed at the *devasthan* only after it is first performed at the older spot behind the *devasthan* where Bhadrakali first resided.

Iyappa *devarakadu* at Iratokkalu (village Kargunda)

This *devarakadu* is spread over 14.11 acres. A *pu prasana (astamangala)* was held here during June 1992. A Brahman *pujārī*, Vasudeva from Kopatti, was invited for the *pu prasana*. The *pujārī* said that a temple/shrine has to be built for the deity. But since Iyappa is never placed inside a shrine, it was decided at the first meeting held on 5 June 1993 to construct a stage for the deity. Normally Iyappa is open to the elements, and no shelter is erected over his head. Hence it was agreed to have a slab shelter resting over four pillars, and to place a stone sculpture of Iyappa riding a tiger on the stage under the slab roof. The people are well aware that rain will not directly fall on Iyappa as it should normally be the case, but they say that since the stage will be open on all sides it would serve the purpose and can still be considered as being open to the elements. There are sceptics, of course, but they are silenced by those who staunchly adhere to the prophecy as revealed by the *pu prasana*.

About twelve trees, big and small, had to be felled in order to clear the setting for the construction of the stage, from around the terracotta deity of Iyappa surrounded by his dogs. The reason advocated for the felling of the trees is that they are going to spend a few thousand rupees for the stage and the stone sculpture and any tree in the vicinity would pose a danger to the deity as it would get crushed if a tree were to fall over the stage during a storm or heavy gusts of wind.

While clearing off the piles of dog terracottas on the northern and southern sides of the east-facing deity, the western side has been left intact; so of the U-shape of the dog terracotta piles the two longer sides have been cleared leaving the semi-circular side intact. At the bottom of these four feet high piles they discovered human terracotta heads and a couple of silver dogs. While the terracotta dogs are encountered quite frequently in many of the Iyappa *devarakadus*, the discovery of the silver dogs is a rarity. That in itself is not surprising as the rich may have made offerings of silver dogs; it is also possible that earlier there could have been a tradition to offer silver dogs when wishes were fulfilled and that gradually gave way to terracotta dogs as an economic measure. But what is surprising is the discovery of human terracotta heads and also human arms and legs. I have never come across anything of this sort in any of the *devarakadus* I visited nor does anyone around the *devarakadus* remember any practice of the offering of human terracotta heads, arms or legs to Iyappa; they all are familiar with the offering of terracotta dogs and bulls for wish fulfilment—what are locally known as *harike nai* and *harike basava*. On my earlier visit to the same *devarakadu* during June 1992 I had a close look at the pile of terracotta dogs but did not have any inkling that anything other than terracotta dogs could be there in the pile. But when I visited the *devarakadu* during the last week of September 1993 the pile had been removed and from the bottom of the pile the human terracotta heads, arms and legs were recovered and kept next to Iyappa along with the silver dogs. Following the guidance from the *pu prasana* the people were warned not to dig any deeper than six to twelve inches around the deity as that may bring to surface quite a few things. Accordingly they have dug only up to six or eight inches where the square stage is to be put up. They were planning to have the deity installed by 15 November 1993 as the annual festival of the *devarakadu* would be during the first week of December. The *asta bandha* was to take place on 15 November when the deity would be fixed to the *pani peetha*.

They had already procured Rs 2,600 from the sale of a part of the felled trees and the rest of the logs were to be sold off soon. The expenses incurred in felling and sawing the trees were around Rs 3,000. They were also on trip to collect donations from the villagers in order to meet the expenses they were going to incur towards the installation of the deity.

Discussion

A number of studies of sacred groves in the Western Ghats have been carried out. For example, Nipunage et al. (1988) point out that sacred groves have been referred to as 'Dev-rai' or 'Dev-Rahat' by Kosambi, and by Gadgil and Vartak. Due to the generally wide-spread practice of not felling the trees or collecting dead wood or leaves from such groves, Nipunage and his associates contend that conservation of natural resources was possible over a period of generations.

Nipunage and his associates 'registered 84 sacred groves protected on religious grounds' (1988: 170) in the Western Ghats in Maharashtra. Besides observing current rituals associated with the sacred groves they also collected folk tales from tribals in the region. The deities are 'placated' with animal sacrifices; but Nipunage et al. are convinced that human sacrifice existed in the past:

> Even today Goddess Shirkai in Poona district in the village Shirkoli is symbolically offered a human victim every year. Originally, the victim must have been sacrificed by being impaled on a hook which was hung on a rope from a rotating pole. Even presently the hook is pressed against the back of the victim, but the man is no longer swung by the hook. He is instead tied to the rotating pole by a *dhoti*. The wound made by the hook is not serious and is rapidly healed. Shirkai has a fine grove of five hectares in which this hook swinging ceremony is annually performed. The original function of the groves was perhaps to provide the proper atmosphere for such primitive rites. There are innumerable stories about human sacrifices offered to the Goddess in the past. At present, however, this custom is substituted by slaughtering a number of cattle and fowl (Nipunage et al. 1988: 171).

They found that the deity is 'generally feminine—an indication of its origin in early times, when birth was still the most miraculous of all events' (Nipunage et al. 1988: 172).

Gadgil and Vartak, who undertook a study of sacred groves in Maharashtra and Goa (1976; 1981a; and 1981b) believe that the sacred groves have 'their origin in the hunting-gathering stage of the society'; they speculate that the sacred groves 'served to create the proper setting for cult rites including human sacrifices'. They also feel that the sacred groves had their origins in 'more secular causes—for the preservation of a valuable tree or climber which was relatively rare in the locality' (Gadgil and Vartak 1976: 157). Such preservation, they feel, could probably have been on from well before the sixth century AD at which time agriculture may have been introduced in the region. They say, 'as befits the cults of hunter-gatherers, the deities are fierce and when aroused are apt to punish the offenders with no less than death'. Except for fallen fruit nothing else was to be removed from the sacred groves in order not to incur the 'wrath of the gods' (Gadgil and Vartak 1976: 159). But they lament that such beliefs have weakened considerably, particularly after 1947, and strong taboos that existed earlier may be true today only as far as the removal of live wood is concerned. According to them 'a number of groves have been completely destroyed. Some of these were so-called *inām* groves, i.e., groves in which no deity resided, but which were preserved for the use of the priests of the deity. These priests derived an income from the fruit and other produce collected from the grove but did not disturb it otherwise' (Gadgil and Vartak 1976: 159).

In another paper, Vartak and Gadgil say 'the sacred groves harbour vegetation in its climax formation, and probably constitute the only representation of forest in near virgin condition. (The border of such sacred groves tends to be distinct even when surrounded by forests from all sides.)' (Vartak and Gadgil 1981: 273)

Nipunage et al., and Gadgil and Vartak, have conducted their studies in the Western Ghats but in the states of Maharashtra and Goa. Kodagu District of Karnataka is also located in the Western Ghats but is in the southern region, north of Kerala, and contiguous with Malabar. While conducting their studies, both teams claim that they have come across strong evidence which points to the existence of human sacrifice in the past. In one of the places a symbolic offering of human sacrifice is carried on even to this day.

In my study of the sacred groves in Kodagu (Kalam 1994) I have not come across any such evidence except for the discovery of the terracottas of human heads, arms and legs, in one sacred grove (discussed in detail in the case study of the *Iyappa devarakadu* in Iratokkalu village). I am still in the process of seeking help and guidance from archaeologists as to the interpretation of the terracottas discovered. There is no doubt a votive intention behind the offering of such terracottas; beyond that, at this stage I would not like to hazard a guess as to the significance of such offerings. The other votive offerings that I have come across in abundance in the *devarakadus* are the terracottas of dogs, bulls, horses, tigers and elephants. The last three are more common in south Coorg than in the north.

In Kirgur village, between Ponnampet and Balele, originally only Iyappa and Chavandi resided in the devarakadu of about 16.5 acres. A few years back a new deity—*kutti chathan* (little devil)—was added and a shrine built for him. But as is usual, both Iyappa and Chavandi are open to the elements. While only fowl sacrifice is made for *kutti chathan*, Iyappa and Chavandi are offered pigs too besides fowl and sheep. On the eastern side is the original entrance to the *devarakadu*; a road which runs all around the *devarakadu* seems to have reduced the extent of the *devarakadu* during recent times; consequently the *devarakadu* can be entered from any side now. However, on the eastern side I come across a platform on which is a pile of terracotta dogs, bulls and horses. Needless to say the older ones are larger and exquisitely crafted compared to the more recent ones which are not only small but also lack in form and details, and not much attention has been given to proportions.

But one interesting aspect about the *devarakadus* in the south is the more frequent votive offerings in silver of miniature human forms, and human hands, legs and eyes. Also found are miniature silver cows and buffaloes. This practice is hardly prevalent today; in the contemporary period only terracotta offerings are made. There is remarkable consistency all around as regards the explanation for this votive offering; that it has to do with the oath, *harike*, taken by people for wish fulfilment when there is a health crisis. A person having an eye ailment would offer a silver eye to the deity on getting rid of the malady; the same thing is done for the hand, leg, etc. For a major ailment affecting the *mai* (Kannada for body) the whole human form is offered. (In Kannada, Tamil and Telugu one always refers to the body when one talks of illness: one says 'body is not well'; one does not say 'I am not well'.) Similarly, when cattle take ill the same practice is observed: miniature cows and buffaloes are objects of votive offerings.

Conclusion

Though the general rhetoric in all circles, viz., the Forest Department, the NGOs and Voluntary Agencies, environmentalists, and academics, as regards discourses concerning the sacred groves is one of conservation and preservation, in practice, and at the pragmatic level, it is not true at all!

While the *devarakadus* were under the protection of the Revenue Department for a period of 80 years, their extent shrunk from 15,506 acres to 6,299.61 acres; a loss of 9,206.39 acres! A further 352.38 acres has been lost due to encroachments. Mostly those *devarakadus* that are in the interiors and away from human predators have survived in near climax or virgin form; those along road sides and close to human habitations have been eroded in various ways and to different degrees. While in general, and in a loose manner, it is fine to say that the *devarakadus* have been preserved because of religious sanctions and injunctions, in practice, and at a pragmatic level, there is very little evidence to support this thesis. In the contemporary context, and also for a period of 80 years (i.e., from 1905 to 1985), the *devarakadus* that were saved, and are in fine fettle, are those that are quite away from human habitations, and where there are no roads or thoroughfares passing through or contiguous to the *devarakadus*.

The argument that sacred groves had their origins in ideas linked to conservation and preservation does not seem to be true, particularly if this argument is situated in the context of the sixth century AD (Gadgil and Vartak 1976), as everything was then in a good state and hardly needed any conservation or preservation. While what happened during the period that the *devarakadus* were under the control of the Revenue Department is one level at which shrinkage of the *devarakadus* took place, events during the contemporary period which are having an adverse impact on the *devarakadus* are, despite being religious, not desirable from the point of view of conservation of the *devarakadus* either. I am not quite sure of the exact extent of loss that occurred between 1905 and 1947, that is, at the time that the British left, but going by the overall loss it can be surmised that encroachments have taken place gradually during the time that the British were here, and also subsequently, i.e., after 1947, till the Notification of 1985 whereby the *devarakadus* were supposedly handed over back to the Forest Department, and declared as Reserved Forests.

Religious activities of a different kind have manifested themselves in the *devarakadus* during the last decade or so; these concern the deities and their 'abodes' in the *devarakadus*. As shown in the case of the Bhadrakali Devarakadu at Kedakal, and the Iyappa Devarakadu at Iratokkalu conscious and concerted steps are being taken to vegetarianise and Sanskritise the hitherto animal or blood sacrifice demanding deities; while situating the deities in such contexts is one level at which changes are being brought in deliberately, the other practice is the attempts that are being made to locate the deities as far away as possible from their erstwhile habitations in real physical terms. In such attempts damage is, of course, caused to the flora in the vicinity of the new niches that are selected to house the deities as per the oracle of the priests who are only too willing to propagate Sanskritic practices as opposed to the crude and primitive religious practices of the tribal and indigenous habitants of the region.

5

Folk-Models of the Forest Environment in Highland Malabar

Rich Freeman

Introduction

The object of this essay is to provide a broad overview of popular attitudes towards the forest and its resources through time in the northernmost areas of the modern Indian state of Kerala. The sources that I draw on are interviews and documents collected from people living in this region, various historical writings, and especially the rich bodies of oral literature that these people and their ancestors have produced in their religious life.[1]

What is fascinating about this region is that many of those in the oldest generation living in the mountainous tracts recall a time when they lived by swidden agriculture and hunting, a way of life that has all but vanished from contemporary India.[2] Accordingly, my broadest goal in this research has been to reconstruct and record the attitudes of people living in this subsistence regime towards the forests and their natural environment.

This mode of life was completely supplanted in some twenty or thirty years by an enormous but little noticed event of internal colonisation in recent south Indian history. From the 1930s into the 1960s, over 70,000 petty capitalist planters from the Syrian Christian

[1] Fieldwork for this project was carried out in Taliparamba taluk of Cannanore District and throughout Kasargod District from June through November of 1993. I would like to thank the French Institute of Pondicherry for their hospitality and financial support of this research, and especially the former director, Jacques Pouchepadass, for his support and encouragement throughout this project. The diligence and companionship of my field assistant, A. Thamban, was, as ever, invaluable.

[2] A survey of swidden agriculture in India is provided in the volume edited by S. Bose (1991) which includes a brief profile of the few remaining acreages under swiddens in Kerala and South Kanara in the article there by P. K. Bose (1991: 139-43).

community of Travancore streamed into the highlands of Malabar (northern Kerala), in an enormous concerted purchase and clearance of the vast tracts of private forest lands there. The transformation effected by that single generation of settlers has destroyed nearly all the natural forest cover of the region and has converted the former jungle lands into commercial plots of rubber, pepper, areca nut, and cashew.[3] With this wholesale destruction of the forests and their fauna, the way of life of those who subsisted from these resources was simultaneously effaced, leaving only the memories of survivors as direct testament to their forest culture. The imperative to record the fading remnants of this earlier life-world, and its links to surviving religious institutions that reach into still earlier times, has formed the substantive agendum of my research.

When I embarked on this study I was of course aware of a burgeoning academic and popular literature on the place of India's forests in the life of its traditional peasant and tribal populations. Informing much of this literature is the thesis that prior to colonialism and industrialisation, India's culture was imbued with a set of beliefs and practices that naturally held human demands on the environment in check, so that populations and their forest environment existed in a kind of ecologically sustainable homoeo-stasis.[4] In particular the religious values and institutions of Hinduism or its folk-variants are

---

[3] An excellent study on the forces driving these mostly small-scale commercial agriculturists out of their native lands in Travancore and into Malabar is Tharakan (1984); see also Kurup (1988). Moench (1991) describes similar forces acting on this community as agents of deforestation in the Cardamom Hills of Travancore. It seems that the inland areas of my region of study had remained largely inaccessible to the commercial exploitation for timber until the arrival of the Syrian Christians in substantial numbers. Thus the District Gazetteer records: 'Lands which were inaccessible for centuries due to thick forest growth have been cleared off and brought under effective cultivation' (Sreedhara Menon 1972: 181). This makes the history of deforestation here rather different from the areas immediately to the south (Kunhikrishnan 1987) and to the north (Pouchepadass 1990), where the blame is usually laid on the commercial exploitation of timber. Due to the absence of roads and rivers to get the timber out for profitable sale, members of the Syrian community reported that they burned the bulk of the timber where it stood as fertiliser for their initial jungle crops.

[4] Greenough (1992) has usefully critiqued a number of the assumptions underlying what he calls the Standard Environmental Narrative. Sinha and Herring (1993) provide an assessment of the larger force of his critique.

supposed to have somehow encoded and transmitted this ecological wisdom across the generations.[5] In its extreme development this religious ecologic is even invoked as nature's mandate for the caste-system. The claim is that the supposed endogamy of castes made them like natural species, and their supposedly caste-exclusive occupational specialisation was like the adaptation of species to different and complementary environmental niches.[6] Of course, virtually all of the anthropological and historical evidence of the past thirty years or so makes such a scenario seem rather dubious, both in its underlying assumptions and as a general thesis. It has indeed become clear that despite official caste ideologies, whether Orientalist or indigenous in inspiration, most castes have demonstrably been characterised by a great deal of reproductive permeability, considerable occupational flexibility, and marked territorial and environmental mobility through time.[7] This is certainly the case with virtually all the castes and tribes of which I have any knowledge in Kerala,[8] and the general scholarly consensus now is so overwhelming on the issue of the fluidity and constructedness of social identity that I shall not belabour the substantive point further.

My intention is rather to point out how the desire for confirmation of modernist ecological doctrines may generate a tendency to

[5] For a succinct statement of these linkages, see the opening pages of Gadgil (1989).

[6] For a recent statement of this, see Gadgil and Guha (1992: 105-6).

[7] The assumptions that castes actually functioned as reproductive isolates and that the members of those castes with an occupational association necessarily, or even usually, practised that occupation were both effectively demolished by Dumont [1970 (1966)], and have not been seriously entertained since by most social scientists. The empirical evidence certainly supports Dumont, and overwhelmingly so in the temporal frame necessary to make any kind of argument for an adaptive significance for caste. The correlative assumptions with regard to fixity of place and of social identity through time have also been thoroughly undermined by many historical studies on particular castes or caste groupings within and across different regions and historical periods (see, for example, Irschick 1994).

[8] Ethno-historical work in Kerala confirms both systematic connubium between castes, and a highly flexible profile of occupational engagements and territorial mobility, leading to a fluidity of identity for the majority of the Kerala communities through time. The many Nāyar castes and sub-castes would provide the most famous and well documented instance of this in the anthropological literature (Gough 1961).

reconstruct idealised scenarios of 'traditional' Indian society that may be at odds with what history and anthropology teach us of these specific Indian societies. This becomes all the more worrisome for a cultural anthropologist, since it often appears that cultural values are being imputed to populations not on the evidence of their actually espousing and expressing those values, but on the basis of inferring that they must hold some such values and beliefs from the requirements of the analyst's own ecological model. Indeed much of the productive tension of my research in Kerala emerged from the constant juxtaposition of what my informants and their cultural documents were telling me, on the one hand, and what the scholarly literature on Indian forest life had prepared me for, on the other.

My own project accordingly attempts a more direct engagement with the express attitudes and beliefs of a people who in their life-times lived in dependence on forest resources, as these are reflected both in their personal memories and in their collective religious institutions. Since one of the main examples cited of the folk's religiously inspired ecological ethos is the institution of sacred groves, I shall begin by briefly characterising what I learned of these in northern Kerala.

The Sacred Groves in Cultural Perspective

The concept corresponding to what we usually find called a 'sacred grove' in the literature is termed *kāvu* in Malayalam.[9] Physically, the *kāvu* is a piece of garden or forest land, but culturally what defines it is that it is dedicated for the exclusive use of particular deities. In this capacity, the groves usually adjoin or are a short distance from an associated structural temple or shrine, though sometimes the structure may be within the *kāvu* itself, and in such cases there need be no connection with structures beyond the grove's confines (C. Achyuta Menon 1943: 10ff.).

In the most well-known pieces by environmentalists, sacred groves have been typically presented as stands of primeval forest, left undisturbed for reasons of deep religious sentiment at their climax stage of floristic succession, preserved in the midst of surroundings otherwise transfigured by human agricultural activity and resource

[9] See the discussion in C. Achyutha Menon (1943: 7-9) and the article in Nambūtiripāṭu (1976: 767-68).

exploitation.[10] While not denying that some *kāvus* may take this form, many others of my experience do not.[11] This has led me to suspect that the modern environmentalist's interest in floristic composition or biodiversity does not inform the institution and maintenance of sacred groves. Cultural practice is not directed according to some hidden ecological imperative. Rather, the manifest cultural concept of dedication to a deity's use is the defining feature underlying a set of otherwise contingent and variable physical forms the groves or gardens may take.

In explaining what 'use' the deities have for such preserves, informants resorted to the more restrictive meaning of a *kāvu* as a garden, particularly a 'pleasure garden' (*udyānam, ārāmam*). The notion here is that deities, like earlier kings, routinely like to sport and have their outings in these preserves. It is of course well known that south Indian conceptions of divinity frequently converge with models of human royalty, and indeed my informants' descriptions of their deities' activities in the forests and gardens clearly reach back, in concept and vocabulary, to folk and literary models of kingship.[12] The

[10] For example, 'Sacred groves are more or less pockets of climax vegetation. . . . These forest patches preserved on religious grounds are the true indicators of the type of vegetation that once existed along these hilly terrains long before the dawn of modern civilisation' (Vartak and Gadgil 1981: 272). The idea that these groves are oriented towards the preservation of biodiversity is developed in the next article in the same volume (Gadgil and Vartak 1981a). This then yields an ideal-typical reconstruction of ancient Indian ecology in which sacred groves, as bio-diverse refugia are envisioned to have been surrounded by common lands of forest and pasture, which the interspersed human settlements and agricultural works drew upon in concert with religious dictates that functioned to preserve the biomass and biodiversity of the ecosystem (see the discussion and accompanying illustration in Gadgil 1991: 20-21).

[11] Over my years of research in Kerala, I have visited several dozen *kāvus* in my capacity as a researcher of folk-religion, but concentrated only in the 1993 field-season on being as systematic as possible in enquiring into the physical conditions, histories, and beliefs attached to a variety of different kinds of grove I encountered. N. C. Induchoodan has undertaken a much more systematic botanical survey of *kāvus* throughout the length of Kerala under a grant from the French Institute of Pondicherry and the publication of his results is anticipated.

[12] For an early example of this model of royal forests from Kerala, see the Old Malayalam commentary on the *Kauṭilīya Arthaśāstra* [Sastri, 1972 (1938), vol. 2: 16-17; 165-70]. For the cognitive and semantic equation of

standard association is that temples are the gods' houses or palaces, and *kāvus* are their gardens. It is thus as the gods' personal property, reserved for their monopolistic use, that encroachment or other use by mundane, human agents is proscribed. It is also as the gods' property, however, that the resources of the groves are there for the gods' use in the sense of consumption to fulfil their culturally perceived needs. And here we see why it is important to attend to actual local conceptions and entailments of practice, as opposed to supplying some external logic derived from an environmentalist's ideal of conservation. For what we actually find is that many examples of what we might regard as human disturbance, resource exploitation, and encroachment are happily accommodated within the cultural framework of the grove as the deities' preserve.

For instance, while some groves may be entered only by worshipping priests, others may have shrine structures in the midst of them that require a regular traffic of devotees through them. While some groves are off-limits to all comers, others may be entered if one removes one's foot-wear and is in a 'pure' condition as mandated for worship in a normal temple. Wood may often be taken as fuel or even felled as timber when the substance or the proceeds are mandated for the deity's use and approved of by temple authorities or astrologers. Some groves have had parts cleared for constructing earthen amphitheatres for the worship of subsidiary deities, and others have had new pathways, shrine walls and other 'improvements' added to them at the expense of standing timber. While in many groves the gathering of fuel or fodder is forbidden, in others one can do this as long as only the hands and no cutting tools are used, and in others the entitled members of particular castes have licence to gather such items for the temple's benefit.

The general point, then, is that physically speaking, various practices are allowed or even enjoined under the same cultural rubric of *kāvu*, because different groves are devoted to different gods who have different needs. Yet all these worshippers are meeting the terms of *kāvus'* charters by reserving the groves or forests exclusively for their deities' use, as those uses are culturally perceived.

---

kings and gods in the ancient Tamil country (including Kerala) during the early centuries AD see Hart (1975: 13ff.). This same equivalence is manifested in the vocabulary of the *Arthaśāstra* commentary (twelfh century) and continues well into the late pre-modern period as attested in Malayalam literature and folklore.

In keeping with this variance at the normative level, the groves, as cultural projects, have varied histories as to their founding and maintenance. While there is certainly a generalised ideal that a *kāvu* should represent a natural state of uninhibited growth, it is hardly possible to view a number of them as pristine relics from a primeval past. For *kāvus* are created by divine fiat, that is, by oracles, and so the trajectory of a particular grove will depend on the previous condition of the land dedicated to this purpose, and on subsequent oracular findings. A *kāvu* may indeed result from the dedication of a patch of virgin forest to a deity, but I also know of those developed from what was once a stand of cultivated toddy-palms, from small stands of shrubbery on laterite hillocks, and in one case, from an old tank in the middle of paddy fields. Similarly, as with temples, *kāvus* may change hands in terms of custody and maintenance through time, and in some the boundaries have changed a number of times. Others were cut over for timber and then subsequently allowed to regenerate.

The end result of these historical contingencies and the inherent tolerance in the cultural category of *kāvu*, is a variety of physical profiles and use-patterns: some consist of stands of a few trees, others of scrub thickets where goats and cattle graze; some are open tree parks where people congregate to picnic, drink tea and play cards; and some are truly thick forests that may never have been exploited. But since all of these are equally entitled in local naming and practice to the designation *kāvu*, it would be a cultural distortion to take only one instance of a stand of virgin forest as the archetype.[13] And it would compound the error to then use this partial or distorted representation as the basis for attributing general cultural postulates of an ethos like modern environmentalism back to the population in question.

The Social Claims on Ordinary Forests

If there are doubts about deriving an indigenous conservationist ethos from the evidence of sacred groves, then even more doubts exist about the extension of such claims to the non-sacred groves and the wider

---

[13] The flexibility of the notion of *kāvu* in terms of its physical profile is clearly seen from the treatment in Damodaran Pillai (1955: 159-61). In terms of the shifting emphasis in the historical semantics, it is also clear from the fact that *kāvu* may refer to a temple that no longer has any associated grove, that the semantic weight of the term rests with the dedication of a site to a deity, rather than with the flora of the site, *per se*.

sphere of nature. These doubts emerged most clearly when I asked informants to distinguish between *kāvus* and ordinary forests, for invariably they said that while the former were subject to various rules, since deities were installed in them, the latter were distinguished primarily by the fact that people can use them in anyway they like. This, they explained, meant that there were no religious restrictions on collecting fuel, fodder, or jungle produce, felling timber, hunting animals or clearing tracts for swiddens.

There were clearly, however, social restraints on use. Here we encounter another common-place of environmental romanticism—the notion that natural resources in pre-capitalist social formations tend to be held in common. I could find no evidence of such 'commons' in the areas where I worked, either in recent memory or historically.[14] There were waste-lands, and people contracted for temporary use-rights over them, but every piece of waste or forest was in principle owned, and those use-rights were granted only in consideration of labour or produce rendered in turn to the owners of those resources.[15] Jungle swiddens were cleared and worked either by labour hereditarily bound to the owner, or by free-agents who rented the jungle plots in exchange for cash payments or a share of the crop.

[14] The complex issues here seem to hinge on whether and how we wish to differentiate between common-property *resources*, as the material 'given' by nature, and property-*rights*, as highly variable socio-cultural conventions for use of those resources. Feeny et al. (1990) provide a good example of an attempt to discriminate between these analytically and develop a cross-cutting typology. According to such a typology, my subjects had common-property *resources*, though all were *privately* vested. But in the more usual understanding of open, or community access to a generalised pool of resources, they do not seem to have had common property, as this is normally understood in the literature, and I adopt this usage in the lines following in the text. A good discussion of common property resources in a number of recent studies is found in Sinha and Herring (1993).

[15] This is the picture suggested by my interviews and the folk-sources. Historically, there is also a strong and consistent argument for private claims over forests and waste-lands in South Canara (Sturrock 1894). Logan (1887) attempts to sketch a more collectivist theory of property for pre-modern Malabar, but most of his material seems to work better against his own argument rather than for it. A recent reappraisal of available documents, settlement records, etc. for colonial Malabar clearly highlights the well-developed proprietary interests held in forests and waste-lands of the region (Menon 1994). See also Note 18.

Similarly, the hunting of animal life was conducted only by permission of the forest's owner, and in exchange for traditionally specified shares of the meat.[16] The oral literature reports poachers being killed in retaliation for breaching these norms, and the killing of elephants by tribals carried a death sentence for them as far back as the twelfth century.[17] Similarly, cesses or tariffs were generally collected on forest produce and timber that was felled.[18] All of these economic relationships seem to reach back well before the colonial presence, and attest to a highly developed notion of forest and other natural resources being vested exclusively in high-caste big men over

[16] Logan's statement that such permission was not required but was an imposition of the English courts seems clearly mistaken (1887: 172). The rights to hunt particular lands were organised, ritualised and negotiated according to a highly developed system of rights and duties around shrines known as *Ūrpalli*, which had particular offices vested in them. Some premodern Malayalam manuscript material on the ritual of the hunt and its elaborate social organisation has been summarised in English by Aiyappan (1937: 45-51), though he also quotes Logan's opinion. Some of this original manuscript material has been subsequently published (Kuññan Pilla 1956). The control of hunting under social hierarchies for Kerala tribes in Vayanāṭu, to the immediate south, is also confirmed for the Kurichiyas (Aiyappan and Mahadevan 1990: 79-81) and the Mullukurumbas (Misra 1971: 56ff.). The folk sources similarly make it clear that rights to hunt animals on a piece of land, or grant those rights to others, were vested in the land's owner. See, for example, the following note.

[17] For example, the brothers of the woman who becomes the folk-goddess, Paṭakkatti Bhagavati, were murdered by their brothers-in-law for failing to inform the latter of a hunt on their land and to present them with the requisite portion of the deer slain. The injunction to kill foresters (Śabaras) who slay elephants is from the twelfth century Old Malayalam commentary on the *Kauṭilīya Arthaśāstra* [Sastri 1972 (1938), vol. 2: 18].

[18] Ownership of forests and their resources as vested in private individuals is confirmed by Sturrock (1894: 124ff.) for South Canara where he discusses the private claims to forest-swiddens (*kumari*), waste-lands (*kumaki*) and forest-easements (*netti-kāṭu*). Logan's reprint of Graeme's Glossary (1887, vol. II: clxviiiff.) gives a good idea of some of the varied particulars for Malabar, proper, as does Kurup (1984). Customs (*cuṇkam*) and taxes (*karam*) and various presentations (*kālca*) were required of all kinds of collections and hunting in the forests, and various kinds of tenures for clearing or developing forest and garden lands (*kuḷikāṇam*, etc.) are well documented, as are particular timber felling agreements around the payment of a stump-fee (*kurrikāṇam*) for each tree felled.

clearly defined and bounded units of territory.[19] Aside from the labour
of clearance, there was little to distinguish conceptually between the
use-rights to forests and regular agricultural lands,[20] and the principal
of socially vesting access to resources and control of labour and its
products followed not from some ecologically mandated primitive
communism but from the same general principles of hierarchy and
coercion that is familiar from the lowlands.

In order to focus in the rest of this paper on the way forest-life was
actually perceived and enacted I will restrict myself to the main
subsistence activities of swidden agriculture and hunting, first looking
at these practices in broad overview, and then considering what we
can document of the religious attitudes associated with them.

The Tenor of Subsistence Activity

Regarding swidden agriculture in the highlands, generally, we must
first recognise that there is scant evidence for the presence of roving
populations of tribals, wandering freely over their own territories and
sowing jungle crops as they liked. Just as was the case with Pulayans
and Parayans of the lowlands, the actual castes and tribes who cleared
and cultivated jungles in the highlands seem to have been traditionally
bound to the estates of particular overlords who owned both defined
territorial acreages and had severe rights of governance over the
labour force attached to those acreages.[21] Similarly, the higher castes
of middle rank who wished to cultivate vacant jungle lands, rented
them from these same overlords under terms very similar to those of
agricultural holdings in the lowlands. [This point is confirmed by

[19] The stock phrases of ownership to the soil and all floral and faunal life
on it are continuous from the ancient grants, into those of the colonial period,
as in Logan's deeds collected in the *Malabar Manual*, vol. II. The development of forest lands in the late medieval period is treated in Ganesh (1991).

[20] This discovery from my fieldwork was clearly confirmed and
elucidated in its historical setting in Pouchepadass (1994).

[21] There are long traditions of indebted bondage and outright slavery
attested for the highlands just as for the lowlands of Kerala. K. Panur has
documented this for Kerala's tribals (e.g., 1963). See also Aiyappan and
Mahadevan (1990) for 'feudal' servitude among the Kurichiyas, and Mathur
(1977: 95ff.) for the continued practice of debtor bondage among various
tribes of Vayanātu. These pledges were secured in oaths before deities, giving
them supernatural sanction, a practice that was vividly attested among my
own informants around their local shrines.

Pouchepadass (1994) and Sturrock (1894) for South Canara; also by Innes (1908: 304) and Menon (1994) for Malabar.]

In terms of the actual activity of swiddening carried out by these tenants or bonded labour, there is little evidence that it was conservationist in its practices or its ethos. There is of course something of a revisionist trend currently underway, as a reaction against the British administration's unilateral condemnation of shifting cultivation. Part of this reassessment hinges on the transparently ideological nature of colonial opposition to swiddening, perhaps more concerned with the governability of the population and the loss of revenues than with issues of forest conservation (Pouchepadass 1994). The other part of the critique points with equal justification to the correspondingly profligate and devastating impact of the administration's own commercial exploitation of timber (Gadgil and Guha 1992: 207ff.). Neither of these issues of the ideology of colonial policy, however, bear directly on what is at issue here—the actual practices and conceptions of the agriculturists themselves.

It was difficult to detect any sensitivity to environmental degradation from my sources on shifting cultivation in this region, either in the spirit of this activity or its practice. The routine of swiddening entailed completely destroying the forest cover over the acreage to be cultivated, along with a good margin around this acreage, through a combination of axe-felling, killing trees through stripping their bark, and burning. The timber was necessarily burned where it stood or fell, since this then provided ash for fertilising the subsequent crop. Surrounding smaller trees were felled for use as rough fences and a variety of millets, pulses and vegetables were intersown with the main crop of hill rice. After cropping once or twice, the area was allowed to lie fallow for a number of years, but the preference was to return and re-use earlier swiddens before larger timber that would require arduous clearing again could take hold. Aside from some variation in the cycles of replanting and fallowing, and occasional light ploughing of some plots, little variation in these basic procedures of cultivation was reported in the colonial records, in descriptions in the old oral literature, or in the recollections of my informants. Again, Pouchepadass (1990; 1994), Sturrock (1894: 208ff.) and Innes (1908: 220) provide more details, and I discuss some specific folk songs treating swidden cultivation briefly later in this paper.

We must also take account of one further aspect of swiddening: hunting. When I naively asked lowlanders who used to cultivate swiddens in the highlands whether they used to hunt in the forests there, they told me, 'To go for swiddening means you have to hunt'. The reason was that the forest animals were the main competitors for the jungle crops. Since the lowlanders could not adequately fence or stay permanently in watch over the fields, the logic of their warfare against the wildlife was to make a pre-emptive strike, the goal being to exterminate all the potential pests from the surrounding forests before the crops were even sown. The standard method of hunting involved a series of nets and hunters armed with bows and rifles strategically deployed around a section of forest. Then beaters and dogs started at the other edge and drove all the game into the lines of nets and waiting marksmen.[22] The aim was quite simply to kill everything possible over that stretch of forest, and these mass exterminations are still occasionally attempted in remaining patches of waste and forest for religious purposes, as I will discuss shortly.[23]

The organisation of the hunt was also in strict keeping with the social hierarchy and control and ownership over the land. The beaters and the net-men and the dog-keepers were of lower caste or tribal status whereas the higher-caste chiefs had the stationary positions with the guns, and they were owners of the game and oversaw its distribution at the hunt's close.

Religious Attitudes

With this as background, I now turn to the express religious attitudes one can document in association with these practices. The major context for information on local religion is the network of shrines to the local deities called *teyyams*, which cuts across and links the

---

[22] These hunts are depicted in numerous folk-songs and accord very closely with the descriptions I collected from informants. I was able to participate in a ritual hunt dedicated to the folk-deity Vayanāṭṭu Kulavan in 1989. Ancestral percussion-cap, muzzle-loading rifles were used and rites of *mantravādam* (sorcery) to protect the hunters preceded the hunt.

[23] The same logic of overkill was also evident in fishing, where the standard method was to dam up, then poison an entire water-source, gathering the fish as they floated to the surface. Again, many folk-sources celebrate this method of fishing, described in the novel *Vishakanyaka* (Pottekkatt 1980: 148). Colonial sources, as usual, lament the practice as wasteful (Sturrock 1894: 46).

highlands and lowlands, and virtually all those communities we call Hindu, from Brahman to former untouchables and tribals.[24] What is distinctive and historically most useful about *teyyam* worship is that the oral liturgies they preserve record the lives, activities and circumstances of their hero-deities from the pre-modern period.[25] Often these represent the apotheoses of various human ancestors of the communities, but even otherwise they contain much information on the social constituency, life-conditions and attitudes of the worshippers. Most pertinent to the present context, there are numbers of deities specifically devoted to or reminiscent of swidden agriculture and hunting, and I shall especially draw on these in what follows.

What are or were the actual religious attitudes towards the vegetation of the forest? Sentiment seems, at best, ambivalent. Insofar as the peoples of Kerala view their vegetation as imbued with aspects of the sacred, those various trees, plants, groves and forests are valued as equivocally as other repositories of sacred power.

Let us first consider the case of individual plants and trees. Though these do not normally harbour spiritual powers or beings, they may, like any physical object, be so possessed. But then, like any other case of spiritual possession or sacred icon, the resident being may be either beneficent or inimical to human interests, and this depends on the nature of the being in question and its disposition towards the particular person in question. Where the human interests focus on the physical utilisation of the species, the ability successfully to harvest and to use the resource may be seen as a power struggle with the being who inhabits it. In other cases, the interest may be more in the being itself, than in the plant medium it inhabits. If a tree, for instance, is in the land adjoining a temple where a deity first came and took rest, offerings may be made there to receive that deity's blessing. On the other hand, when one unknowingly goes to cut such divinely inhabited trees or pluck their flowers or tap their toddy, the supernatural resident may turn on one and bring about illness, demonic possession or death. In such circumstances one may thus need recourse to protective rites, initially, or to more powerful beings, subsequently, to subdue the occupying force in order to seize its material substance or channel its spiritual powers for use.

---

[24] See for instance Kurup (1977), Ashley (1979), and Freeman (1991).

[25] Kurup (1973) gives summaries in English of a number of the prominent *teyyam* deities' narrative liturgies.

There are common legends of demonesses (*yakṣis*) who live in palmyra or toddy palms and lure men, siren-like, up their trunks and to their deaths. There are also demonesses who haunt particular bowers where they wait, especially at night, to feed on the blood of hapless passers-by or to enter the wombs of pregnant women to feed on their foetuses. The folk-lore and sacred texts also record instances of supernatural struggles with the inhabiting spirits of particular trees to wrest their timber from them for making a particular bow or for constructing a fortress. There are also gardens where women go to pluck flowers that turn out to be inhabited by demons who possess them when the blossoms are placed in their hair. Higher deities are then invoked to void these supernatural pests.

Modern ecological discourses occasionally invoke another vegetal complex as evidence of the positive folk-values attached to the forest and the preservation of its biodiversity. This concerns the purported medicinal value of many plant species. In spite of being totally at odds in principle and practice with Western, scientific medicine, there is enormous popular faith, backed by official government investment, in Āyurvedic and other folk-pharmacopoeias. Many of the species used are found in the forests (though others are also cultigens), and forest officials told me that they regularly allow gatherers of medicinal plants license to harvest these from otherwise protected forests. Partly overlapping this quasi-professional nexus, there were (and still are) various tribal and other specialists who are also supposed to be gifted in curing snake-bite, skin-diseases and many other maladies by drawing on their knowledge of forest plants and their properties. Despite the modernist, pharmacological veneer given to government sponsored Āyurveda, however, the theory and practice of Kerala folk-medicine is thoroughly enmeshed with principles of Frazerian sympathetic and contagious magic, as well as implication with supernatural beings and agencies. Indeed, traditional medicines (*marunnu*), their properties, their gathering and their application, are closely tied up with the worship of the godlings of sorcery (*mantravā dam*).[26] Accordingly, there is also a negative side to the quasi-magical 'medicinal' properties of plants. From ancient times the forest has also been the source of powerful poisons and magical potions connected with sorcery and black-magic. The same tribal or low-caste masters of

---

[26] On the intimate relation of indigenous medicine (*marunnu*) and sorcery (*mantravādam*), see Viṣṇunambūtiri (1979: 41-48).

this jungle pharmacopoeia have thus also been seen as trafficking in the noxious supernatural beings, powers and substances of the forest, which has often led to their being suspected, accused and even executed for practising sorcery. [27]

In terms of forest fauna, a similar complex has been well documented regarding the medicinal value of animal products at the pan-Indic, Sanskritic level (Zimmermann 1987), with many corresponding folk-references to such preparations as monkey-'paste' (*-lēhyam*) or python-'lard' (*-ney*) in popular lore and literature. Again, though, the associations of these preparations and the people who traffick in them are sinister and tinged with the demonic.

Given the ambivalent estimation attached to individual plant and animal species, it is not surprising that at the aggregate level of the forests as a resource base for swiddening, I have encountered little concern for the scope of human destructive impact in either forest clearance or the accompanying hunting practices I have reviewed. The songs that describe the clearing of forests are matter-of-fact as to the actual process of chopping down and burning the timber, and the description accords quite closely with the accounts of colonial sources and living informants. The overwhelming sentiment in the *teyyam* songs is not one of reverence or gratitude towards nature, but reflects struggle in terms of the labour of wresting a living from the site, and apprehension of the dangers, natural or supernatural, that accompany this process. Again, as with particular trees and plants, the corresponding religious attitude was one of the harnessing and mastery of potentially inimical supernatural powers. The destruction of forest cover for the swiddens by fire is described in the sacred texts and informants' testimony with little sentiment or sense of loss concerning the natural environment. By contrast, there is a marked concern for the dangers to humans and their habitations from these fires. One *teyyam* deity, for instance, commemorates the death of a shifting cultivator, caught and burned alive in his own conflagration. (I return on page 75 to the social and religious implications of the

---

[27] In the section on the royal forests and their useful produce from the *Arthaśāstra*, just after the brief mention of medicinal herbs comes a much more explicit list of poisons as a prominent resource of the forest [Kangle 1963: 149; Sastri 1972 (1938), vol. 2: 167-68]. Indeed the entire fourteenth book of the *Arthaśāstra* is devoted to means of sorcery against ones enemies, many of which entail elaborate preparations of forest and other organic products (Kangle 1963: 573ff.).

circumstances of his death.) Several other *teyyam* deities also seem to wield fire as a potent weapon with which they burn forests and threaten the lives, homes, and dwellings of their worshippers and of their higher caste antagonists. The fire they carry is primarily associated with swiddening, and as great hunters, they are equally efficient destroyers of wildlife as well. It thus seems that their destructive powers, as demonstrated in their abilities to lay waste to the forest and its inhabitants, are a major factor in their celebration and worship. At any rate, the main religious attitude shown towards the vegetal life in these songs is one of ambivalence about whether the supernatural agencies harboured in particular species or in aggregate forests are noxious or beneficent. The main religious efforts are directed towards alleviating human labour and hardship, enhancing the expectation of a good crop, and the hope that social superiors will leave their subordinates a fair share at harvest.

Aside from an obvious concern with the food-crops themselves, and with the occasional danger from forest demons and wildfire (*kāṭṭutī*), the other major focus of attention was on wild animals and their depredations. While many *teyyam* gods and their liturgical songs are directed to the hunt in isolation from other activities, a few do relate hunting directly to a livelihood from shifting cultivation. The song of worship to the swidden god, 'He of the Mountain Slopes' for instance, begins by describing a long range hunt in which the killing of deer, boar, and panther in the surrounding forest is celebrated in preparation for clearing a swidden. A predatory panther later invades the sown field at one point and is dispatched by a huntsman. The final scene of this song has the watchmen of the fields gleefully slaughtering with their slings thousands of parrots that come to feed on their crop, and declaring they have been exterminated from the whole country.

A major source or concern, however, lay not just in protecting the crops, but also, as this previous song indicates, in preventing predation on livestock and human beings.[28] Informants recalled how

---

[28] This state of affairs is dramatically confirmed in the statistical information given in Sturrock (1879, vol. 2) for South Canara. For instance between 1888 and 1893, on average more than 3,000 head of cattle per year were lost to wild animals. In most years more than half the cattle deaths were due to predation: in one year, this rose to 80 per cent (Sturrock 1879: 171). In the years 1882 through 1892, 813 people were killed by wild animals, an

the dwellings and the barns of their youth gave little provision for either light or air, since they were built as virtual stockades against the perpetual threat from tigers and panther. They also recalled the frequent loss of livestock to such attacks and the subsequent hunts these losses instigated.[29] In the case of a successful kill, the cat was carried on display, impaled and spread-eagled on a framework for presentation before the god at the local temple. Here the hunt was assimilated to a ritual presentation before the god (*kālca*), which was periodically required for a number of deities, as we shall see. In short, an attitude of antagonism and fear was still manifest in the memory of informants towards the faunal life of the forest, as is also amply attested from the corpus of folk-literature.[30] I was surprised to find among those original inhabitants who live in the highlands today, that however much they may resent the incursions of the Christian settlers, many remarked what a benefit it nevertheless was that one could move around the countryside now without fear of attack by wild animals.[31]

A clear complex of rites is focused on animals and hunting, but this seemingly has more to do with human or divine regimes of prestige and power than with the animal populations as a resource to be rationally managed. Forest meat was and is a kind of booty, divided up in ritual shares as honours accorded to the deities, hunters, shrine authorities and owners of the forest-lands. The *teyyam* songs recount bloody feuds resulting from slights to the honour of hunters or landlords in matters of meat distribution, and there is still a cult of the hunt dedicated to *teyyam* gods, in which the traditional shares are jealously apportioned as tokens of prestige. In keeping with the earlier

---

average of 74 deaths per year (Sturrock 1879: 94). (A small portion of these figures may include deaths to humans and livestock through snakebite.)

[29] Hunting of the big cats was officially encouraged by the British authorities, who, for instance, from 1888 through 1892, paid out bounties of Rs 10,718 in South Canara for the killing of 380 tigers, panthers, and leopards (Sturrock 1879, vol. 2: 186).

[30] Something of this animosity is also suggested by the account of the extended torture that was indulged in by the Mullukurumbas when they successfully trapped live tigers (Misra 1971: 59ff.).

[31] The thesis that the kind of attitudes I have documented here with regard to the mortal dangers from and animosity towards wildlife were likely widespread in pre-modern India has been lucidly argued and documented in Greenough (1992).

mentioned assimilation of human to divine authorities, the ultimate lord to whom the meat is first presented as his share is the deity, and the subsequent apportioning of the meat to the hunters and worshipping community is given out as grace of the god.[32] I was surprised in tracking down and visiting the shrines of a particularly famous hunting *teyyam*, to find how many shrines still have annual hunts (despite legal sanctions), and that the system of apportioning the various cuts of meat as given in the *teyyam* songs is still known and, in the main, followed.[33]

Hunting was clearly also linked with martial endeavour, since the same skills with weaponry were applicable in both pursuits, and since huntsmen were often recruited into the military service of chieftains.[34] This led to a militarisation of the hunt along two dimensions. First, there developed an agonistic cult around predatory animals in which warriors tested their skills by having 'duels' (*ankam*) with them, and in which both the animals and such warriors might later become deified as *teyyams* in testament to their valour. This kind of assimilation of the hunter-warrior to the prey is seen in the group of tiger-*teyyams* (Pulidaivaṅṅal), where one of their number is in fact the apotheosis of a great warrior who sought to slay them when they predated on his king's cattle. The warrior himself was killed by the tigers, after he killed one of them, and he then took on the partial form of a tiger and became one of their divine troop. That the thematics revolve around the issue of the warrior's manhood and valour is

---

[32] The mythical origins of many hunting deities in Kerala trace themselves to a Sanskrit prototype (an episode called the Kirātārjuniyam) that recounts the forest feud between the great god Śiva (in the guise of a tribal hunter, a Kirāta) and the epic hero Arjuna over which of one of them has the right to a wild pig they have both shot. One of the traditional modes of hunt in Kerala was even named in commemoration of this episode.

[33] Misra shows that this system of formally naming and apportioning shares of forest meat is (or was) also current among the Muḷḷukuṟumbas (1971, Appendix: 110-11).

[34] Gods like Vēṭṭakkarumakan ('The Hunter's Son') and Vayanāṭṭu-kulavan clearly typify this pattern for they are both great hunters, originally, but are then drafted into regular military service and leadership in the lowland kingdoms. Again, this mythical template is exemplified in the aforementioned narrative of the Kirātārjuniyam (Note 35), since Arjuna and the hunter Śiva are both depicted as bellicose warriors. In the Kerala version, Vēṭṭak-karumakan is indeed the son of this Kirāta, Śiva.

shown by the fact that he is not just dispatched by the tigers in the ordinary manner; rather, he is castrated.

The second aspect of militarisation of the hunt, is the fact that traditionally hunts themselves were explicitly declared as a form of warfare against the animals who were mythically and ritually assimilated to the status of human or demonic enemies. Each village ideally had special shrines where these hunts were organised and ritually dedicated, and the earlier mentioned hunts for *teyyam* deities are clearly a remnant of this complex.[35] This assimilation of warfare and the hunt to a divinely mandated sacrifice was once more common and widespread among the higher castes: even in Brahmanical temple festivals there is a scripturally required ritual of a mock-hunt, mythically justified as the commemoration of the gods slaying those demons who fled to the forest in the guise of wild animals.

The Forest and Social Struggle

Some of the ambivalent or even antagonistic attitudes towards nature that I have so far documented doubtless stem from the arduous labour and dangers entailed in wresting a subsistence from the tropical forests. What is far more evident in the folk sources and informants' accounts, however, is the social dimension of struggle in these swidden regimes. On the one hand, the various elites and their military agents battled each other over lands and tribute, an arena of competition that demonstrably shifted back and forth across the highlands and lowlands, as well as between the various major coastal kingdoms. On the other hand, we have eloquent testimony to the vertical dimension of these relations, realised in the highlands by the domination by these same elites over their lower-caste and tribal labourers, countered by the latter's attempts to secure a livelihood and modicum of social justice in these conditions.

As a prototype of this religiously inflected social agonism, we need look no further than the serpent deities or *nāgas* who are the commonest godlings inhabiting and guarding the sacred groves. They seem to symbolise quite clearly the supernatural extension of the forest's fertility into the human realm, for *nāgas* are the deities primarily responsible for assuring human fertility and childbirth. But

---

[35] Again, see Logan (1887, vol. 1: 171-72) and Aiyappan (1937: 45-51). I hope to treat at greater length in the future some fascinating information on these hunting organisations (*nāyāṭṭu saṅgams*) dedicated to particular *teyyam* deities at their shrines.

there is an ethno-sociological dimension to their identity as well, since they are said to represent the former inhabitants of Kerala who were conquered by the Brahmanical order and consigned to the groves. They show their consequent resentment at this subjugation by visiting sterility and disease on those who offend or fail to propitiate them.[36] Their rootedness in this oppressed, autochthonous complex of the forest is also clear in the accompanying mythology which attributes *nāgas* with the creation of the first forest game and the institution-alisation of its ritualised hunt.[37]

A similar theme emerges at the more individuated level of certain *teyyam* deities who also seem to represent not only the fertility of the forest but also a social pollutedness and violence which pose a threat to the established caste order. The stock narrative tells of childless, high-caste couples who adopt foundling children from the forest. Initially, life seems happy, but as these children mature, their wild, lowly and impure natures reassert themselves as an assault on the social order, and they are eventually either banished or killed, prior to their divinisation as *teyyams*. In these tales, the children's natural parents may interchangeably be either tribals or animals, for from the upper caste perspective, there is little difference in their natures. For instance the divine tribal child, Kuṭṭiccāttan, adopted by a great Brahman temple priest, eventually reverts to his inner animal nature when he leaps like a beast of prey to the back of the household bull and eats it alive. This interchangeability between the lower castes and dangerous animals is more literally rendered in the case of the chief *teyyam* of the Pulayan community, a sorcerer who has the ability to change himself at will into a tiger, and who is eventually banished permanently to the forest in this form. To the elites of settled agricultural regimes, then, the forest becomes a symbolic repository for the demonic, antinomian and antisocial qualities of all those lower castes and tribals with whom the higher castes were dependently, but ambivalently tied.[38]

---

[36] Forest demonesses (*yakṣis*) display a more overtly vicious depiction of this side of the forest, as does a *teyyam* goddess, Kariñcāmuṇḍi, who poses as a midwife to eat the foetus of a young mother as she tries to give birth.

[37] This myth is recorded in the earlier mentioned Malayalam manuscript (Kuññan Piḷḷa 1956: 212ff.).

[38] The impurity that Brahmans received from travelling about in the open, for instance, was known as 'forest-pollution' (*kāṭṭuśuddham*) (Viṣṇu-nambūtiri 1982: 63).

The obverse attitudes of the lowly towards the elite were similarly reflected in their relations with the forest. I noted in my discussion of sacred groves that they were considered the exclusive personal property of particular deities, and suggested that this mirrors what we have also seen of how ordinary forests and their resources were vested as exclusive property in human overlords. If this observation is valid, then the supernatural defiance to this order depicted through the gods of the lower castes may come as no surprise. Indeed, we find that there are a number of *teyyam* gods who are clear violators of the sacred groves and their temple precincts. For instance, the great hunting *teyyam* of the Tiyya caste, Muttappan, is recorded to have killed his Brahman adoptive father when the latter forbade him to hunt and cook his jungle meat in the temple's environs. Similarly, the *teyyam* Vayanāṭṭu Kulavan was blinded and banished from Siva's presence when he defiantly hunted in the god's sacred grove and drank toddy from the pots left there as an offering. Relatedly, it turns out that the earlier mentioned *teyyam* who burned alive in the fire he set to clear a swidden, had undertaken this clearance in a grove of sacred serpents, and by implication had died in punishment for this socio-religious dereliction. His charred corpse is subsequently revived and his person divinised through the power of this last named Vayanāṭṭu Kulavan, and the two deities then proceed around the country as a stock pair, the one apotheosised for his hunting in and despoiling the offerings of a sacred grove, the other for putting another such grove to the torch for a swidden.

These and many other *teyyam* deities celebrate more directly incidents or movements of lower caste or tribal resistance to upper caste domination. Individual instances are those like the divinised forest colonist of the Maṇiyāṇi caste who was murdered by one of his untouchable labourers in the fields, or like the famous Poṭṭan, who was an untouchable notable put to death in the highlands when he volubly and openly defied the behavioural norms and ideology of caste. At a more collective level, the earlier mentioned Muttappan is also reported to have led tribal rebellions in the hilly regions of Kōṭṭayam and Vayanāṭu against the oppression of its overlords. Similarly, after the demonic Kuṭṭiccāttan was put to death by his Brahman foster father, his spirit, through his possessed mediums, continued to be responsible for wide-spread looting, arson, and murder in upper-caste settlements in the highlands.

The Social Implications

With the last part of this paper I have shifted further away from the forest and its resources *per se,* towards the often conflicting social interests that converged on these resources. Indeed, the emphasis of the *teyyam* songs and mythology does seem to be as much concerned with social contests as with natural ones, and I hope this essay has shown how little there may have been historically in the 'Hindu' culture of traditional Kerala society that mandated any particular restraint or harmony in the relations with nature. It is my thesis that such a restraint was probably environmentally unnecessary, or was, at any rate, not perceived as necessary. To the extent that any sort of pre-modern ecological 'balance' existed in traditional highland Kerala, I think it was because resources were plentiful, population was relatively sparse, the technologies of exploitation and transport rudimentary, and because there were few traditional incentives for the intensification of resource extraction much beyond the needs of subsistence.[39] On the other hand, the express cultural values of society towards nature as viewed through religious beliefs and institutions reflect exactly the kind of antagonisms we might expect to be generated in a social order predicated on a coercive caste hierarchy underwritten by armed dominance. Rather than nature somehow informing the caste system with its supposed ecological imperatives, the convergence of socially created and conflicting human interests on the resources of the forest is more likely to have informed this society's view of nature. To the extent that nature herself may have provided the raw symbolic material for this socially informed world-view, my sources from Kerala seems to confirm Paul Greenough's thesis (1992) that we have too long ignored the real and present danger from forest animals in shaping Indian views of nature. I would add, though, that this stuff of natural experience is itself thematically

---

[39] Paul Hockings suggests, however, that even under the pre-modern regimes of swiddening practised by tribals and migrant Badagas in the Nilgiris, extensive tracts of forest were burned over and transformed into grasslands for agriculture (1980: 45-69). This suggests that we may need to be more cautious in our discounting of colonialist complaints on the destructive impact of swiddening. Buchanan [1870 (1807), vol. 2: 197ff.] attributed the lateritic wastes in our region to depletion from swidden practices. His testimony and that of other travellers may need to be reconsidered, despite their political agendas.

elaborated within a socially driven complex of armed dominance, warfare and blood sacrifice that survives as a central paradigm of popular religion down to the present.[40] This historically long-lived social order, informed by a figuratively predatory model of caste, has perhaps been naturalised by being read as the logic of the cosmos and of nature itself.

Lastly, in recognition of the value of those authors whom I seem to critique, let me say that my intention is not to take issue with the highly destructive regime of forest depletion inaugurated under colonial rule, or its devastating legacy in terms of a despoiled environment and inherently conflicted policy. I am rather suggesting that for social scientists, this issue needs to be kept discrete from the actual attitudes and practices otherwise held by those we study, since these attitudes and practices ought to be a matter of direct enquiry through historical, folk-loric and anthropological investigation. My hope is that the present study might provide an example of one such attempt.

I also have no intention of undermining what I regard as the critical imperative to preserve and to restore India's forest resources, wherever this is socially feasible, in light of current ecological understanding and through marshalling popular support. As an anthropologist, however, I hope to have shown that at least in the case of this particular region, such ecological projects cannot be legitimately construed as drawing upon or returning to some well-spring of folk-wisdom or religious belief for their inspiration or public appeal. To the extent that there is an increasing ecological awareness in Kerala, it derives in my experience not from a mystical legacy of Hinduism, but from the common-sense perceptions of an observant people that under the social and material technologies of capitalist development, they do indeed have the capacity to undermine and destroy the sustainability of their environment in a very short time. Most of those living by agriculture today in northern Kerala have borne witness to the rapid course of their landscape's transformation, and an increasing number of them at the official, intellectual, and popular level wish to bring a halt or even a reversal to this process.

---

[40] Roy Ellen (1993) has shown how even those 'natural' classificatory activities in relatively primitive subsistence interaction with the biotic environment are fundamentally informed by the social interests of actors. This seems even more to be the case at the level of broader cultural typifications and value schema that I have attempted to treat here.

The question in my mind thus becomes whether the theme of restoring a supposedly lost and distinctively Indian eco-wisdom, implicated as it is in dubious reconstructions of 'Hindu' values and caste, will prove either necessary, desirable or effective in marshalling the political will and support needed to implement ecologically sound policies for the future. My sense is that in Kerala, such myths will hold less weight with the general populace than they might with academics.

6

Forests in Garhwal and the Construction of Space

Antje Linkenbach

Introduction[1]

The Himalayan forests came world-wide into focus in the course of the environmental debate, which gained momentum in the late seventies in academic circles as well as in the general public. Himalayan forests were recognised as an endangered part of the natural world which needed to be saved from total destruction because of their stabilising capacity within the whole Himalayan ecosystem and because of their importance as provider forest for the local subsistence-oriented communities. Local struggles for forest protection like the Chipko movement in Garhwal and Kumaon received widespread international prominence. In explaining people's involvement in the forest-related struggle many authors stressed the special commitment of the hill population, especially women, to their forests: it was argued that religious and economic linkages, as well as biological dispositions in the case of women, lead to a feeling of affection and responsibility and to a conservationist attitude.

One of the central problems in scientific as well as in public discourses on Indian forests is that descriptions of people's relation to their forest are often marked by generalising statements and assertions and are not based on concrete and detailed research. It seems

[1] This is a revised version of a paper presented at the Forest Panel of the 13th European Conference on Modern South Asian Studies, Toulouse, 31 August to 3 September 1994. It is based on field research in Garhwal (District Uttarkashi and District Chamoli) conducted in 1993-96 and financed by the German Research Foundation, Bonn. I thank all those who contributed to my research, especially J. S. Chauhan who was my research assistant, and Martin Fuchs, who partly joined me during my field research, for discussions and critical comments while writing this article.

especially problematic that such *a priori* generalisations are adopted in debates on modernisation since they act as guidelines for developmental strategies and practices. Here I address two inter-related questions: In what ways do people relate to their forest? How can these be analysed and how can they be represented? But first I consider some of the (epistemological) dangers and difficulties inherent in a 'traditionalist' and 'textualist' attempt to re-construct the agents' original relationship with their forest.

The Relation between People and Forest— a Question of Ontology?

> (Forests) have always been central to Indian civilisation. They have been worshipped as Aranyani, the Goddess of the Forest, the primary source of life and fertility, and the forest as a community has been viewed as a model for societal and civilizational evolution (Shiva 1988: 54).

> The forest thus nurtured an ecological civilisation in the most fundamental sense of harmony with nature (Shiva 1988: 55)

These quotes epitomise Vandana Shiva's characterisation of the basic relationship between human beings and forests in India. In her approach the forest is a sacred and providing space, a place for religious contemplation; it is associated with a harmonious life, with people's capacity to merge intellectually, emotionally and spiritually with the rhythms and patterns of nature. Shiva argued that the knowledge about the forest was not only the subject of the *Aranyakas* or forest-books (which are part of the ancient Vedas), but also of the everyday beliefs and practices of tribal and peasant societies. Because nature is considered as a female principle[2] women have a specially close relation to it; consequently they show a particular responsibility and nurture a conservationist attitude towards the forest. This affective relationship is challenged by the patriarchal project, expressed in modern (colonial and post-colonial) sciences and economics. The Chipko movement is Shiva's central case.

Several shortcomings can be discovered in Shiva's approach. She deduces the special nature of the relationship between humans and forest from Sanskritic texts and claims their validity for everyday life

---

[2] The word translated as nature is *prakriti*. It is 'an expression of Shakti, the feminine and creative principle of the cosmos' (Shiva 1988: 38).

in all parts of India, for all communities, for the past, the present and the future. She argues for an ontological opposition between men and women and attributes to each certain patterns of thinking and acting, valid for all times. The relation to the forest and the relation to nature are made equivalent: forest acts as *pars pro toto*. Traditional ways of life guided by the feminine principle are predefined to be in harmony with nature, while modern ways of life following the patriarchal project are seen as nothing but destroyers of nature.

Shiva's essentialist argument obviously does not aim to grasp the particular relations people have developed to their environment at a certain place and at a certain time. Moreover it serves as a pseudo-scientific foundation (legitimation) to push the environmental issue, and especially women's role in it, onto the most general level. I do not want to deal with Shiva's argument more intensively.[3] What is more interesting is that from the same Sanskritic texts to which she refers when drawing her picture of harmony between humans and forest, the *opposite picture* can also be deduced.

Indologists, also working on a general conceptual level, have shown that the dichotomy of *grāma* (village) and *aranya* (forest) is omnipresent in the Vedic literature: 'Le *grāma* et *l'aranya* se partagent la totalité du monde habitable' (Malamoud 1976: 4). It is discussed as a duality between wilderness and civilisation, nature and culture and so has the status of a basic, fundamental opposition. According to this concept, forest always remains *outside*, distanced and more or less detached from the sphere of human praxis. The relationship between forest and people, nature and culture is not described as a state of harmony but rather as a state of tension and ambivalence.

The basic opposition remains undisputed, though a closer look at the old texts allows one to question the seemingly static character of the relationship between the two zones, or, as Sontheimer would have it, to see it as a 'continuum' (Sontheimer 1987: 128, 164). Malamoud and Sprockhoff take up another conceptual pair, namely that of *vana* (forest) and *ksetra* (fields, inhabited space). Often *vana* and *ksetra* are used in the Sanskritic texts as equivalents to *aranya* and *grāma*, but Malamoud and Sprockhoff argue that there is evidence that the interpretation of *vana* and *aranya* as equivalents and synonyms can be

---

[3] Shiva's approach reflects an extreme position and has been heavily criticised (see, e.g., Bina Agarwal 1992), but nevertheless it has gained broad international publicity, especially in European feminist circles.

found only in late Vedic and post-Vedic literature.[4] Both draw
attention to the etymological origins of *vana* and *aranya* and their
usage in the earlier Vedic literature. They come to the conclusion that
both terms have different connotations. *Aranya*, translated as
wilderness, desert, sometimes also as forest, is linked etymologically
with *arana*—alien, distant; it is the dangerous, the frightening space,
inhabited by demons, wild animals, but also by brigands, it is the
space which one tries to avoid, it is linked with death. *Aranya* and
grāma appear as reciprocally exclusive categories. This is *not* the case
with *vana* and *kṣetra*: they *interact* with each other and this
interaction is seen as positive. *Vana* is the forest which supplies
villagers with timber for house construction and tools; here herbs and
wild plants are found, single trees may get special ritual significance
as *vanaspati* ('Lord of the trees', Sprockhoff 1981: 39). But the
boundaries between *vana* and *aranya* are fluid: the same space, which
was seen as *aranya*, as wilderness in previous times may become
vana, utilisable forest, or land for cultivation later.

The dualism of forest and inhabited area seems to constitute an
explicit form of conceptualising one's life world in religious,
economic and spatial aspects (see Sontheimer 1987: 127). The two
opposed but related zones apparently indicate the co-ordinates of at
least one way to structure cultural space.

Even though the recent Indological interpretation of the relevant
texts suggests a certain dynamic in the relation between forest and its
opposed 'other' the approach remains on a general (ahistorical) level
and does not relate the *conceptions* of forest to modes of social *praxis*.
Therefore we need a more *contextualised, relational perspective*:
forest should not be talked about as an abstract category. Instead one
should look at forests in a particular region and time to which
particular communities relate in their social praxis. Accordingly, the
relationship between people and forest has to be analysed and
described in its *specificity, complexity and processuality*. And to do
this properly one has to concentrate on the perspective of the social
actor him- or her-self. To put the question in that way means also to
ask whether forest is a central category for organising space in the

---

[4] As a non-Indologist I refer only to secondary sources in which the
authors have systematically dealt with the dichotomy of forest and village
(*vana, aranya* and *kṣetra, grāma*): see Malamoud 1976; Sontheimer 1987;
Sprockhoff 1981 and 1984.

imagination of villagers. How far does the dualistic construction of space known from the Sanskrit tradition meet with a lived reality?

Recent discussions of space in human geography and in the social sciences—starting from different theoretical assumptions—try to conceptualise space as a social category.[5] In particular, anthropological approaches challenge a static and passive conception of space. Instead of relating space simply to the situatedness of practices, to see it only as 'container' for action, they concentrate on the 'social construction of the spatial through both discursive and non-discursive practices' (Low 1994: 47). The concept of cultural construction of space includes some important analytical premises, which I will summarise briefly:

(1) Priority is given to the viewpoint of the social actors, vested with agency and interpretative capacity.
(2) Individuals and/or collectivities in (or relating to) one locality are recognised as having different *landscapes* of action and interpretation; acting and interacting with and within these landscapes as well as transforming them by performing different

[5] So-called postmodern geography points out that increasing globalisation in the modern world has helped reciprocally to increase the significance of the *local* and the *different* (locality, local identity). To cope with this complex situation the interdependence of place, culture and sociality has become one focus of research. Such an approach asks for an interdisciplinary perspective, and recent debates in the social and cultural sciences gained importance in the context of postmodern geography, especially debates which concentrate on hermeneutics and on the theory of action (see Jackson 1989, Rodman 1992).

Clifford Geertz, one of the main representatives of contemporary cultural anthropology, has stressed the hermeneutic aspect of social praxis ('culture as text'): to see the world as an always already interpreted, meaningful world (see Geertz 1973). Whereas Geertz favours a monolithic view of culture, recent discussions focus on a perspective which sees culture as more pluralistic or fragmented, where the emphasis is laid upon a variety of interpretations, relating to the perspectives of different social actors.

The revision of the concept of culture is related to modern sociological theories of action, which build upon the concepts of agency and social interaction as processes of structuration. Giddens strongly stresses the relevance of time-space relations 'inherent in the constitution of all social interaction' (Giddens 1979: 3), focusing on the different perspectives of various agents managing and controlling one *locale* or *setting* in their everyday interactive practices, bringing into view power relations and struggle.

contextualised practices (religious, economic, social), in which special places get importance; and having different and sometimes conflicting *perspectives* which are linked with these practices. [6]

(3) The different landscapes and perspectives are negotiated in the field of social interaction and in this negotiation process dimensions of power and control come to the fore.

Forests in the Local Praxis: The Multidimensionally Appropriated and Meaningful Domain

From an observer's point of view the landscapes of social action and interpretation of the hill people of Western Garhwal are diverse. They are composed of the village with its different internal regions, the fields, the forest and the pastures, the hill tops, but also the neighbouring villages and—dependent on the mobility as well as on the geographical, social and religious horizon of the village people— the more or less distant localities of cities, villages of the affinal kin, sites of pilgrimage and religious festivals. Forest is only one part of the landscape but, I presumed, a central one. As I aimed to con-centrate on the ecological crisis and people's perception of it, my fieldwork was guided by the idea of learning about people's relationships to the forest. Having read about the Chipko movement I started with the strong premise that villagers in Garhwal relate in very basic and essential ways to their forest. I also expected people to have an explicit or at least implicit discourse on that issue. To avoid misunderstandings: I did not intend—as is the case in cognitive anthropology— to collect the mental maps of individuals describing their individual landscapes of action. What I was interested in was to learn about any discourses (including probable counter-discourses), interpretations or narratives which guided activities in regard to the forest and which might also show how forest plays a central role in the spatial conceptualisation of the world. I considered that the best way to approach the issue was to focus on the *practices* of local people. Taking the dichotomy of forest and inhabited space as a heuristic model I tried to find out how far the forest is a cultural appropriated

---

[6] 'Landscape' is used as another category which indicates a cultural interpreted and appropriated space, although it is less experiential from an individual point of view. Landscape 'tends to be something more external and objective than our personal sense of place; and something less individual, less discrete, than the usual named place' (Meinig 1979: 3).

and significant space. Here, by appropriation I refer not only to economic practices, but also to social and mental appropriation in
different forms of praxis *and* interpretation.

In the following I discuss primarily a village (and its surrounding
region) in western Garhwal, where I lived during my field research.
The village, to which I give the pseudonym Nakoli, is located at an
altitude of about 2200 metres in the hills of Rawain. It is surrounded
by well terraced fields and comparatively dense forests of oak, pine
and spruce which mark (at the moment) the boundary of the cultivated
and inhabited area. Agriculture and animal husbandry are the main
sources of livelihood, with cash crops (apple, potatoes) playing an
important and increasing role for income generation. Nakoli is
inhabited by Harijans and Rajputs.[7] According to their lore the
dominant Rajput clans migrated into the area 8-9 generations ago. On
arrival, they met with other groups, who are believed to be the
ancestors of today's Harijans.

In the perception of the local people forest is the land outside the
village which is covered mostly with trees and shrubs of different
varieties and in varying density. Whereas fields and other cultivated
places are distinguished by names, forest is the space without a special
name, it is just forest (*jangal* or *vana*).[8] But certain places in the
forest—clearings used as grazing ground, *bugyals* (high altitude
meadows), cross-roads, peaks, sacred places around a temple—are
also named and so a greater closeness and significance seems to be
indicated. The boundaries of the forest that is perceived by the
villagers as their own are known to a certain extent and can be
indicated, at least by some members of the community. But the forest
area as a whole is of less relevance for the villagers in their everyday
activities: in different contexts and times (seasons, but also historical
times) different parts of the forest were and are relevant for different
actors. Additionally, forest is always a *shared* space: no community
enjoys exclusive rights and access. It is primarily shared with other

---

[7] One of the remarkable features of the settlement pattern in this area is
that Brahmans and Rajputs preferably live in separate villages, together with
Harijans. Harijan is the term the respective *jatis* themselves as well as the
other inhabitants of the region use as a cover term. *Dom*, the term which is
more usual in anthropological literature, is seldom used by the villagers
because it is seems more pejorative.

[8] The classical meanings of *jangal* are discussed by Zimmermann (1986).
Dove (1993) describes how the term is used in everyday life in Pakistan.

human beings (those of one's own as well as neighbouring villages), who use and appropriate certain parts of the jungle. It is also shared with non-human beings: animals, gods *(devtas)*, evil spirits *(matri, bhutas)*, who normally occupy those more dense and remote parts of the forest which are at higher altitudes. The forest also has had to be 'shared' with paramount political institutions, who claim access to it, control and regulate the local appropriation.

Forest seems to be meaningful not as a concept or as an abstract idea, but as the real forest, the forest that people are surrounded by and which they appropriate in their everyday life; they refer to it as *hamāra jangal* ('our forest'). When relating to their forest by acting, interpreting, talking, they relate to it as a bundle of significations. Every single practice is implicitly or explicitly overdetermined by other meanings. But for the purposes of representation one has to split the interrelated praxis into isolated segments. So people appropriate their forest in ways which can be *analytically* grouped according to the observer's perspective: the forest is meaningful as economic, symbolic (religious), political, gender-related space, also as 'free' space and, in recent times, also as space for leisure time activities (space for recreation).

Forest as an Economic Space

Forest is a setting for subsistence activities. As far as production and reproduction are concerned the hill economy depends on the forest which provides fuel, fodder (leaves, pasture) and fertiliser (dry leaves). In certain other communities herbs for medical purposes are collected as well as wild vegetables, fruits, mushrooms. Local timber is used for house construction and agricultural instruments. The forest is frequented by men, women and children (of all status groups); here regularly-used paths and cattle tracks as well as a few temporarily used stables *(chanis)* are to be found.

According to the seasonally varying tasks the places in the forest which are economically significant also vary. For example, a woman intending to collect firewood or lop a tree for fodder goes to the oak forest, and she prefers the most nearby parts to keep the walking distance with a heavy load as short as possible; for collecting litter for the animals she will go to a mixed jungle of oak, pine and rhododendron. A man looking for firewood normally takes a mule and will bring in larger pieces from more distant parts of the jungle; if a tree for house construction is needed he will move to higher altitudes to fell a cedar or a silver fir. For the grazing of the animals different parts of the jungle are frequented according to the seasonal change (e.g., oak forest in spring, *bugyals* in the rainy season).

Until recent times the hill population in Nakoli and the surrounding villages probably did not put too great a strain on the resources. This was possible partly because the population was low, partly because people explicitly cared for the regeneration of the commons (e.g., by collectively extinguishing forest fires, lopping techniques that allowed the trees to regain foliage, and by cautious clearing of forest land for cultivation). The economic use was interrelated with symbolic practices; for example villagers said that in former times people used to ask one of the main local deities [*Baukhanaga*, god of the hills (*pahāron ka devta)*, associated with water and forest] for permission before felling a tree. They burned some incense (*dhup*), fixed a coin (as *tikha*) and sometimes also a ribbon on the tree growing next to the one they intended to fell, and by doing so people recognised the god's supreme right to the forest. But besides the respect people showed to the forest, it was recog-nised as something to which humans had legitimate access and which had to give way to human settlements and agricultural land. Accordingly the borderline between forest and field has always been flexible and the cutting of trees has to be seen as a 'traditional' practice.

Regarding all this it seems that 'traditionally' people's relation to the forest in the context of subsistence production was a relation characterised by a certain ambivalence and tension: a pragmatic, instrumental attitude combined with a preserving ('ecological') one, primarily rooted in social responsibility; additionally it was interwoven with a symbolic dimension which led to a an overall *attitude of respect* towards the forest, forestalling its exploitation and unnecessary destruction.

The balance between instrumentalism and preservation is a precarious one and can be disturbed easily. At the end of this essay I will argue that the instrumental view, though always existent, seems to have gained predominance in the last decades, with many consequences for the forest.

Forest as Symbolic Space

The religious significance of the forest discloses itself to the observer through the places which are meaningful in the religious landscape of the villagers. Approximately 150 metres above the village the hills form a saddle, where a temple is located, faced by a huge cedar tree (*deodar*). In 1993/94 this marked the northern upper borderline of the inhabited and cultivated space and from here paths run in different directions into the adjoining forest. These paths are normally used by people when they go for firewood and fodder as well as on their way to neighbouring villages and to the Yamuna river valley. Here, as well as at similar cross-roads, travellers used to pay reverence to local deities to secure safety on the road by inserting coins or fixing ribbons on certain trees or bushes. The forest is not only inhabited by wild animals, but also by demons and evil spirits (*bhuta*, *matri*) who try to harm human beings and therefore need to be controlled by more powerful deities.

Three main local deities are worshipped in the region. Each god occupies a village temple, but two of them, *Baukhanaga* and *Ludeshwara*, own an additional temple, located on thickly wooded hill-tops amidst the jungle. The forest temple is only used occasionally and local Brahmins explained that the deities would prefer to stay permanently in the forest temple, but because they need daily worship (*pujā*) performed by a Brahmin priest, they (are forced to) live in the village. The forested hill tops, so the Brahmins say, are the favourite abodes of the deities because they are clean and calm, therefore just the opposite of the village, which is dirty and noisy. But apparently the high altitude is especially associated with purity and calmness, the forest only providing an additional quality. Each god is brought to his forest temple only for the annual fair, which is a highly appreciated festival and visited by thousands of people of the surrounding region. On this occasion the deity demonstrates its power by possessing one of the Brahmin priests (the one who is chosen by the god as his *mali*[9]), creating a nearly ecstatic atmosphere, in which other subordinate spirits also may appear in human beings. Many stories show how each of the gods controls his forest area: he punishes wrongdoers, but mostly helps men against evil spirits or wild animals, grants water, shows the right way to people who get lost on their journeys and who proved themselves as real devotees of the deity.

In case of *Ludeshwara-devta* a strong relationship between ritual and politics is symbolised in the forest area. In front of the forest temple of *Ludeshwara* is a platform which traditionally was used as a

---

[9] In the Pahari language of western Garhwal and the neighbouring parts of Himachal Pradesh *mali* denotes a priest, possessed by the god.

place for the seat of the local *thokdar* (the political representative of the Raja of Tehri Garhwal), who also functioned as 'minister' (*wazīr*) of the deity.[10] According to J.-C. Galey, in the region of the former princely state Tehri Garhwal political networks were dependent on religious identification. Galey argues that the religious foundation of political power is inherent in the constitution of royal as well as of local authority (Galey 1990). When acting as *wazīr* of the local deity and when occupying the platform in front of the temple the *thokdar* claims his political rights mediated through his religious authority. Elders described a rivalry between the local *thokdar* and one from a neighbouring *patti* (an administrative unit), whose inhabitants also worship *Ludeshwara-devta*. The other *thokdar* equally claimed his right to sit on the platform (i.e., to underline his political supremacy by religious authority), which was in the end granted to him.

A connection also exists between the cult of the Pandavas and the forest, which seems to be the space where Pandavas have a special affinity and can exert a special control. Pandavas are worshipped as divine ancestors by the Rajput clans in Garhwal. In some of the western parts (especially in the area of Bangan between the rivers Tons and Pabar) an epic tradition of *Mahabharata* is still alive, but elsewhere in the region different forms of *Pandavalila*, dramatic performances from the life of the five Pandava brothers and their wife Draupadi, are celebrated.[11] Around Nakoli people show the Pandava *nrtya* (dance of the Pandavas), mostly in short performances which can be seen on several occasions all around the year and where people get possessed by individual brothers of the Pandavas (Arjuna and Bhima preferably when I was around) or by Draupadi. Harijans as well are involved in the Pandava worship, and men from this group get possessed by *bana-devta*s. The identity of a *bana-devta* is unclear: some think of it as *vana-devta*, a deity living in the forest, who meets and helps the Pandavas in their forest exile; the more likely explanations which the local villagers and especially the Harijans

[10] A *wazīr* has to look after the 'finances' of the deity, he is responsible for the organisation of the god's journeys (*yatra*) and in former times was expected to accompany him. In each of the cases of the two main deities in the research area a Rajput from an influential lineage functions as *wazīr*.

[11] In Bangan local versions of *Mahabharata* are recited by local bards. One elaborated version, the *Panduan*, was recorded, translated and interpreted by C. P. Zoller (1996). For the tradition of *Pandavalila* see, e.g., Sachs (1991).

themselves give, refer to the meaning of *bana* as an arrow, which is interpreted as a symbol of strength and power (*shakti*). In this version a Pandava and his *bana-devta*—which then is synonymous with his *shakti*, his mental and physical strength—are seen as a symbiotic unity.

The most outstanding Pandava ritual is *Navratra* (in 1993 it took place in November), where Pandava dances continue for nine nights. Every second year on the eighth day the Pandavas and the *bana-devta*s proceed through the jungle to the bank of the Yamuna on a night's journey. Here they meet with other Pandava-groups from neighbouring villages, fires are lit and they dance for several hours in the light of the flaring flames. Then, in the first glimmer of the dawn, they dip their weapons in the holy river Yamuna. On their night journey through the forest the Pandavas pass several villages, where they dance for a short while, then receive and eat pure food and fruits (*ghī*, yoghurt, apples, walnuts). On the last day of the whole ritual the Pandavas spend half the day outside the village at the edge of the forest, where they prepare and eat *khir* (rice cooked with milk); afterwards they return to the village and the great 'finale' starts. Scenes from the life of the Pandavas are performed: in 1993 the main scene showed the hunting of a *gainda*.[12]

One more example shows the Pandavas' relatedness to the forest and their special capacity to control the negative powers inhabiting it. Amidst the dense oak forest a big stone is hidden in the undergrowth facing the village from the northern hills. From this spot a direct line could be drawn to the top of the village temple. People believe that the area surrounding the stone is full of danger because it is the dwelling place of evil spirits and of wild animals. The stone itself is said to have the potential to destroy the whole village or at least to threaten its inhabitants seriously. Only the Pandavas and their *bana-devta*s are vested with the power to control the bad energies of that stone. At regular intervals, but especially when the villagers face certain problems (illness, natural hazards), Pandavas and *bana-devta*s move into the forest taking with them a big iron nail (*khil*). Having

---

[12] For a discussion of the hunting of the *gainda*, which is a common motif in folk literature and drama not only in Garhwal see Zoller 1994. People also told me that in other years the ritual was more elaborated. For example, villagers masked as animals entered the scene. But generally the performance is only accompanied by drumming, neither songs are sung nor texts are recited.

reached the stone they try to drive the nail into it, each Pandava and *bana-devta* giving one blow. Rusty, half-broken nails fixed in the chinks of the stone as well as traces of the powerful hammer blows testify to the continuous and obviously successful efforts of the Pandavas to protect the village and its inhabitants.

The forest is a space with strong symbolic expressiveness and in this special quality it is in a certain sense opposed to the village. It is linked with gods, spirits (helpful and dangerous ones) and the divine ancestors, the supernatural beings claiming and obtaining rights to at least parts of the forest. The opposition is best expressed by the sounds of the *dol*, the big drum which is beaten every day after sunset and in the first glimmer of the dawn to mark the boundaries of the village in order to keep the evil spirits out. Human beings not only have to share the jungle with non-humans, but the forest is also a space where humans are dependent on the guidance and benevolence of supernatural beings and interact with them. The symbolic power of the forest also plays a constitutive role for the political and social integration of the community. The forest is an important space for keeping up and strengthening the collective memory as well as for the stabilisation of identity for the different status groups.

Forest as 'Free' Space (or Backstage)

In his plea for the integration of space-time relations in the theory of human agency Anthony Giddens refers to the distinction of regions into front stage and back stage, which was first made by Erving Goffman.

> The spatial and social separation of back and front regions, as distinguished by Goffman ... can be connected in an illuminating way to practical consciousness and the operation of normative sanctions (Giddens 1979: 207).[13]

---

[13] Giddens gives several examples for behaviour of individuals in the back and in the front region on the lines of Goffman: 'Performances in front regions typically involve efforts to create and sustain the appearance of conformity to normative standards to which the actors in question may be indifferent, or even positively hostile, when meeting in the back' (Giddens 208). He refers to the difference of behaviour of workers in a shop-floor and in the office area; and he mentions slum areas of a city, which are 'hidden away' from the time-space paths of others living in the city (Giddens 1979: 206-19; 1984: 122-26). Gerald Berreman (1993) used the difference of back

Differentiating between front and back stage—i.e., the region with strong normative control, where people try to behave according to the dominant social norms and role expectations, and the region where these norms are temporarily repealed—is useful because in the hill villages of western Garhwal people's behaviour mirrors perfectly such a regionalisation. An important back stage for men is the 'hotel', where they can sit and talk, drink and smoke. For women there is no such an opportunity for retreat *within* the village.[14] In the village area women are under strong normative control, for example young women always are watched by their mothers-in-law and by other elders. So they enjoy working in the forest, because by going there they can withdraw from social control at least for some hours.[15] I accompanied the women into the forest many times; when going to the forest they first stop near the upper temple and wait for others, then they start together (the 'official' argument for going together is safety), talking, joking, laughing, singing. They usually take care not to be accompanied by men. On the way, during and after work they rest, smoke *bidis* and if available eat some groundnuts or roasted rice. Songs, jokes and talks are often provocative and teasing. Difficulties with husbands and mother-in-laws are freely communicated to female friends in the forest. Girls sometimes also use their forest-work to gain an opportunity to meet and gossip with each other, so they avoid going together with the elder women. All in all, besides the heavy work females have to carry out in the jungle, the forest is a space of secrecy, joy and relaxation, where for a limited time-span one can disappear from the sight of other village people and behave more freely.[16]

The forest also provides security and protection in times of conflict. The implementation of strict forest legislation under the reign

---

and front stage and reflects on his field experience in another part of Garhwal and especially the relation between anthropologist and his 'object'.

[14] During fieldwork my room also functioned as backstage or 'free space' for women and girls, and—due to my research assistant—sometimes in the evenings the kitchen was backstage also for young men.

[15] The normative difference between village and forest was mentioned by Sontheimer in analysing tribal practices as well as classical (especially Tamil) literature: 'From the point of view of the settled people ... the normal rules of social behaviour did not apply in the *vana*, ... there was a relative freedom in the *vana*, often associated in poetry and religion with eroticism' (Sontheimer 1987: 138).

[16] For the behaviour of women in the forest see also Krengel 1989.

of Narendra Shah (Raja of Tehri, 1919-46) resulted in the closing of the forests and the curtailment of formerly legitimate rights of access of the villagers and provoked serious conflicts between Raja and people especially in the *parganah* Rawain (see later). It is recorded that in those times village people withdrew into the safety of the jungle when persecuted by the king's officials.

During my research several times young men disappeared into the jungle for a couple of days after a serious quarrel. Having learned that the opposing party had consulted the local police the boys thought to escape any possible enquiry by diving into the jungle. In each case they silently returned after the police had left the village and sometimes after their families had paid a certain amount as a fine. Then nobody openly discussed the matter again.

Forest as Gender-related (Male) Space

Certain activities related to the forest are carried out exclusively by men. The most obvious 'male' activity in the forest is hunting. Even though hunting without a license is strictly prohibited today as it was from 1929 in the former Tehri State (Rawat 1989: 123), the practice is kept up in my research area and at least a few men who possess or have access to a gun go for a hunt sporadically. Successful hunters were and still are highly respected persons of whom co-villagers talk with pride. Previously as well as today hunting is a good opportunity to get meat—and most probably it also carries on the Kshatriya tradition: by hunting men can prove themselves as true Rajputs. According to local villagers, after the ban on hunting in 1929, Raja Narendra Shah granted, to his subjects living in villages situated in higher altitudes, one hunting-day per year. People had to apply officially for that day before, and after a successful hunt they had to provide one leg of the prey to the local forest ranger. This very day, I was told, was celebrated as a festival (*airi*). The male population of the village set out for hunting, and animals were allowed to be killed only with the *dangra* (a battle-axe) to demonstrate individual bravery. After a successful hunt festivities started in the village, especially if a tiger had been killed. After independence the hunting-day was prohibited.[17]

---

[17] Villages in lower regions were not allowed to celebrate *airi*, they met for a fishing festival, *maun* (fishing also was prohibited in 1929; Rawat 1989). Whereas the *airi* was stopped after independence, *maun* is still celebrated and I participated in it during my fieldwork. The difference

The strong hunting tradition is also indicated by the existence of a hunter's temple *(sikhar mandir)* in the village of my research. The temple is visited frequently and after a successful hunt men may offer, for example, the horns of the dead deer. The temple is dedicated to a divine hero, formerly a Rajput boy, who died very young in the forest after he had hunted and killed a large number of forest animals.

Another male activity related to the forest is *pabin*, a *puja* carried out only by Rajput men in the month of *baisakh* (April/May). The worship is dedicated to *Baukhnaga*, the local god related with the forest. The men stay overnight in the forest near the temple without eating, women are not allowed to participate because of the danger of possession, mental disturbance or being killed by the *matri*. The forest, although a space for female activities as well, holds many dangers for women and girls. Non-human beings like wild animals and spirits, dwelling and roaming in the forest, cannot be controlled by them. Therefore females have to avoid especially the dense forest and should not stay in the jungle at night.[18]

Forest as Area of Recreation

To experience a landscape primarily focusing on its aesthetic qualities seems quite unusual for villagers. It is not that they are unable to appreciate a delightful scenery but, taking the case of the forest, its beauty cannot be seen detached from its role in everyday life as well as in the religious conceptions. Only recently a different perspective is slowly developing: a few younger and educated people, born in Nakoli or surrounding villages but now studying or living and working in local small market towns or in the district capital, have started to enjoy the forest as space for vacation and recreation. Individual young men or even girls (mostly college students) go trekking and mountaineering, young married couples on a visit in the girl's home may spend some hours walking and also having a picnic in the forest accompanied by friends and relatives.

---

between *maun* and *airi* may indicate two different ecological zones: one, where villagers in their whole life-style are more oriented to rivers and valleys, and one where they are oriented to high altitude and forests.

[18] A woman coming from the forest is not allowed to look at a small child less than three months immediately after her return; she has at least to sit briefly near the fire before approaching the child. An evil spirit may have accompanied her silently and unnoticed and might try to harm the baby.

Those people often have a certain ecological awareness in the current sense. They have heard about the stabilising functions of the forest in nature's economy and about the danger of deforestation, some came into contact with NGOs engaged in certain forms of ecodevelopment and talk in a more sophisticated language arguing for forest conservation and against tree felling.

The Local Concept of Space and the Role of the Forest

I will now turn from social practices related with the forest to discuss the social significance of the forest, and ask how far it plays a crucial role in the spatial conceptualisation of the world.

Three things struck me most during my fieldwork in respect to people's relation to the forest. Firstly, the local villagers obviously cut their forest (although in a comparatively moderate way) to prepare new agricultural fields for cash crops. Ideas and concepts of forest protection as well as activities like the Chipko movement are either unknown or are treated with indifference or even hostility. Secondly, despite the importance of forest in daily life as well as in ritual I could find no explicit discourses focusing on the forest. In many stories the forest is referred to, but the forest itself is never the subject of these stories. The forest is known as the area where supernatural powers exist, but a forest has no supernatural quality itself nor is it vested with supernatural powers. Thirdly, from the practices of the local population one could infer an underlying concept of ordering space along the lines of village versus forest or human versus non-human space, but again the discursive praxis does not make it an issue. To sum up, the forest forms a vital and meaningful part of people's life-world but the forest does not have a special immunity nor is it a main point of reference in the representations and interpretative concepts of the local population.

In contrast, the discursive praxis suggests another spatial conceptualisation of the life-world. Instead of focusing on the relation between people and nature the spatial concept is constructed in terms of territoriality and power and thus lays emphasis on sociality. In this concept forest is just *part of the territory*, though a very essential part. It is necessary to concentrate briefly on this mode of constructing human space in order to understand why Nakoli people perceive and handle their forest in a certain way, and to understand how villagers react to the legal claims made by the state to the forest. In the following discussion I use individual and group discussions for information, interpretations and narratives of, many of them provided by members of the dominant Rajput lineages.

In the Nakoli area specific practices as well as discourses are related to territory and power. They deal with (historical) processes of land acquisition and settlement; relations with neighbouring villages and the political centre; and the ritual sphere and the realm of influence of the main local deities.

Nakoli apparently represents a place of junction of ritual and political activities in the region. Strong territorial identifications of the villagers exist but they differ not only according to the individual or group status but first of all with respect to social fields. The political geography and the religious geography of the villagers are not congruent: they are overlapping, joining into a dynamic concept of power, control and socio-ritual space.

Nakoli is located in the upper part of a valley carved out by a tributary of the Yamuna river in the hills of Rawain. Geographical landmarks as represented in collective memory provide the main patterns through which territory and boundaries are constructed *politically*. The imagined territory may be but is not necessarily congruent with contemporary administrative units. For example, the imagined territory of Nakoli includes a few villages which are today administratively and sociologically separate, but which are perceived as historically linked with or even dependent on Nakoli.

A densely forested mountain range helps to distance Nakoli spatially and politically from the neighbouring *patti* in the east and south-east. Differently, the northern borderline cuts through an existing administrative unit. The *patti* to which Nakoli belongs is seen as divided into two parts: *alli* and *palli* (this side and the other side). The perception is strengthened by the local geography. A mountain ridge which runs from east to west separates the villages located on the northern slope which gently falls away to the Yamuna Valley from those situated in the interior hills on the southern side. Despite social and political relations today as well as in recent history (the *patti* was an administrative unit already in the princely state of Tehri Garhwal), a territorial distance between the inhabitants of Nakoli area and those from the other side exists. In the south-west no geographical point can be used as a territorial mark. Here certain village and field names indicate a boundary, which can only be understood when listening to the narrative reconstructions of local history. Moreover, through these reconstructions the whole concept of territorial claim reveals itself immediately.

Local narratives of all status groups mention two brothers named *R* and *G*, who according to genealogical data (*vamsavali*) are the ancestors of the still dominant Rajput clan. They entered the area nine generations ago. The newcomers met resident shepherds and agriculturists who are considered to be the ancestors of today's Harijans. The Rajputs, who belong to the Panwar *jati* and who claim a relationship to the former kings of Garhwal, established themselves by defining a certain region with more or less clear territorial landmarks as their own—exactly the same as I tried to depict. The territory was densely forested and parts of that forest in different altitudes were cleared for cultivation. The legitimacy of this act of land acquisition is still questioned by the Harijans. They complain that their forefathers, as shepherds for longer periods far off in the jungle, have been expelled from parts of their land and socially become dependent on the dominant Rajputs.

R and *G* apparently enjoyed a central political role: they functioned as *thokdar* or *sayana*—the language of the villagers oscillates between the two terms—for the area they laid claim to. In the north, east and south-east separated by natural landmarks, the territory in the south-west ended where the realm of influence of two other *sayana*s (or *thokdar*s) began. An important issue in the narrations of the villagers is that *R* and *G* as well as *B* and *S* (the two other *sayana*s) from the neighbouring region had at their disposal a *hadi bedi*—a certain instrument of torture, which they could use for punishment in cases of minor offences. The official position of the *sayana* or *thokdar* and the power of jurisdiction in certain cases indicate that *R*, *G* and *B*, *S* apparently functioned as 'big men' and local power holders of the Raja of Garhwal in their area of control.[19]

[19] The narratives do not mention the time of the events. Genealogies and oral histories suggest that the land settlement occurred before the invasions from 1791-1804 of the Gurkhas from west Nepal. In those days the royal *Durbar* was located in Srinagar (Garhwal, now Pauri Garhwal District). In 1815 the Gurkhas were defeated and driven out by the British. Sudarshan Shah was installed as ruler of the area west of the Alakananda (except two *parganas*, one of them Rawain). The princely kingdom was named after the new capital, Tehri Garhwal. Rawain was ceded to Tehri Garhwal in 1824. A member of the royal family received a *jagir* of nine villages in the Yamuna

Whereas the political geography originates in the collective memory of an act of appropriation the key to the religious geography is continuous mobility: the deities of the region have to confirm their territory—which is at the same time their realm of influence and power—by moving around and visiting the villages included in it during the annual *yatra*. Three deities are of importance in the region, and according to the oral tradition each of them has his own history as well as his own place of origin. Their initial struggles for power resulted in a division of the region into different spheres of influence and in the hierarchisation of the gods along a model which allows them to relate as elder and younger brothers. Each god is worshipped as a main village deity by a certain number of different villages: only in Nakoli do the spheres of all three deities overlap.

In a most conspicuous way the religious spheres of the gods relativise the geographical boundaries drawn by political interests. If one roughly visualises the spheres of the deities as three concentric circles overlapping in Nakoli, each circle transcends the political boundaries of Nakoli and covers parts of the neighbouring region: *Baukhanaga devta* in the east, *Ludeshwara devta* in the west and *Daheshwara devta* in the south. So altogether the spatial concept of villagers in my area of research is perceived as a double one: the territory of socio-political relations and dependencies is transcended by the territories of ritually based solidarities. In a certain way religion joins what politics separates.[20]

How does the territorial concept of space relate to the specific way in which the local population of the Nakoli region deals with its forest? Three aspects seem of crucial relevance: forest is a vital part of the local socio-economic and cultural life; forest is part of a certain territory in which local political power is exercised or which is defined by religious solidarity; and the territorial perspective nourishes a certain feeling of regional autonomy.

As forest is part of a political or religious territory those who lay claim to the territory also lay claim to the forest. In this sense the right to control and to use the forest and the forest products is vested with the community. But this exclusive right of the community has been

---

valley under Raja Pratap Shah (1871-86) and he and his descendants (the last of them one of my informants, who died in 1995) functioned until 1949 as *thokdar* for the *patti* in which the village of my research is located.

[20] One example: the Brahmins who act as *pujāri* and as *purohit* in Nakoli come from the regions outside of the area of Nakoli.

challenged by the state and therefore the forests in Garhwal have become a *contested domain* in recent history. As a state monopoly the use of the forest is regulated by the state through forest legislation. Here is laid down how far forests can be commercially exploited and how far access can be granted to the local population. All the recent conflicts which have emerged around the forest and which became known under the label of ecological conflicts are primarily struggles for the right of management and control. Local communities see the forest as part of their territory and as essential basis of livelihood and try to defend this 'property' against the often exploitative and destructive grasp of the state. Local people call for the right to relate to the forest according to their own decisions—and this may result in conservation and pragmatic use but also in destruction of the forest.

In the following I develop this point by discussing how in Nakoli area the assumed legitimacy of forest access is defended against the demands of the state. First I concentrate on the Dhandak of Rawain, a historical uprising of the local hill people against the closing of forest by the Tehri Raja; then I return to today's practices to show how the claim for forest control and self-determined forest use finds expression in everyday life.

Forest as Contested Domain

The Dhandak of Rawain

In the princely state of Tehri Garhwal the ownership of the forest was vested with the king, but *de facto* control was exerted by the local village communities who obtained the customary right to use the forest as well as the forest products. When forests became a valuable good of high economic interest in the eighties of the last century this situation started to change.[21]

In the territory of Tehri State large parts of the forest had been leased by an Englishman, Frederick Wilson, for around 25 years from 1840 to 1865.[22] He extracted forest produce (musk, fuel timber, animal hides) and felled *deodar* and *chir* in the Bhagirathi Valley Forest and sold them to the British Railway Department. After the expiry of Wilson's lease the Raja of Tehri leased out the Gangotri

---

[21] The history of the territories of Tehri Garhwal and British Kumaon is documented in Guha 1983 and 1991; also Rawat 1989 and 1992; Pant 1922.

[22] Wilson's first name is mentioned only in Trivedi 1995: 156.

Valley, Tons Valley and the Shivpuri Forests to the British Government. The leases ended in 1885 and in 1925 respectively. By 1885 the Raja realised the commercial value of forests, and started to work and use his forests released by the British. In 1897 systematic forestry, following the British model, was started in Tehri State with the help of Pandit Keshva Nand. Under his control the best forests were demarcated and the access of village people was restricted. In 1908 the then Conservator of Tehri Garhwal State Forest, Pandit Ram Dutt Raturi, established an even more efficient system: the forests (proclaimed as state monopoly) were divided into the three categories of Reserved, Protected and Village Forest and severe restrictions minimised the customary rights of the local people. The closing of forest by legislation went along with the erection of boundary posts (*munarbandi*) and the control of forest areas by forest guards. In 1928/29 the Tehri Durbar engaged the services of Franz Heske from Germany as Forest Advisor of the State and a further even more restrictive management of the Forest was based mainly on his reports and advice.

The so called scientific forestry of Tehri State (which was legitimised by the preservation of forest including flora and fauna), de facto served commercial interests and led to exploitation and extensive felling of forests. The control of the forests by the Tehri Forest Department did not allow a *sharing* with local villagers, rather the forest became a space from which they were forcible expelled and alienated. The previously enjoyed customary rights of village people were simply erased, formerly legitimate practices (like cattle grazing or building of *chanis* in the forest, felling of trees for the preparation of agricultural instruments, etc.) turned out to be an infringement of law, provoking severe punishment. In the region of Rawain villagers did not tolerate the new forest policy but opposed it, resorting to a traditionally legitimised, non-violent means of protest, the *dhandak*.[23]

The *Dhandak of Rawain* (1929/30) is still present in the oral tradition of Nakoli and the other villages of both sides of the *patti* as well as in villages of the neighbouring *patti*s. I collected various local narratives dealing with the uprising, amongst them a version from Jot Singh Rawalta, village Kanseru. He is the son of Dayaram, one of the leading figures in the *dhandak*. Jot Singh's narrative, which he

[23] According to Guha, the main forms of protest in the *dhandak* are non-co-operation and protest marches to the capital; see Guha 1991: 67ff.

himself had also put down as a text, idealises the time of Raja Kirti Shah (1892-1913) and stresses the worsening of living conditions under his successor Narendra Shah.[24] Faced with the increasing unhappiness and discontent of the villagers, Jot Singh, the village heads and elders from the region founded a committee to mobilise the people as well as to co-ordinate the then emerging movement. As this committee was declared illegal by the state officials, its members chose a place near Lakhamandal (a very nearby village on the western bank of the Yamuna which belonged to the Dehra Dun *parganah*, British Garhwal) for their monthly meetings. One incident seems to be very lively in the collective memory. The villagers met in Barkot, collectively lodging a complaint with the state officials about the restrictions, and explaining that they needed the forest as grazing ground because the cattle was their main support. Divisional Forest Officer Padam Dutt Raturi answered: 'If you like, throw your cows and buffaloes down the hills and butcher your sheep and goats.' The sentence was perceived by the villagers as a severe disregard of their rights of subsistence. When the conflict escalated the Raja was on a journey to England and his officials were not interested in compromise with the villagers. The *dhandak* was crushed by military force on 30 May 1930 in Tilari, a level ground at the banks of the Yamuna River near Rajgarhi. In the tumult at least 33 men died, and a further 17 were seriously injured.[25]

The *dhandak* and its local representations are proof that the forest is highly esteemed as a nucleus of economic and cultural life and that access to the forest is seen as a customary *right* which cannot be withdrawn without provoking severe resistance. In the course of the movement people also succeeded in creating new solidarities by transcending existing or imagined political territories—probably also with the help of the religious links. Today inhabitants of the region repeat, not without satisfaction, that although the protest was suppressed with brutal force, at least some of their old rights had been re-granted to them by the Raja. The political target which had guided the *dhandak* was the restoration of previous conditions; it was not aimed at social or political transformation.

[24] I refer to the written version: *Tiladi goli kand ke sambandh me*, by Jot Singh Rawalta, Village Kanseru (received from the author in 1993).

[25] Jot Singh Rawalta provided the estimates of the number of people who died and were injured at *Tilari Maidan*.

Forest: A Space for Everyday Resistance?

After independence no major change occurred in the forest policy of India, which is usually recognised as an extension of the British model. Forests, predominantly seen as commercially valuable resources, remain a monopoly of the state. Administrative control is exercised by the Forest Department and appropriation rights of the village communities are limited by legislation.

When discussing forest as a contested domain in contemporary India one has to take into consideration not only the forest policy of the new Indian state but the processes of social and economic modernisation as well, which did not leave the hills and its people unaffected. After the Indo-China border conflict in the early sixties the formerly marginal Himalayan hill regions were increasingly seen as a natural borderline to China. In the following years the Indian state built a large network of roads and bridges, and installed electricity, predominantly to facilitate military operations. On the one hand the new infrastructure allowed the use of the forest resources of the Central Himalayas with a 'new aggressiveness' (Rawat 1991: 315) and the exploitation of forest wealth through commercial felling increased. On the other hand infrastructural measures facilitated the penetration of the market economy and the expansion of communication media. Even though this was a very slow process, the needs of the local population underwent changes. In areas where increasing market orientation and the growth of population met with an ongoing exploitation and degradation of the forests it obviously had a considerable negative effect on the local subsistence economy, leading to a high migration rate of the male population with all its consequences for the local social structures.

In parts of the Districts of Tehri and Chamoli the increasing exploitation of Himalayan forests by private contractors,[26] together with the severe restrictions which villagers had to face, resulted in open discontent of the population in the early seventies. The state was accused of misusing its supreme rights in the forest without taking sufficiently into consideration the economics of rural life. Especially in central and eastern Garhwal, Gandhian workers as well as political party activists succeeded in mobilising local villagers to save their forests from large-scale commercial felling. The tree-saving

---

[26] The private contractors bought their plots in public auctions held by the Forest Department.

activities—well-known as Chipko movement—had a clearly economic and political target: to stop exploitation by outsiders, to grant local people the *autonomy* to manage and to use their forests and the forest produce as well as to generate local employment. In the first years of protest forest *conservation* was not an issue, only later the ecological role of the forest came into the fore. The demand for management rights and forest use for local villagers was enriched and in course of time even superseded by the claim that forests need to be saved as a stabiliser of the sustenance-providing Himalayan eco-system.[27]

The Chipko movement created a general awareness of the ecological role of forests, which resulted in an alteration of the forest policy of the state. The Forest Conservation Act of 1980 introduced a ban on green felling for 15 years in all parts of Uttarakhand above an altitude of 1000 metres and an angle of 30° from 1981. But the new environmental policy of the state already seems to contain the seed for new conflicts, because interests in forest conservation and interests in local development could not be harmonised.[28] The local population feels that forest protection and an environmental sound policy are implemented at their expense, since these policies hinder what villagers perceive as life-improving projects. In their opinion, to give environment priority results in delaying or marginalising development projects like construction of roads and water pipelines, the implementation of income generating programs and marketing schemes. Many people of eastern Garhwal are critical of all attempts to tie them down to a so called 'traditional' life style and to deny them their legitimate share in modernisation in the name of ecology, especially when others are profiting.[29]

In Nakoli and the surrounding villages similar attitudes can be discovered. Strategies as well as discourses display a critical stance towards the ecologically instructed state forest policy and towards the

---

[27] For a discussion of the Chipko movement see, e.g., Weber 1988; Linkenbach 1994 and in press.

[28] See 'Has Chipko finished what it set out to do?' cover story in *Down to Earth*, 30 April 1993; also see Rangan 1993.

[29] This problem is discussed at more length in Linkenbach 1995. Local villagers are not simply captured by a blind desire to follow modern ways of life. On the contrary, they self-confidently want to select from its values and achievements according to their own needs. This will become clearer in the remaining part of this chapter.

environmental 'messages' spread by Chipko protagonists like Sunderlal Bahuguna. The actual practice of forest conservation is considered to cause severe injustice: besides the legal felling of dry trees illegal practices of commercial logging are still common, with the profit mostly flowing 'into the plains'. The forest policy is accused to work in favour of communities in lower altitudes (due to the logging moratorium of 1981), whereas the chance to use the forests for the sake of local development is denied to the population in higher altitudes.

In Nakoli region villagers had found their own way to participate in the ongoing process of modernisation and 'to improve' their lives. In order to get monetary resources they have started to grow apples, potatoes and peas as cash crops. Additional land is required especially to produce apples, so villagers claim the right to use the 'commons' (*panchāyat* forest, waste land, pasture) as a space of self-determined appropriation, which includes felling trees to acquire new fields. In principle to acquire land is possible for all families of the village, but whether it is done or not depends on social prestige and economic status, but not necessarily on formal caste membership. The strategy is based on a consensus of certain individuals and groups, including Harijans. Women also support the strategy and do not oppose it out of ecological sentiments.[30]

The cutting of the forest in Nakoli area has to be interpreted in a twofold way. On the one hand it serves local economic interests. Most villagers see growing cash crops on an extended agricultural expanse as the only way of earning money under the existing social and cultural conditions, and without too heavily affecting social structures and social life. Money is valued as the basic condition for 'standing on one's own feet', for gaining the strength and 'power' to work for the improvement of one's own family but also of village life. To show social responsibility for the future generations now also includes to

[30] Women are at best ambivalent. Cash cropping is a male activity and with its increase the production of 'traditional' agricultural crops may get devalorised; additionally it tends to concentrate monetary income in the hands of men. Women profit to some extent only if this money is used for household improvement, education, health care. In the long run cash crops will lead to differentiation within the local population cutting across the caste hierarchy. The inhabitants of villages which are located in the territory controlled by Nakoli and who therefore do not have direct access to the forest are most likely to be marginalised.

ensure a monetary income for oneself and one's heirs, so that they will survive in the market economy.[31]

On the other hand cutting the forest may be interpreted as a form of local protest against the prevailing forest policy which denies control and management of forests to the local population. By felling trees and cultivating new plots villagers try to demonstrate and to defend their customary rights to the forest, which they consider as a legitimate part of their territory. But at the same time such a praxis may be seen as a repetition of the initial act of land acquisition and therefore as a subtle way to lay claim to the territory based on a historical construction of space.

[31] The responsibility does not only apply to economic aspects, it includes also education, health care, and a say in political matters. The contemporary struggle for autonomy in Garhwal and Kumaon (Uttarakhand) should be seen in the light of responsibility as well.

7

People's Rights in a Bird Sanctuary: The Case of Bharatpur

Stig Toft Madsen

The Problem

What are the rights of people living close to one of the major protected areas in India, i.e., the Keoladeo National Park, also known as Ghana Bird Sanctuary or, simply, as Bharatpur? Prior to becoming a bird sanctuary, this area was used for hunting by the rulers of Bharatpur. Bharatpur, therefore, is one of the few places in which people's rights have been crystallised and circumscribed well before modern conservationist efforts were initiated. As Saberwal notes:

> [T]he best known, and most successful, of India's protected areas—Bharatpur, Dachigam, Gir, Kanha—were originally hunting preserves of the Maharajas of small princely kingdoms, and lacked substantial human populations to start with. Establishing these protected areas did not require the displacement of large numbers of people (Saberwal 1995).

The question remains, however, whether or not the park should meet some of the economic needs of the people living in its vicinity. If a national park should meet, at least to some degree, such needs, and if Bharatpur fails to do so, it may be said that the rights of the local people are violated. This is what Kalpavriksh, an environmentalist action group, has claimed. The question merits a more detailed analysis than I am able to provide. My aim here is restricted to identify the major parameters of the situation in terms of the rights and interests involved.[1]

---

[1] I gathered information for this case study during visits to Bharatpur in from 1977 onwards and in March 1993. I may have overlooked important persons and events during these short and informal visits. I would like to thank A. S. Brar, Siri Chand, Petri Hottola, Akbar Hussain, Bholu Khan, Sohan Lal, John Liep, Dhanajai Mohan and Raj Singh for help and advice.

In this paper I describe how the Indian state has succeeded in gradually establishing a hegemony of rights over the area. When the park was formally closed to grazing in 1982, however, a violent confrontation took place. In its aftermath, the Forest Department (FD) devised some modest, but significant, innovations to reach a working agreement with people living in the vicinity of the park.

In India, environmental policy-makers tend to view 'local communities' as well-defined and stable sets of local villagers. This view lies behind the forest act proposed by the Narasimha Rao Government in 1993 (see Kulkarni 1994). In the case of Bharatpur, this presumption is not entirely misplaced, but, as I shall show, the meaning of 'local communities' has expanded to include different sets of locals with evolving interests in the park.

History of the Park

The Keoladeo National Park is located in the eastern part of Rajasthan near the city of Bharatpur on the highway between Jaipur and Agra. It comprises just 29 square kilometres, but it is one of the world's best heronries, and a major wintering area for ducks and geese during which season the park hosts about 200,000 birds. A total of 369 species of birds have been identified in the park (see, e.g., Kumar 1992). The park is the only known wintering ground in India for the almost extinct western population of the Siberian Crane (*Grus leucogeranus*).

The natural vegetation of the area is dry deciduous savannah forest and rainfall averages 688 mm a year. Though the park is situated in a natural depression, this location is not sufficient to support the extensive wetlands which attract most of the birds. Instead, the wetlands are sustained mainly by human design.

Already by 1755 the Jat ruler of Bharatpur, Maharaja Suraj Mal, had constructed dikes and fenced the area to provide grazing land for buffaloes, and to protect agricultural crops from feral cattle (Pandya 1992). Feral cattle were a major problem. During periods of political instability they raided fields forcing agriculturists to turn pastoralists (Haynes 1992: 20-21). In 1795, the then ruler of Bharatpur decided to capture the 'woodland cattle' (*van gāy*).[2] Many were caught, domesticated and sold before it was decided to concentrate the remaining cattle in the extensive jungles which surrounded Bharatpur

[2] See Rackham (1990: 38-39) for the history of 'wild bulls' in Britain.

till the 1820s (Maan 1992). They seem to have survived there despite floods and carnivores.

Traditionally, Indian rulers had not considered duck-shooting a royal pastime. The advent of the British changed this, and in 1899 during the regime of Maharaja Kisan Singh, the area was turned into a duck-shooting preserve by Harbhamji, the administrator of the state (Ziddi 1984: 15). To attract more migratory ducks and geese, the habitat was developed by diverting the waters of two smaller seasonal rivers, Gambhir and Banganga, to a flood-control weir called the Ajan Bund.[3] The Ajan Bund is close to the sanctuary. Water is distributed from the dam through the main and some smaller canals into the eight sections of the wetlands from July onwards.

At present, additional water may also be led into the park from further away. The FD buys such water from the Irrigation Department. A total of 500 million cubic feet of water is required to create and maintain the wetlands. In recent years—especially after a drought in 1979—tubewells inside the park have yielded additional water to secure the survival of turtles, fish and smaller organisms in the dry season. Many of the breeding birds feed on these organisms, some of which are brought into the sanctuary by the canal water.

As the wet areas gradually dry out in the hot season, most birds leave the sanctuary, but the next good monsoon brings back thousands of birds to nest in the crowns of the Babul trees (*Acacia nilotica*) planted systematically on small mounds in the wetlands, or on the floating grasses and water lilies.

Transfer of Rights

In what follows I will concentrate on the developments in the 1980s, but it is worth noting that the recent phase is a part of a longer history of transfer of ownership and management from the local ruler, whose superior rights appear to have been strongly asserted to the FD in pre-colonial times.

The renowned ornithologist Salim Ali was the first to study the area in 1935 when it was still a very prestigious duck-shooting preserve of the Bharatpur Maharaja. The Indian royalty lost its

---

[3] Jain (1995) claims Ajan Bund was constructed by Maharaja Suraj Mal in 1760 to protect the town of Bharatpur. According to *The Statesman* (1991), the dam is less than fifty years old. Apparently, the dam has been constructed in stages.

political powers in 1947. The decline of the princely order encouraged anti-feudal forces in the state to press the demand that the reserve be opened to the farmers for agriculture, and that the waters in the area be utilised for farm irrigation. According to Salim Ali's own account, he got wind of this plan and together with two non-Indian ornithologists, a Quaker and the Chief Engineer of the army, he approached Jawaharlal Nehru, whom they all knew personally. 'It was', writes Ali, 'Jawaharlal's prompt and positive response that saved the teetering Ghana [Bharatpur] from the brink' (Ali 1985: 150). Within the FD, Kailash Sankhala worked to preserve the area, and in 1956 the area was notified as a sanctuary and transferred to the FD (Sankhala 1990: 118). This prevented the area from being converted into agricultural land, but the Maharaja retained shooting rights in the reserve as a part of the deed of transfer. Hunting was practically stopped in 1964 or 1965 after Salim Ali and others had coaxed the Maharaja to surrender his personal shooting rights. This completed the overall transfer of rights from the old order to the new.

In August 1981 the sanctuary was upgraded to a national park. This meant that people's rights in the form of concessions and privileges were to be reviewed. In practice the Government of India, which is always involved in the notification of a national park, often fails to settle claims before an area is formally declared a national park. In this case it appears that the FD did enter into negotiations with the surrounding villagers regarding their fodder requirements.[4] The Conservator of Forests (Wildlife) claimed that only 119 of the villagers grazing cattle in the area owned less than five *bighas* of land (Kalpavriksh 1986). The implication was that all others would be able to feed their cattle with products from their own fields. No agreement had been reached about established rights when the FD closed the park for grazing on 7 November 1982.

Clash over Grazing Rights

Villagers living outside the park apparently reckoned that the authorities would let the *status quo* continue, park or no park

---

[4] The population of the surrounding villages consists mainly of caste Hindus, such as Gujjars and Jats. The scheduled caste population mainly belongs to the Jatav or Chamar caste. The major caste-related political conflicts in the area occur between Jatavs and Jats, and between Jats and Rajputs. The number of Muslims in the area is small.

(Kalpavriksh 1986: 446). When it became clear that the FD meant business, a group of villagers immediately staged a confrontation to press their right to graze cattle in the park. According to official sources on the day the park was closed some 3,000-4,000 people from Aghapur, one of the nine villages bordering the park, broke through the closed Aghapur gate, led their cattle into the park, and surrounded police and forest staff.[5] After failing to control the crowd by teargas, the Assistant District Magistrate ordered the police to open fire on the legs of the protesting villagers, but to avoid shooting at women. Despite this order, six or seven people died either near the gate, or after the police entered the village itself. Among the dead, according to villagers, was a village priest. The villagers further claimed that they were arrested at the park headquarters when they were taking the wounded to the hospital, and that the wounded were left unattended. Apart from Aghapur, none of the other villages near the park seems to have openly protested the closure of the park.[6]

Legally, the FD could claim the authority to revoke grazing rights after the sanctuary had become a national park under the Wild-life Protection Act of 1972. As seen by Kalpavriksh, the question was whether, and under which circumstances, the FD had a right to deprive resource-poor villagers of their established rights. According to Kalpavriksh, these rights included the right to life, which generally has been interpreted as the right not to be unlawfully killed by state force. This right is guaranteed in Article 21 of the Constitution. The same Article, however, has been reinterpreted to cover a much more comprehensive right, i.e., the right to livelihood. In their argument on behalf of the villagers, Kalpavriksh referred to this right as a 'right to a means of livelihood' accruing to land-poor farmers with a need for fodder for their cattle. Kalpavriksh further argued that the villagers had a customary right to graze: they had been allowed to do so earlier

[5] Aghapur is located near the only paved road in the park. This road runs parallel to the canal from Ajan Bund, which is near Aghapur (see map in Ewans 1989). In 1993, the FD staff in the park consisted of a Park Director, a Research Officer, 2 Forest Rangers, 8 Foresters, 35 Forest Guards, and 60 or more casual labourers.

[6] Apart from Kalpavriksh, Gadgil and Guha also mention the clash, but they do not go into details (Gadgil and Guha 1992: 235). Sankhala (1990) and Ewans (1989) fail to mention the confrontation although Sankhala apparently was Chief Wildlife Warden of Rajasthan at the time. Sankhala died in 1994 (Rangarajan 1994a).

on payment of Rs 16 per buffalo and Rs 8 per cow. The villagers, therefore, held a group-specific customary right to certain resources, or, at least, a right to be compensated in case of withdrawal of their customary right.

Rights to Collect

According to Bholu Khan, a Forester in the park, 40,000 heads of cattle—mostly zebu cattle but also water buffaloes—were grazed in the sanctuary before it was closed to grazing. This was some 10-15,000 more than the official records showed. The park authorities alleged this level of grazing was harmful. They were supported in this view by the Bombay Natural History Society (BNHS), which started a project on the ecology of the sanctuary in 1980. The Principal Investigator of this project, V. S. Vijayan, reckoned that around two thousand buffaloes would be optimal for the entire area, but that some 6,000 buffaloes were grazed in an area of about 8.5 square kilometres. These animals, it was said, destroyed the floating nests of certain birds, besides causing inconvenience to the increasing number of visitors to the park by blocking the roads.

Whatever the ideal and real level of grazing in the wetlands, within a year the ban on cattle grazing led to a rapid growth of grasses. The grasses formed a thick layer on a large part of the surface of the water. As a result, the number of diving birds decreased. According to the BNHS, the main problem was the grass *Paspalum distichum* which grows faster but decomposes slower than several other marsh grasses (Bombay Natural History Society 1988). To leave the grass to decompose naturally meant the gradual siltation of the wetlands. The FD admitted that it had been a mistake to impose a ban on grazing, and started searching for a way to eliminate the grass in the wetlands after these areas dry up.

For a period the FD used bulldozers to remove the grass and also to clear firelines. This management technique was both expensive and disliked.[7] In 1989, the FD changed its policy. Each household in the surrounding villages was allowed to cut and carry out grasses growing

---

[7] Villages allegedly let loose some of their cattle as a mark of anger, thereby increasing the population of feral cattle. As the number of feral cattle grew, while the population of wild ungulates such as Nilgai (*Boselaphus tragocamelus*) and Spotted Deer (*Axis axis*) also grew, grazing was not eliminated, but only reduced, by the shift in departmental policy.

in the wetlands from around 1 April till the onset of the monsoon at a fee of Rs 15 per month for two people or a household. The FD also agreed that the farmers could cut grasses growing above the surface of the water from September onwards.

In addition, villagers were allowed to cut grass in the dry parts of the jungle from later in the year till February, when the local birds start to breed. This grass was used for thatching, etc.[8] The villagers were also allowed to take home the grass they cut while making fire lines. The FD further agreed to villagers selling the grass they cut rather than feeding it to their cows and buffaloes. *Paspalum* grass from the wetlands has a low market value because it is believed to cause certain diseases to the cattle for which only local villagers know the cure. Be that as it may, the grass seems to have helped both to tie over the cattle in the hot months, when fodder is otherwise scarce, and as a marketable commodity.

Thus, the Park Authorities judged that a phased and controlled exploitation of certain resources was ecologically viable, socially acceptable and also workable in practice. Though the BNHS researcher, V. S. Vijayan, had argued that 'It is as difficult to control thousands of people as it is to control buffaloes' (Pandya 1992: 16) he concluded, nevertheless, that 'Selective harvesting of some blocks potentially is the most economically, socially, and politically acceptable way to control Paspalum in the Park' (Bombay Natural History Society 1988: 5).

Water hyacinth or jal kumbhi (*Eichhornia crassipes*) and water lily, nāri or kamodini (*Ipomea sp.*) are other plants that make the wetlands less attractive for ducks and geese. The FD also wants to control the spread of these plants, and even to eradicate water hyacinth. However, villagers do not have an economic interest in these plants. The FD, therefore, has to employ casual labourers from the surrounding villages to remove them.

While the villagers won the right to cut grass in the park, the FD has maintained a monopoly on rights to fuelwood and timber. Charcoal burning, one of the major wood-based trades, was terminated around 1972. Felling of mature trees is prohibited, though

[8] According to Ewans (1989: 132), the right to harvest khus grass (*Vetiveria zizanioides*) used to be auctioned. A perfume is extracted from the roots of the grass, but the local production of this perfume was brought to an end in 1981.

it does take place. At present, however, the focus is on smaller trees and bushes. On its side, the park management has a strong interest in controlling certain 'weeds'. Several of these, including vilayati babul (*Prosopis juliflora*), vilayati kikar (*Prosopis chilensis*) and *lantana*, have spread rapidly. The Park Director in 1993 was inclined to let villagers cut *P. juliflora* to prevent it from spreading further. However, the FD retained its ingrained and not unfounded suspicion that villagers would take the opportunity to cut and damage other trees and bushes while moving about in the denser parts of the jungle eradicating weeds. The FD, therefore, continued to hire casual labour at Rs 22 a day, and to sell the brush-wood as fuelwood.

Wilder Animals and the Boundary Wall

In the mid-1970s a stone wall was constructed along the perimeter of the park (Kalpavriksh 1986: 444). Because the park is relatively small, this wall has been relatively easy to maintain. While the boundary wall is instrumental in keeping out domestic cattle, the nilgai (antelope) is able to jump over it to feed on wheat and pulses in neighbouring fields. As the population of nilgai has increased to about 600, the biotic pressure on the fields caused by nilgai has also increased. The wild boars (*Sus scrofa*) are also able to leave the park, through the holes in the wall meant to allow rainwater to pass. The pigs may also cause damage in the fields. Unlike the nilgai, which are rarely hunted, the pigs are hunted and meat of wild boar is said to be on sale locally. Illegal pig hunting may have caused a decline in the pig population (Petri Hottola, personal comm.).

One method suggested to ameliorate the problems caused by nilgai is to raise the wall to twice its present height. Another possibility, suggested by the Park Director in 1993, was culling of wild ungulates, but this would require a major change in wildlife management policy. A further proposal would be to control the population of ungulates and pigs by introducing major predators, such as leopard (*Panthera pardus*), into the park as was suggested by no less an authority than Kailash Sankhala, who has been Chief Wildlife Warden of Rajasthan (Sankhala 1990: 23, 116 and 123). In my judgement this would be a serious mistake, because it would turn the area and its vicinity into a much less user-friendly environment. Sankhala was aware that people will try to kill leopards who stray outside the sanctuary at night, but suggested that trees be planted *outside* the wall to allow leopards to return safely to the sanctuary in the morning![9]

Generation and Spread of Employment and Skills

Problems relating to parks and sanctuaries are not confined to questions of sustainability, access to natural resources, and people-animal conflicts. The actors involved in the equations themselves change. In Bharatpur, the very importance of the park from an ornithological point of view has created new stake-holders. One such group are the rickshaw-drivers, many of whom are Sikhs who have settled in the area after 1947.

In 1981 the then Park Director, Captain Soni, initiated a three-months project to train a number of rickshaw-wallahs in bird identification. The idea apparently came from his staff. Since then, around sixty rickshaw-drivers have learned to identify the common birds of the area and to name the species in English, Hindi, and, occasionally, in French and German as well. Several have their own binoculars which they have been given by foreign visitors. These visitors have also donated binoculars and a telescope to some of the FD staff members. In the FD such gadgets are usually reserved for the superior officer. The transfer of these gadgets across status lines is in itself a minor revolution.[10]

---

[9] The leopards introduced in the Sanjay Gandhi National Park in metropolitan Bombay also seem to me to stretch Indian notions of peaceful coexistence too far. The park plays host to around 47 leopards on 103 sq. km. and has three million visitors a year. The park is surrounded by one million people living in huts or slums. The location of this park comes out clearly on the map of Bombay in McCarry (1995). No wonder that occasionally leopards 'mistake a playing child for a goat and catch it and become man-eaters' (Sanzgiri 1993: 40). But, one may say, this is just another instance of forcing people to live with major feline predators: why should the urban population be spared the experience if forest inhabitants are not? One proposed solution is to raise a concrete wall around the park at the cost of Rs 70 million.

[10] Among the most radical mechanisms through which 'status-equalisation' and 'status-inversion' occur in South Asia today are international labour migration, foreign projects and aid, tourism, and crime. Sanskritisation, education, mainstream entrepreneurship, legal reform, reservation policies, land reform, etc., are more pervasive and deep processes of change, but they are slow and incremental compared to the first mentioned mechanisms.

The rickshaws were equipped with signboards identifying them as authorised by the park, divided into three groups and assigned three different stands (the Main Gate at the periphery of the park, the Forest Lodge and the Barrier near the wetlands) in rotation by dividing the month into three parts. The fare in 1993 was Rs 20 per hour, which meant that a rickshaw-driver cum guide could expect to earn Rs 40-60 a day or more from August to April. They had to pay Rs 5 per day to enter the park. Other rickshaws plying in the park during peak-loads had to pay Rs 5 every time they entered the park. As ordinary vehicles were no longer allowed beyond the Barrier—though VIPs continued to be given jeep rides—ordinary visitors were likely to hire a rickshaw, if they did not prefer to walk, or hire a bike, one of the two horse-drawn carriages, one of the two electrical vans, or one of the boats operated by the FD.

The trained rickshaw-wallahs cum field guides of Bharatpur are unique. As long as visitors to the park use their services, the system is bound to increase the stake of this particular section of the local population in the park.

Apart from the rickshaw-drivers, ornithologists also trained a number of young, male graduates as naturalists. The training program, which was started in 1976 or 1977, was announced through the newspapers and therefore open both to locals and to outsiders. Most of the respondents apparently were from somewhere in the vicinity—Bharatpur not being the kind of a town to which graduates would happily shift unless assured permanent service. In 1993, the naturalists so trained charged around Rs 40-50 per hour for groups of four people or more, or Rs 400 for a day.

The above developments contributed to an increasing interaction between ornithologists from around the world, the FD, the tourist trade, and the local population. The few FD staff members, who took to field-ornithology in a more sustained manner and whose low departmental rank meant they were not transferred, attained a much higher degree than their superiors not only of local or embedded knowledge, but also of context-free or disembedded knowledge. This development was initiated by Salim Ali, the prime mover of the BNHS. When Ali surveyed the area, Bholu Khan attracted his attention by localising the nest of a mottled wood owl (*Strix ocellata*). Bholu Khan later entered the FD as a Forester through a competitive exam. His father, Habib, had served in the army during the Second World War in Poona, where he met Mahatma Gandhi, who was imprisoned in the Agha Khan Palace because of the Quit India agitation. Habib later left the army, returned to his birthplace, and was employed by the Maharaja of Dholpur as a cook. From 1961-62 he was a cook for the Maharaja of Bharatpur. Later, he was employed by the FD as a cook in Shanti Kutir, the old hunting lodge in the sanctuary. During his career he served dignitaries such as Jawaharlal Nehru. One of his sons, Iqbal, was later employed in the Shanti Kutir. Two brothers, Siri Chand and Sohan Lal, from Jatoly (or Jatwalee) village located very close to the Shanti Kutir rest house and the Barrier also entered the FD, but as Forest Guards. They, too, had the occasion to work with Salim Ali. Together with Bholu Khan, they have become the 'hard-core' ornithologists of the FD in Bharatpur.

Conclusions

The point I want to make is that some local people of more or less humble background have been employed by the FD and have managed to attain considerable skills. They also have a surprising degree of influence, as witnessed by the fact that the Government of India has sponsored Bholu Khan to participate in an international crane conference in Pakistan (for which Pakistan apparently denied him a visa). These skills were not due to training imparted by the FD, but due to a personal interest, which was nurtured by encounters with ornithologists from around the world. These skills, however, have not been rewarded with a commensurable rise in departmental rank. This points both to the strengths and to the weaknesses of government in South Asia. The attention to local talent is not absent: the forest guard who 'knows the tiger's time-table', or the cook who knows the taste of the officer will certainly be appreciated. As this minor case study has shown, families—or 'service-families' as Bayly (1975) calls them—may share a common departmental fate over generations. But the system is relatively stiff, and it suffers from one of the major managerial weaknesses found practically all over South Asia: the unwillingness and fear of delegating power. It insulates itself against change by keeping the amount of in-service training and the scope for advancement negligible. In a small place like Bharatpur, it is not at all surprising that skilled ornithologists may be low in departmental rank, and that some are, indeed, illiterate. The FD does trace local talent and it does offer some scope for permanent employment, which is not to be discounted. For example, the department may allow a poor widow to succeed to her deceased husband's position. But it does not nurture departmental talent systematically below the highest levels.[11]

A similar argument holds for the benefits the FD offer to the villages. Yes, villagers have been allowed to cut grass, and one may speculate that the park is likely to continue to produce a large amount of fodder because grazing has decreased. But in and by itself the management of grass-harvesting does not offer much scope of economic development for the villagers. The positive-sum outcome of the bargain struck by the villagers and the FD has been contingent on the willingness of the villagers to cut and transport the grasses manually. In 1993-94, official figures stated that villagers took out 228,600 headloads weighing an average of 30 kg. During this year the FD issued some 3,810 monthly permits of Rs 15 earning an income of Rs 57,150 for the department. As has been said, 'This is how the management keeps the villagers happy. They get their work done without paying'. In other words, the carrying capacity of the park is sustained by the 'carrying capacity' of the villagers. Were the villagers to insist on being paid not simply the minimum daily wage, but according to an ecological audit, the bargain struck might look different.

The idea of training people to perform a service like guiding is comparatively more innovative. It is less of a concession to custom, more of a way of creating a new occupation. It links up with tourism, which clearly has an employment potential. The park is close to major tourist centres. and many tourists pass the area on their way between Agra, Fatehpur Sikri and Jaipur. Those who halt at Bharatpur generally only stay for a few hours. However, private entrepreneurs have opened approximately fifteen hotels, and the employment opportunities here have to be taken into account when making a cost-benefit analysis of the park. It has been suggested that each national park should have a committee comprising of the Park Director, hoteliers, tour operators and the tourism department to manage

---

[11] The entry requirements for Forest Guards has been raised to six or eight years of schooling, and it may be raised to ten (Indian Council of Forestry Research and Education 1991-92: 73). Some states recruit a number of women on the lowest level, i.e., as Forest Guards, and at the highest, i.e., as IFS officers. At the middle level, such at that of Rangers, the number of women are few, because they are subjected to transfer without being offered 'acceptable' facilities (see also Sarin 1992).

tourism (Akbar Hussain, personal comm.). As far as I know, the FD in Bharatpur has not been involved in such a development.[12] No scheme exists to earmark a portion of the income derived from tourism for the development of the area. In Nepal, it has been planned that 30-50 per cent of the income earned in national parks should be utilised in community development (Brown 1995: 17).

This is only one among several sins of omission on the part of the FD. The park management does not seem to have initiated any schemes of agro-forestry or social forestry in the nearby villages alone or in co-ordination with others to increase the ability of the villages to meet their firewood demands. The Lupin Rural Support Programme successfully operating in Bharatpur district also does not appear to have been involved in work on the periphery of the park (Sen 1993). Further, the FD does not seem to have recognised a need for improving husbandry in the villages surrounding the park. Around 1991, the FD started capturing feral cattle and translocating them to Chambal Valley near Dholpur, where they have been let loose. In 1992-93, 407 heads of cattle were shifted in this way bringing down the population of feral cattle in Bharatpur to perhaps 800. The latter figure, however, must be taken with a grain of salt: despite the ban on cattle grazing, an unknown number of domestic cattle appear to be grazing unofficially in the park.

The conclusion is that the FD in recent years has enhanced the use-value of the park for an increasing number of local parties in several ways, a few of which are positively innovative. As regards grazing, the strategy of the FD has changed from one excluding both cattle and people to one allowing people to harvest fodder for their cattle manually. This strategy accommodates local interests without, however, evolving a more comprehensive eco-development plan for people living near the park.[13] The FD has so far only enhanced the

---

[12] In some parks, the FD makes tourism a paying proposition. Some FD staff in, for example, Corbett National Park have tried to extract personal benefit out of a situation in which they control the limited accommodation facilities within the park. Tour operators allege that they have been forced to bribe FD staff to book or 'block' these facilities in order to secure access for their clients. Transaction costs have further increased by competition and queue-jumping by Delhi-based diplomats and Indian VIPs.

[13] More ambitious eco-development plans are being made for a number of National Parks in which Project Tiger is implemented. These include Corbett,

utility of the park for the surrounding villages if this has furthered its own conservationist objectives at no great cost. Thus, rights of access still play a central role in park management though it has often been said that all rights of access were extinguished by the British. Apart from usufruct rights, the relationships between people and the FD are shaped by the economic and ecological considerations of the FD as well as by employment considerations. A final dimension of the equation is the generation of new skills, and even departmental reform.

Keoladeo National Park is a World Heritage Site. According to Herring (1995: 15), UNESCO has threatened India that the park will be deleted from the list of World Heritage Sites ostensibly because Siberian Cranes did not winter there in 1994-95. Though the ongoing project to rear Siberian Cranes from eggs collected in the wild has not enjoyed full support from the Government of India, it seems unreasonable to blame their decline on Bharatpur (Nordin 1995: 20). It might be more constructive on the part of the monitors of the World Heritage Convention to suggest how the management of Bharatpur can be further improved. In this regard, a study of the impact of pesticides and other toxic material on food chains in and near the park should be of high priority (see *Oriental Bird Club Bulletin* 1995).

Bandipur, Kanha, Palamau, Simlipal, Sunderban, Periyar, Namdapha, Melghat, Valmiki, Pench and Ranthambhore (*The Times of India* 1993). The World Bank has proposed other schemes (Thapa and Brijnath 1995).

8

NGOs and Forest Management in Karnataka

David Potter

In this paper I report some findings from field research in 1993-94 on NGOs (Non-Governmental Organisations) working to influence the development of JFPM (Joint Forest Planning and Management) policy in Karnataka.[1] The research aims to explain why this major change in forest policy is taking place, with particular attention to the advocacy work of FEVORD-K (Federation of Voluntary Organisations for Rural Development—Karnataka), the principal NGO coalition in the state. I begin with a short account of FEVORD-K, summarise the new forest management policy announced in 1993 and FEVORD-K's immediate response to it, and then comment briefly on FEVORD-K's work in relation to this policy in terms of agenda setting, policy choices, and implementation processes (in Uttara Kannada District) up to the end of 1994. I argue in the paper that the extent of FEVORD-K's influence has varied between these three phases of policy making.

[1] I am indebted to my research associate in Karnataka, A. P. Kripa, and to many other people in Karnataka and elsewhere who generously gave their time to educate me about FEVORD-K and JFPM. Special mention must be made of: Bangalore, E. Raghavan (*Times of India*), Shobha Raghuram (HIVOS), Madhav Gadgil (Centre for Ecological Sciences), Aloysius Fernandez (MYRADA), M. K. Bhatt (NOVIB), Gerry Pais (Oxfam), Dhirendra Singh (former IAS Secretary, Forest Department), A. S. Sadashivaiah (Chief Conservator of Forests); Dharwad and Uttara Kannada districts, S. R. Hiremath and Shoba Karjagi (SPS), Ranjan Rao Yerdoor (IDS), Sheela Khare (Vikasa Rural Development Society), Shivappa Poojari (Siddi Development Project), Prabhakar Bhat (Centre for Ecological Sciences, Sirsi Field Station), Rajaram Hegde (Sahyadri Parisara Vardhini), Panduranga Hegde (Parisara Samrakshana Kendra–Appiko Movement), Susairaj Reddy and Theresa Reddy (Karwar Rural Women and Children Development Society), T. H. Mallakarjunaiah (Deputy Conservator of Forests–JFPM); elsewhere, Eric Hanley (ODA, British High Commission), R. Sudarshan (UNDP), H. N. Mathur (SPWD), James Manor (IDS, University of Sussex), Murray Culshaw and Tricia Fenney (Oxfam).

FEVORD-K

Although non-governmental initiatives in rural development activities had featured in Karnataka for a long time, there was a marked increase in this activity in the 1970s for a variety of reasons. It was triggered partly by the national 'Emergency' of 1975-77, when AVARD (Association of Voluntary Agencies for Rural Development) was blacklisted. One person who helped to found FEVORD-K said to me that 'the Emergency had a great effect on us all, pushed us to start organisations at state level'. Other factors included widespread disillusionment with the Government's Community Development Programme, continuing rural poverty, availability of funding for NGOs from international donor agencies, and an increase in the number of people from varied professional backgrounds moving into voluntary work in rural areas. By the end of the 1970s some of these NGOs started to meet from time to time to share experiences and consider common collective effort on matters or mutual concern. One possibility was to form a state chapter of AVARD, but those involved in the early discussions believed this format tended to be strong at the top and weaker at the bottom and they wanted an arrangement the other way round. A state-level convention of NGOs was held at Magadi (Bangalore District) on 16 and 17 January 1982, when the decision was taken to form FEVORD-K. A Board of Directors was constituted representing most regions in Karnataka. By mid-1994 FEVORD-K had about 120 member organisations ranging from small activist groups to large hierarchical organisations.

It is an unusual 'federation'. FEVORD-K has only a very small office in Bangalore with two and a half full time staff who act mainly as a post box for information going to and from the members. FEVORD-K is not involved in the internal functioning of member organisations. It does not evaluate member organisations or fund them. It does not have projects of its own. The life of FEVORD-K is primarily in the countryside amongst the members. If the members are not singly or jointly active, FEVORD-K is not active.

All major decisions of FEVORD-K are made at the Annual General Meeting. These occur each time in a different part of Karnataka. About 30-55 attend, each person representing a FEVORD-K member organisation. One day is for business, the second for workshops. The AGM sets the broad direction of FEVORD-K action for the following year. It also constitutes the Board of Directors and various Standing Committees. The Board has 21 members and meets about every three months. The President of the Board and other office bearers in FEVORD-K cannot hold office for more than two years, nor can they be active in party politics. There were fourteen Standing Committees in 1993 on different aspects of FEVORD-K work, e.g., community lands and forests, rural health, women, training, and liaison with the Government of Karnataka. Committee chairpersons are usually selected by a nomination committee formed before each AGM. FEVORD-K members join the committees that interest them (not more than two). Each committee meets several times during the year in a location convenient for the members.

Certain member organisations tend to be prominent on a particular FEVORD-K Standing Committee for a period of years. The Forestry and Common Lands Standing Committee is an example. In 1993-94, the Chair of the Committee was S. R Hiremath, a leading figure in SPS (Samaj Parivarthana Sumudaya), an NGO in Dharwad District. Also prominent in the affairs of the Committee and FEVORD-K's work in relation to the new forest management policy is IDS (India Development Service), an NGO at work on rural development projects in Dharwad and Uttara Kannada districts. For example, IDS appointed a full time worker in November 1993 to act as FEVORD-K's 'inter-development services co-ordinator' for JFPM. IDS pay his salary. He has been travelling throughout the state alerting NGOs to the implications of JFPM for their work, providing training programmes for NGOs about JFPM, and encouraging the development of new NGOs needed to assist effective implementation of the new forest policy. This example underlines how the life of FEVORD-K, even the financing of new initiatives, lies with individual member organisations of the Federation.

Networking and dissemination of information are obviously features of FEVORD-K activities. Beyond that there are perhaps two other aspects that stand out. The first is the emphasis on shared training programmes. Many NGOs in FEVORD-K are small. Each also has particular expertise not shared by others. Training programmes are organised through FEVORD-K to allow such expertise to be shared with other members. In this way the quality of the work of individual NGOs in FEVORD-K can be enhanced at minimal cost.

The other major activity involves advocacy work in relation to government policy. A conventional approach to this subject is to see NGOs like FEVORD-K as either 'insider' or 'outsider' pressure groups. Insiders liaise regularly with government and are part of government policy networks; outsiders do not co-operate with government and attempt to influence government policy by mobilising pressure from outside the state, in civil society. FEVORD-K obliterates this conventional distinction because its advocacy work is both 'insider' and 'outsider'

It was clearly involved in 'insider' dealings when a delegation of FEVORD-K met the Chief Secretary of the Government of Karnataka in June 1982 'to explore the possibilities of co-operation between the government and voluntary agencies' (Ramaswamy and Prasad 1990: 9) which led in December 1989 to a government decision to henceforth make available to FEVORD-K member organisations all Government Orders, circulars and policy papers. Subsequently in 1984 a consultative group of NGO (including FEVORD-K) representatives, the Karnataka Development Commissioner and heads of government departments was set up and has met from time to time. This arrangement was extended to each District in 1989 when district consultative committees were set up by the Chief Secretary of *zilla parishads* (District Councils). Also very 'insider' in character was the establishment in 1989 of what amounted to policy advisory groups ('sub-committees') on certain subject areas of government activity, each advisory group comprising both NGO representatives and personnel from relevant government departments. This arrangement has had mixed results; the 'sub-committee' for Forest and Wasteland Development, for example, has rarely met.

'Outsider' action and protest has also been a feature of FEVORD-K member organisations. Best known is the long struggle from 1984 to 1993 to return 30,000 hectares of village forest and common lands to village communities, lands which had been acquired by Karnataka Pulpwood Ltd (KPL) (51 per cent shares owned by the Karnataka Government, 49 per cent by a Birla company Harihar Polyfibres) set up to plant eucalyptus plantations for the exclusive use of the Harihar Polyfibres factory on the Tungabhadra River in Dharwad District. The struggle involved village people together with FEVORD-K organisations and others engaging in non-violent direct action against KPL (i.e., the Karnataka Government) including the Kittiko Hachchiko (Pluck and Plant) *satyagraha* in 1988 during which various *satyagrahis* including FEVORD-K people were arrested. The struggle also involved a FEVORD-K organisation (SPS) filing a public interest writ in the Supreme Court of India, which issued a Stay Order against the Government of Karnataka. The campaign to wind up KPL went on for years and was ultimately successful The whole story was written-up and published by SPS and others for FEVORD-K (Kanvalli 1993) Other 'outsider' action includes FEVORD-K members lobbying the World Bank and the ODA (UK), which have funded Karnataka Government forestry programmes. They have lobbied these inter-national bodies about what they see as the adverse consequences of certain forestry programmes, hoping in this way to put powerful out-side pressure on the Karnataka Government.

The fact that FEVORD-K engages in both 'insider' and 'outsider' activity in its advocacy work with the Karnataka Government is symptomatic of a certain lack of overall coherence within the federation. Such problems are perhaps intrinsic to an NGO federation lacking centralised control. Some member organisations in FEVORD-K are small action groups, regularly receiving attention from the police and other enforcement agencies of the government, and very 'outsider' in orientation. Other member organisations, larger and better financed, consult with government departments as 'insiders' on a fairly regular basis. The former tend to feel that 'FEVORD-K has not done much to benefit them' (Ramaswamy and Prasad 1990: 18). The latter are concerned that the 'outsider' action orientation of some members hinders their efforts to work co-operatively with government as FEVORD-K representatives. Both groups sense that this problem of overall coherence may help to explain why a number of NGOs committed to rural development are still not part of FEVORD-K. Despite such problems, however, FEVORD-K is without question the single most important NGO presence in Karnataka. and is recognised as such by the government.

The New JFPM Policy and the FEVORD-K Response

A major shift in policy is currently underway to bring 'people's participation' to forest management practices in India. Since the nineteenth century management of forests has been handled essentially by officials in forest departments (Guha 1989; Gadgil and Guha 1992). The new policy sets up joint management schemes involving forest officials, village communities and NGOs. Its main premise is that poor land management is causing environmental degradation in the forests and that regeneration of forests cannot be achieved without the active participation of the local population in their management. These changes are currently being implemented across India. Between 1989 and August 1993, thirteen state governments issued enabling orders or resolutions setting out the details of the particular joint forest management scheme to be established in their state: West Bengal in 1989; Bihar and Haryana in 1990; Gujarat, Rajasthan and Tripura in 1991; Andhra Pradesh, Jammu and Kashmir and Maharashtra in 1992; and Himachal Pradesh, Karnataka, Orissa and Punjab in 1993. Karnataka's Government Order (G.O. AHFF 232 FAP 86, dated 12.4.93) is one of the longest and most detailed. Its provisions can perhaps be summarised briefly in terms of six main features.

First, JFPM in Karnataka is restricted to: (a) degraded areas of forest where the canopy cover is less than 25 per cent; (b) certain other non-forest government wastelands formally under the control of the Revenue Department: and (c) plantations raised over foreshores of tanks, road sides and canal banks. Forests with better canopy cover are excluded from JFPM.

Second, Village Forest Committees (VFCs) are to be formed, consisting of beneficiaries of the scheme in a village (or a group of villages) in or adjacent to JFPM forest areas. One member per family is eligible to become a member upon payment, normally of Rs 2. When a VFC is established and registered as an association under the Karnataka Society's Act, a number of *ex officio* members also join. A VFC will consist of *mandal panchāyat* members from the village, the village accountant, local officials of the Agriculture and Animal Husbandry Departments, local foresters, the school teacher working in the village, and one representative from a local NGO (nominated by the relevant Deputy Conservator of Forests). A VFC has a number of duties and responsibilities, e.g. to help the Forest Department in preparing the Joint Management Plan for the area, to approve the plan, to protect and develop the forest areas and other government waste lands assigned to it, and to be entirely responsible for the full protection of the forest and plantations raised on such lands after three years (preferably through its volunteers or through paid watchmen employed by the VFC out of its resources).

Third, each VFC has a Managing Committee elected for a period of five years by the members: a chairman, ten other elected members (nine from scheduled castes or tribes, two women, one landless labourer, one artisan, four general category members), and four *ex officio* members (the village accountant, *mandal panchāyat* secretary, NGO representative, and a forester—who acts as the member secretary). The Managing Committee is expected to meet at least once a month. It has various powers, e.g 'to apprehend the forest offenders and hand them over to the forest authorities'; 'to seize wood illegally cut'; and 'to impound cattle engaged in unauthorised grazing' in the forest.

Fourth, all members (and thus beneficiaries) of the VFC are entitled to grasses, leaves, fuel wood (including lops, tops and prunings) from the JFPM areas free of cost. The Managing Committee is to supervise the distribution of such produce, ensuring it is 'fair and equitable'. When disposing of minor forest produce/fruits, timber and fuel wood, 'the requirement of the local village should be treated as a first charge on such final produce', and any surplus 'shall be disposed of by the VFC at open public auction or local sale'. The proceeds from such transactions are shared: 50 per cent to government; 25 per cent to beneficiaries on the VFC; 25 per cent to the Village Forest Development Fund.

Fifth, a 'tree *patta*' scheme is provided for, enabling private landowners adjoining the JFPM area to enjoy the usufructs from trees on roadsides and canal sides free of cost 'providing he maintains the trees at his own cost after the third year of planting'. A rent of Re 1 per tree per annum is charged. These cannot be cut without prior permission from the Forest Department. If no such private landowners are interested. then the tree *pattas* are available to members or beneficiaries of the VFC.

Sixth, the Government Order explicitly gives voluntary agencies and NGOs 'with proven track record' a role in JFPM, but not a very central one. NGOs 'may play a supportive role in assisting the Forest Department and VFCs', may assist in disseminating Forest Department information, and can act as 'an extension agency between VFCs and Government Departments'.

Several months after the Karnataka Government Order of April 1993 was made public, the Chairperson of the Committee of Forestry and Common Lands of FEVORD-K drafted a response to it. (The following summary of this NGO position is based on the unpublished written draft response and my interview with the Chairperson on 5 December 1993 at Rennibennur, Dharwad District.)

Although the NGOs in FEVORD-K generally welcomed the Government Order as an important step forward, they urged the government to revise a number of its detailed features in order to improve the JFPM scheme and its chances of success. First, they questioned the restriction of JFPM to only degraded areas of forest with 25 per cent canopy or less. They urged the government to consider extending the scheme to less degraded lands also. They argued that many tribal and other forest dwellers lived in less degraded areas and would be unable to benefit from JFPM. They also suggested that the restricted coverage of the Government Order would create an incentive for excluded communities to degrade their own forests in order to become eligible for JFPM; they said this was a view shared by a number of experienced foresters.

Second, they made a number or detailed suggestions aimed at relaxing the exclusive and rather tight control over the scheme exercised by the KFD (Karnataka Forest Department). For example, they recommended that the power to nominate NGOs to the VFCs and Managing Committees should be moved from the Deputy Conservator of Forests to the Deputy Commissioner of the District in which the village is located. They also recommended that other powers lodged in the KFD (e.g., powers of nomination, appeal, dissolution of VFCs) be transferred to another Government Department or to that existing structure of state and district level committees (mentioned earlier) created to provide government consultation with NGOs.

Third, the NGOs advanced detailed proposals to amend the position of the VFCs and Managing Committees. Their main concern was that women, who are the most involved in using forests on a day to day basis, are poorly represented on the VFCs due to the provision in the Government Order that only one adult member from each household is eligible for membership. That person has usually turned out to be the male head of the household. They recommended that two adult members from each household be eligible, one male and one female. They also urged that the reserved categories for the ten elected members of the Managing Committee be revised as follows: scheduled castes/tribes, two; landless labourers, two; small and marginal farmers families, two; village artisans, two; general category members, two; and that 50 per cent of all these categories must be reserved for women.

Fourth, there were detailed proposals related to the functioning of the Managing Committee and the tight control over it by the KFD. For example, FEVORD-K members were critical of the provision that the forest officials had the sole right to call a meeting of the Managing Committee. They argued that the Management Committee ought to be more accountable to the VFC that elects most of its members. They recommended that provision be made that if, for any reason, some members of the VFC are dissatisfied with the performance of the Managing Committee, they should be allowed to petition the Member Secretary to convene a general meeting for open discussion of the issue.

Fifth, the NGOs drew attention to the complex arrangements for sharing and disposal of produce from the forest lands under JFPM. They made several suggestions aimed at making this arrangement simpler and more transparent to VFC members. For example, they recommended that the VFC should simply decide how its 50 per cent share of the produce is disposed of, and it should set the rates for any produce that it sells.

Sixth, they urged the abolition of the 'tree *patta*' scheme on the grounds that it amounted to the privatisation of common lands. They recommended that trees on roadsides, canal sides and similar places, and the right to plant trees in such places, should not be offered to landowners in the area but instead should be considered as part of JFPM, with the VFC being responsible for them.

It is clear that both FEVORD-K and KFD share a common interest in the broad outlines of JFPM, but they are also in *conflict* about the content of the actual policy in various ways. Such conflict between interest groups and organisations is, of course, a normal feature of policy making. Furthermore, the conflict between KFD and FEVORD-K summarised here amounts to only a momentary exchange in a historical *process* that can be said to have started at least 20 years ago and will go on for years to come. Also, there are many more *interests* involved in JFPM than just these two. Conflict, process, multiple interests—these three must figure centrally in any analysis of NGO influence on public policy.

The Main Question

Have NGOs in FEVORD-K been influential in affecting the development of JFPM policy in Karnataka? The question raises a number of complexities, not all of which can be pursued here. My focus is on a feature which is largely ignored in the literature on the influence of NGOs on development and environmental policies (e.g., Clark 1991; Holloway 1989; Khator 1991; Tandon 1989; Hulme and Edwards 1992; Farrington and Lewis 1993). Any major policy change, like the shift to JFPM, involves a continuous process with three distinguishable phases—agenda setting, policy choices, implementation processes—and the influence of NGOs in affecting this continuing policy process is variable depending on which of these three phases is being considered.[2] In the remainder of the paper I illustrate the argument briefly by referring to aspects of the JFPM story in Karnataka in terms of these three phases.

Agenda Setting

The JFPM policy details in the Government Order of April 1993 did not suddenly spring *de novo* from the brains of policy élites in Karnataka. The policy was profoundly shaped by a process of agenda setting that can be said to have begun in the early 1970s. The process was not confined to Karnataka nor even to India. It was a truly global process, during which the discourse about forests, and how they should be managed, gradually shifted.

Tracing all the events and processes world-wide that moved the agenda on forests and rural communities during the 1970s and 1980s would be a gigantic task, and one not really necessary here. However, by way of illustration, several events in the 1970s can be singled out as important markers that set the shift in motion. One was the energy crisis of 1973 which drew attention to energy resources generally and the dependence of rural people in developing countries on forests for fuelwood. 'For more than a third of the world's people', Eckholm (1975) remarked, 'the world energy crisis is a daily scramble to cook dinner'. The fuelwood crisis became linked to the escalating rates of deforestation in tropical forests. which began to receive prominence in the media at this time. The dependence of the rural poor on trees and forests for fuelwood, food and other household needs was seen as contributing to environment problems of deforestation and land degradation. All this connected with another trend in the 1970s towards paying increased attention to rural 'basic needs'.

These events and processes began to influence the thinking of some people who mattered in the world of forestry and who determined the content of development projects related to the forests. In 1978, for example, the theme of the Eighth World Forestry Congress was 'Forests for People'. This marked the increased importance being given to the subject in teaching and research in the forestry schools throughout the world, and may have influenced

---

[2] For a general discussion of development policy in terms of agenda setting, decision making and implementation, see Grindle and Thomas 1991.

professional foresters trained in the schools who began to fill the forestry departments of governments and international agencies. The World Bank (1978), for example, published a forestry sector policy paper signalling a perceptible shift in project priorities from industrial forestry toward some attention to protection of the forest on environmental grounds and meeting the needs of local communities who depend on forests. Whether this meant an actual shift in Bank priorities is debatable. In the same year, the main UN agency concerned with forests and rural development published a policy paper on 'community forestry' (FAO 1978). Community forestry meant providing 'fuel and other foods essential to meeting basic needs at the rural household and community level', providing 'food and the environmental stability necessary for continued food production', and generating 'income and employment in the rural community'. 'Forestry for community development', they said, 'must therefore be forestry for the people and involving the people. It must be forestry which starts at the "grassroots"'. Such ideas became more prominent globally during the 1980s (for example, as summarised in FAO 1991).

These ideas began to have consequences for forest policies in India. For example, various 'social forestry' policies were set in motion in many states during the 1980s. They tended to comprise two main components: farm forestry (private farmers encouraged to plant trees on their land, with the government providing as an incentive free or subsidised seedlings); and community forestry (forest departments planting 'forest crops' on public property such as river banks, canal sides, along railway tracks) meant to provide fuel and fodder for nearby rural communities, with such communities then being made responsible for the care, maintenance and distribution of these 'forest crops'). Unusually for a development programme, as much as half of the entire cost of these projects was financed internationally. In Karnataka, for example, the World Bank and ODA (Overseas Development Administration, UK) financed half the total cost of social forestry between 1983 and 1988. Governments in India claimed social forestry was a success, while independent observers were more negative and some called it a disaster (for an analysis of these contrasting views, see Khator 1991: Ch. 5).

FEVORD-K was one such independent observer. It expressed serious concerns about social forestry. One concern was the predominance (over 80 per cent) of eucalyptus species in farm forestry, the problem of eucalyptus replacing food crops, and issues related to eucalyptus being forced on the rural poor. FEVORD-K addressed a joint memorandum, dated 28.11.85, to the Chief Minister of Karnataka, the President of the World Bank and the Head of ODA, suggesting a number of improvements to the social forestry project in respect of eucalyptus and other issues. Another concern centred on the lack of provision in the social forestry project for the active involvement of local people in the management of forests and other local resources. FEVORD-K shared this concern with the Centre for Ecological Sciences at the Indian Institute of Science (Bangalore), the Save the Western Ghats Movements, Sahyadri Parisara Vardhini, and others. These groups together worked out some proposals in 1988 for involving local people in the management of village forests. These proposals were subsequently debated during 1988/89 in a number of meetings at which government officials, other NGO people, technical experts, and people from the news media were present. There appeared to be broad agreement with the arguments advanced by FEVORD-K and the others as to why involving local people would contribute to better management of natural resources. These included (SPS 1991):

(a) the quality or life of local people is intimately linked to the health of the resource base. Hence they are likely to be better motivated than any impersonal machinery operating from a distance to manage the resources well.

(b) local people have considerable location-specific knowledge of the resource base of value to its good management.

(c) local people can continuously and closely monitor what is happening to the resource base, and how the various interventions are affecting the environment.

(d) involving local people in a proper sharing of the benefits of the resource use is vital to the alleviation or rural poverty, our most serious social problem.

(e) involving local people actively in managing resources of their locality could help get them out of the syndrome of dependency on government handouts for everything and confer on them some community responsibility and personal dignity.

So the discourse on forest management practices locally and globally was shifting, at least in more enlightened quarters. But setting an agenda for reform had not yet translated into actual policies leading to action. What triggered that step in Karnataka were definite statements in favour of such action by the Government of India. A new National Forest Policy, presented to Parliament in December 1988, clearly indicated that a move in that direction would be desirable. The report in 1989 of the Steering Group on Environment, Forests and Wasteland Development for the Planning Commission considering the Eighth Five Year Plan (1990-95) stated quite bluntly (GOI 1989: 134): 'it is necessary to empower the local community at the village level and ensure that each settlement will clearly have a locally defined environment and a natural resource base of its own to protect, care for, and use'. This emphasis was subsequently built into the Eighth Plan (GOI 1992). Most important was a circular of 1 June 1990 sent from the Secretary, Environment and Forests, Government of India to all the Forest Secretaries of all states setting out the details of a new policy called 'Involvement of Village Communities and VAs (Voluntary Associations) in the regeneration of degraded forest lands' (reprinted in SPWD 1993). These and other Government of India statements and policy directives contain the results of political work by policy élites in New Delhi in the 1980s who succeeded in redefining government policy on forest management practices (a story not pursued in this paper). In doing so, they drew upon ideas in the changing discourse about sustainable forest management, linking these ideas to events and political forces in India in order to make a case for JFPM.

FEVORD-K's role in the agenda setting for JFPM is not easy to assess. It certainly expressed views on joint forest management which were considered by forest officials and others in government. But it did so in company with others, notably the Centre for Ecological Sciences headed by an internationally renowned ecologist. That association was no doubt a consideration for the Karnataka Government. But neither FEVORD-K nor the Centre set the agenda for the Karnataka Government. They were only two of many NGOs and other institutions at local, national and global levels that helped to orchestrate the changing discourse in the 1980s about forests which policy élites in the Government of India drew upon when framing directives to state governments. It was the Government of India which most directly set the agenda for the Karnataka Government.

Policy Choice in Karnataka

The Government of India's Directive to all state governments on 1 June 1990 set in motion the detailed discussions within the KFD resulting in the JFPM policy announced on 1 April 1993 and summarised above. The policy choice phase of JFPM in Karnataka can be said to have occurred essentially between those two dates. (One informant thought an early draft of a JFPM scheme may have been circulating within the KFD before June 1990.) The evidence from interviewees and other sources suggests provisionally that, of the array of agencies involved in the detailed policy choices, those within the state were profoundly influential, those outside the state less so.

Within the state generally, there was the pressure bearing down on the Karnataka Government from the Government of India. The general provisions of the Seventh and Eighth Five Year Plans were part of that pressure. The directive of June 1990 from the top civil servant in the Ministry of Environment and Forests to the top civil servant in the KFD put pressure on more directly. The proof of the importance of this national directive lay in some of the language of the Karnataka JFPM policy when it emerged in 1993: for example, both documents refer to NGOs 'with proven track record'.

Within the Karnataka Government the Council of Ministers during this period gave broad political direction to the KFD to produce a JFPM policy but left much room for detailed policy choices within the broad remit. These choices were made basically within the KFD. Their content reflected the agreement reached after a series of meetings marked by tension and some open conflict between what can crudely be described as 'progressive' and 'traditional' foresters. The former were keen on community and NGO participation in forest management and the latter were more resistant or wanted to proceed very cautiously, retaining as much control as possible over JFPM in the hands of KFD officials. The bureaucratic politics within the KFD during these years explains much of the detailed content of the JFPM policy decisions.

External influences appear to have been less important in influencing the policy choices made. The main external influence that needs analysing is the development of the Western Ghats Forestry and Environment Project of the ODA (Overseas Development Administration, British Government) and FEVORD-K's advocacy work in relation to the project.

The background is as follows. In July 1988 the KFD requested project funding from ODA for extensive tree planting activity in the Western Ghats and support for related management, training and research activities. That request was known as the 'Red Book'. A draft Project Report was circulated early in 1989 to various interested parties, including FEVORD-K. This led to a seminar at Dharwad in June 1989 organised by KFD to discuss the draft. One of the major suggestions made by FEVORD-K and others was that there was no provision for people's participation: rural people were involved only as beneficiaries or labourers, not as active participants. The KFD people asked that these suggestions for people's participation be made more specific. That led to a seminar at the Centre for Ecological Sciences in September 1989 attended by senior people in the Karnataka Government, representatives of NGOs, and scholars from research and academic institutions. The seminar considered a draft on 'people's participation in the management of natural resources' which had been prepared by FEVORD-K and others for the seminar. A revised draft ODA project proposal document was circulated in Karnataka in September 1990: the 'Green Book'. It differed considerably from the 'Red Book' and included the idea of people's participation in the implementation of various aspects of the project. FEVORD-K responded to this draft at the end of 1990; they drew attention to a number of problems in the 'Green Book' and made various further suggestions to strengthen the role of local communities and NGOs in the project.

Also during 1990 FEVORD-K went international in relation to the ODA project. They worked to put pressure on ODA in London to ensure that their suggestions were built into the final project agreement. They sent their 'response' to the 'Green Book' to the Minister of Overseas Development, Lynda Chalker, and to the Prime Minister, Margaret Thatcher, by way of 'co-signatories'—Friends of the Earth, IIED (International Institute for Environment and Development), World Rainforest Movement, ECOROPA, and the editors of *The Ecologist*. Oxfam and Survival International declined to join this 'coalition' but wrote separately. (Aubrey Meyer, then working for the 'Save the Forests, Save the Planet' campaign in London, helped to co-ordinate this effort.) The international campaign had some temporary effect: ODA postponed signing the agreement and top KFD officials complained publicly that FEVORD-K had 'thrown a spanner in the wheel', as reported in the *Times of India* (Bangalore), 7 September 1990.

The ODA appraised the draft project once more in early 1991 and the final project document, dated April 1991 (cyclostyled), was produced by KFD and approved. The project aimed to assist the long term conservation of the biodiversity of the Western Ghats and to find ways, on a sustainable basis, to assist those whose livelihoods depended on the forests. The project would establish a new range of management practices to include more flexible approaches to planting, an extensive research programme, and speedier and more effective monitoring of changing forest conditions and work activities. It would also set up JFPM in the project areas; as part of this, there would be provision for training teams of local forest officials in the new participatory techniques, with the training being done by MYRADA, a large NGO in Karnataka (also a member of FEVORD-K). Project funding for all this would be substantial. The main grant of £18 million (mostly for planting, plus some for training, monitoring and research) plus over £5 million for technical co-operation (e.g. consultancies, foreign training) would support the project for a period of six years. (It was then ODA's largest project in India.) Operations would focus on two circles in the Western Ghats area starting with Kannara circle, which roughly covers the Uttara Kannada District in the north-west corner of Karnataka immediately south of Goa. Although the start date for the project was 1 April 1991, the main work involved in setting up village forest committees, agreeing forest plans and all the other JFPM aspects could not start formally until a legal basis for it was promulgated by the Government, which of course happened when the Government Order came into effect in April 1993.

The final project document of April 1991 referred to JFPM as 'the fundamental instrument' for delivering the project and said JFPM builds on practices already being developed by KFD and other Forest Departments in India' (KFD 1991: 5). The document referred generally to local people playing 'a major role in the planning, management and protection of the forest' and NGOs having 'an important role in assisting the JFPM process'. However, no details were given. The details emerged in April 1993 in the Government Order (summarised earlier in this paper), developed by KFD separately from the ODA project.

The fact that KFD sought and obtained major funding from ODA does not mean that ODA then had a directing influence on KFD. ODA were clearly keen on joint forest management schemes involving local communities and NGOs. No doubt this was one of many influences on KFD's thinking during the period 1990-93. But this influence was hardly decisive, for the agenda had already been set and a JFPM scheme was already being developed in KFD and forest departments in other states. Furthermore, when the Karnataka JFPM scheme appeared in 1993 the details did not reflect altogether what the ODA people close to the project had in mind. For example, ODA were unhappy about the restrictions in the JFPM order to areas only with 25 per cent or less canopy cover. The relationship between ODA and KFD is basically co-operative: when disagreements do emerge, they are discussed at length and compromises or adjustments are agreed in due course. 'Sometimes we are exasperated', one ODA person remarked, 'but we cannot order them about'; instead, 'we have to box clever'. JFPM figures in the ODA project, but the details of the JFPM features within it were hammered-out separately within the KFD.

FEVORD-K may appear at first glance to have been a prominent influence on the JFPM decision by the KFD. One can point to 1989-90 when the draft 'People's Participation in Management of Natural Resources', prepared by FEVORD-K and others (reproduced in SPS 1991) was considered by the KFD when preparing the revised draft ODA project document in September 1990. It is true that this revised project draft did include, for the first time, the idea of people's participation in forest management, but only in a general way. Significantly, the specific proposals in the FEVORD-K draft were *not* included. In any event, the Government of India circular had already arrived earlier in the year and, as we suggested above, the KFD's detailed decisions on JFPM, even some of the language used, came from that circular. In December 1990 FEVORD-K renewed their effort, drawing attention to what they saw as important omissions in the revised ODA project draft of the previous September. But these suggestions did not appear in the KFD's final project draft of April 1991, nor were they included in the Karnataka JFPM order of April 1993.

An assessment of FEVORD-K's impressive effort in London, by way of friendly NGOs there, appears to point to the same general conclusion. The effort in London may have put 'a spanner in the wheel' momentarily and may have educated some ODA people in

London about existing forest practices in Karnataka, but these efforts did not decisively affect detailed policy choices about JFPM being made at that time in Bangalore.

The set of detailed decisions about JFPM contained in the Government Order of April 1993 has been summarised earlier in this paper, together with FEVORD-K's critical response to them. That 'exchange' in 1993 illustrates FEVORD-K's continuing unhappiness about the details of the KFD's approach to JFPM; the exchange also underlines the inability of FEVORD-K to have a major influence on the KFD's policy choices during 1990-93.

Implementation Processes

FEVORD-K and other NGOs in Karnataka have been more influential in the implementation phase of the JFPM policy. This is clear from provisional conclusions drawn from our field research in Uttara Kannada District, one of the two districts receiving ODA project funding. Although the JFPM order of April 1993 applied to all Karnataka, implementation of JFPM has moved ahead in Uttara Kannada and, more recently, Shimoga districts because a whole structure of JFPM officials has been appointed, using ODA project funding, to work only on JFPM in those two districts. Most of these officials have been trained by MYRADA. This new structure parallels the existing KFD hierarchy of officials in these districts.

Uttara Kannada is in the Western Ghats and is the most heavily forested district in Karnataka: 80 per cent of the total area is forest land, and roughly 30 per cent of forest revenue comes from this area (Government of Karnataka 1985; Giriappa 1993). The humid tropical forests of the Western Ghats have been described by noted ecologists as 'of considerable significance for India' because they 'constitute an economic resource, protect watersheds of all the major rivers in the Southern Peninsula, support livelihoods of substantial peasant and tribal populations and are a depository of biodiversity surpassed only by the Eastern Himalaya'; and it is 'a matter of considerable concern therefore that the Western Ghats have suffered substantial outright loss of forest cover, loss of standing biomass in areas retaining forest cover and loss of biodiversity'—forest cover in Uttara Kannada specifically having declined from eight thousand square kilometres to six thousand square kilometres during the past 40 years (Daniels, Gadgil and Joshi 1993: 16). The reasons are various, including over-utilisation by logging industries and poaching, overgrazing and general overuse by local people. Seventy-five per cent of Uttara Kannada's growing population is rural, most of whom are peasant and tribal peoples living in or adjacent to the forests and dependent on them for their livelihoods.

Field research in rural Uttara Kannada in 1994 was conducted in all five of the district's forest divisions. This involved interviewing people in all ten NGOs there working on JFPM, sixteen forest officials in the district (one Conservator of Forests, seven DCFs and eight RFOs); and people in twenty-five villages: five villages where an NGO was active and JFPM had been implemented; nine with JFPM and no NGO; six where an NGO was active and there was no JFPM; and five where there was no NGO and no JFPM. Care was taken to ensure that no forest guards were present when villagers were interviewed. Further interviewing in the district took place in 1995 and 1996.

The main provisional finding from the 1994 interviews in Uttara Kannada is that FEVORD-K and the local NGOs there appear to be having an important impact on the implementation of JFPM. For example, in those villages where JFPM had been implemented and NGOs were active, the people interviewed in 1994 had a noticeably clearer understanding of JFPM and more enthusiasm for it than in JFPM villages where no NGO was present. Villages where there was no JFPM and no NGO either had not heard of JFPM or were less interested in taking part in it than villages with whom NGOs were involved. Also, it was particularly noticeable that women were more involved in JFPM where NGOs worked than in villages where they did not. In Sirsi Division, where the local NGOs were not keen on JFPM, implementation of the programme via the KFD without active NGO involvement appeared to have been less successful. Also, in Hanovar Division where there was no NGO involvement, village people interviewed were either unaware of JFPM or, where it had been implemented, were less enthusiastic or knowledgeable about it: one NGO there had repeatedly approached the local KFD officials wanting to get involved but had been rebuffed.

Throughout the district, it was striking that where NGOs were present in JFPM villages, the VFCs tended to give more emphasis in their plans for their JFPM plot to long-term ecological conservation, e.g. the planting of a variety of different types of trees, including fruit trees. Where no NGOs were present, the tendency was for the VFC to emphasise considerations like the planting of only trees giving timber intended to provide financial benefits for the members in the shorter term.

These findings were strengthened by what the interviews with the local forest officials suggested. Most were fairly or very positive about JFPM and recognised the importance of NGOs in helping to achieve its successful implementation. One local forest official said he had now become 'a servant of the people', going from door to door, conducting meetings. trying to encourage people to form a VFC and construct (with the Forest Department) a forest management plan.

A major problem is that village people know the past history of the Forest Department, and may not believe what is being said. This is where NGOs come in, the forest official said, and where they are crucial to the successful implementation of JFPM. 'NGOs can urge the people to support the Forest Department'. They can 'play a major role as a bridging group—creating confidence, awakening the people, encouraging sharing, helping formulate the plan, keeping everything in the open'. 'A forest officer is still a forest officer: he will plan to suit his needs. He may dupe the people. If an NGO is there, it can ask the important questions that village people will not think of'.

In Uttara Kannada, however, there are very few NGOs, the forest official said. Before JFPM most NGOs were not playing a role in protecting the forests, but one of confrontation with the Forest Department. They were also making war on industries, for example, the West Coast Paper Mills. Some, like IDS, were engaged in economic uplift, but this, he thought, had no noticeable effect on deforestation in Uttara Kannada. Before JFPM there were no NGOs in Uttara Kannada 'with a proven track record of the sort we would like to see'. So the ODA project includes a contract with Oxfam to appoint someone 'with missionary zeal' to the district to build up NGOs. New NGOs need to be encouraged. Also, the Oxfam person would recruit people who would work with existing NGOs and interest them in forest issues.

NGO people in Uttara Kannada have a rather different view of all this. An NGO person in FEVORD-K underlined the difference by saying 'neither the Forest Department nor ODA have responded to our critique of the Government Order'. He said many of the problems of JFPM lie in the rules laid down in the Order. Too much power rests in the hands of the Forest Department, hindering the development of genuine joint forest management. Working to such rules, forest officials have tended to 'define everything', have tended to assume responsibility for all decisions: the general approach has been: 'I do, you participate'. Village meetings, for example, have been organised by Forest Department officials at their convenience. Such scheduling 'should not be left to one side only'. Various particular features of the Government Order which FEVORD-K criticised were still posing problems. The role of women is one such problem. When VFCs are formed, forest officials 'will call two women and make them sit there'. Usually later it was eventually agreed that women could be members. Another example involves the procedures for collecting Rs 2 from members; the money must be sent registered post and a receipt obtained. Such procedures pose no problem for bigger farmers, but they can be troublesome for the poor. But foresters usually 'have found it easier to work with big farmers'.

Another issue of contention involved the choice of Uttara Kannada and then Shimoga as the locations for the ODA project and the main initial sites for implementing JFPM. The reason given by ODA and forest department people for choosing Uttara Kannada initially was that this area contained some of the best forest in south India, one where considerable degradation was occurring: the ODA project aimed to arrest that process and contribute to sustainable forest development in this important ecological zone. The FEVORD-K person thought there was also 'lots of scope there for the forest department to make money'. He also believed the forest department preferred Uttara Kannada because there were only four or five FEVORD-K NGOs there. It would therefore be 'easier' for the forest department to implement JFPM. He admitted that the NGO presence and networking in Uttara Kannada was 'poor at the outset, but we are making that up now'. That the 'NGOs are weak' criterion may have been important in the KFD's choice of site is supported by the choice of Shimoga as the second site. FEVORD-K preferred Mysore District where NGOs were strong and plentiful, but Shimoga, where NGOs are weak, was the district selected. A choice consistent with the criteria used for choosing Uttara Kannada, that is on ecological grounds, would have resulted in Dakshina Kannada (immediately south of Uttara Kannada) being chosen, not Shimoga.

Not surprisingly, Oxfam's role in Uttara Kannada was viewed critically by the FEVORD-K person. He thought Oxfam had strayed from its proper role as a donor agency to a dubious role involving definite programme functions. Inevitably, they would be sucked into local politics. The KFD were attracted to Oxfam, he said, because

Oxfam could neither criticise them nor bring any pressure to bear. Oxfam were being given VIP treatment by the KFD, and that had created 'bad feeling' among the rural poor. Helping to build up the NGO sector in Uttara Kannada should be FEVORD-K work, rather than the work of an 'outsider' like Oxfam.

Although these and other criticisms were firmly expressed, the FEVORD-K person also said that relations with KFD had been gradually improving in 1994. He thought 'pressure from NGOs at all levels' had helped. He also said there was a growing recognition in FEVORD-K circles that there were at least *some* very good forest officials in Uttara Kannada committed to JFPM and keen to see it succeed. Even some ordinary forest guards were becoming enthusiastic about participatory methods, instead of 'relying on coercion as of old'. Such people in the KFD appreciated that NGOs were needed to implement JFPM successfully in the longer term throughout Karnataka. and that Oxfam's role could only be comparatively temporary and confined to Uttara Kannada. The work of FEVORD-K in strengthening NGOs and training them in JFPM methods was bound to strengthen their position vis-à-vis the KFD. More importantly, the successful implementation of JFPM *depends on* the work NGOs can do that the KFD cannot do with local rural communities. As that dependency relationship is increasingly recognised by both the KFD and FEVORD-K, then the latter's influence on the details of the implementation phase of the JFPM policy process is likely to become increasingly important.

Conclusion

Have NGOs in FEVORD-K been influential in affecting the development of JFPM policy in Karnataka? I have briefly essayed this question in terms of agenda setting, policy choices and implementation processes. The evidence comes from research currently in progress in Karnataka, so the answer to the question is necessarily provisional. It does seem, however, that FEVORD-K's influence may vary as between these three phases of policy making. Agenda setting involves numerous NGOs and other organisations and groups at local, national and global levels whose work over time helps to shift the discourse within a particular policy arena: by itself, FEVORD-K can be said to have had minimal influence, but in combination with others outside the state at different levels articulating a new direction for forest management policy they appear to have had some influence in setting the agenda. Policy choices are made by what for NGOs can be called 'target organisations' at which an NGO's advocacy work is directed; for FEVORD-K the KFD was the main target on which they worked while specific JFPM policy choices were being made during 1990-93, but despite their efforts FEVORD-K did not have a major influence on these policy choices. Implementation processes are also part of any policy, the details or which can be affected by NGOs; FEVORD-K and other NGOs are currently working hard on this phase of JFPM policy and they are likely to become increasingly influential as time goes on because the JFPM policy cannot effectively be implemented throughout Karnataka without them.

In short, it appears that FEVORD-K may have been least influential when they tried their hardest directly to influence JFPM policy choices by the KFD during 1991-93; together with many other organisations and groups they may have been a bit more influential in helping to set the agenda for JFPM during the 1980s without perhaps fully appreciating that they were doing so; and our field research suggests they are most influential in affecting the implementation of JFPM in Uttara Kannada and are likely to become even more influential as JFPM policies and practices are gradually implemented throughout Karnataka.

9

Autonomous and Joint Forest Management in India's Jharkhand: Lessons for the Future?

Sarah Jewitt

Since about 1980, rapid forest loss stemming largely from increased industrial demand for timber, conversion of forest land to agricultural use plus growing rural and urban requirements for fuel and construction wood has been recognised as one of India's most serious environmental problems.[1] It is only since 1988, however, that the Indian government has acknowledged the failure of many of the forest policies pursued since Independence to resolve this problem.

Although attempts at forest conservation have succeeded in slowing the rates of deforestation from about 1.5 million hectares per year in the early 1980s to an estimated current rate of 47,300 hectares per year (Palit 1993), over 37 million hectares of India's 75 million hectares of so-called 'forest land' is still classed as degraded. Out of this total, over 24 million hectares requires afforestation, and much more land needs to be planted with trees if the Indian government's aim of achieving 33 per cent forest cover is to be met (Indurkar 1992; Palit 1993).

The reduction in environmental quality that is caused by a loss of forest cover has had severe implications for those members of the Indian population that are dependent on forests in some way. For many rural communities, forests are a source of fuelwood, house construction materials, timber for making agricultural implements, fodder, land for cattle grazing or shifting cultivation, food, medicinal herbs and other (potentially saleable) non-timber forest products

[1] Although the cutting of forests for firewood and construction timber has a fairly minor impact on forest loss compared to commercial timber exploitation and agricultural encroachment, its necessity for subsistence at the local level has made it an issue of national importance.

(NTFP). For some communities it is also a place of great socio-cultural and religious significance (Roy 1970 and 1985).

So what is responsible for forest decline? Although the pressure of increasing human and animal populations on declining areas of non-Reserved Forest has undoubtedly exacerbated forest loss by forcing people to use forest resources unsustainably, this 'official' view of the causes of forest decline is not the only explanation. Indeed, deforestation in India has been a rather more complex process than that suggested by the population-based models of 'open access' or common property resource degradation (Shepherd 1993; see also Hardin 1968 for a more 'traditional' perspective).

Guha (1983), for example, describes how in Uttarakhand, many local communities became alienated from what they had previously thought of as 'their' forests, following the reservation of forests for commercial production by the British colonial state in 1878. In many cases, this loss of control discouraged local people from protecting and nurturing forests that were being 'scientifically' managed, policed and felled by frequently corrupt Forest Department employees and contract cutters.

But not all communities reacted in this way. The actual process of forest exploitation by outsiders often encouraged local communities to protect nearby jungle areas by means of village-based forest protec-tion committees. Some of these have been operating successfully since before the independence of India in 1947. In several more recent cases, Forest Department officers (and sometimes NGOs) have sought the active support and involvement of local villagers in forest management. This, in turn has stimulated further interest in community-based forest protection (Kant et al. 1991; Mehrotra and Kishore 1990).

Of particular interest are 'joint forest management' initiatives in which control over local forests is shared by the state and local communities. By 1996, 16 of India's 25 States had issued notifications institutionalising joint forest management systems; most of these contain provisions for the establishment of locally-based forest protection committees. Currently, over 200,000 hectares of state-owned and community forest land are being managed as common property resources by such committees (Kant et al. 1991; Mehrotra and Kishore 1990; Sarin 1993).

Using the Jharkhand region of Bihar as a study area, I will examine the dynamics of forest management and forest policies in the British and post-colonial periods. I will then take up questions of autonomous (villagers') forest protection and management strategies in Ranchi District, Bihar, dawing heavily on fieldwork that I carried out in two villages in 1993 and 1995. The following section considers the development of 'official' forest protection committees in India (with particular reference to Bihar), and discusses their likely utility and probable shortcomings in relation to the autonomous committees.

Forest Policy

British Forest Policy

At first, Britain did little in the way of managing what it considered to be India's 'inexhaustible' forest resources. By the mid-nineteenth century, however, concern about declining forest resources and the need to secure future supplies of timber for railway construction, ship building and military purposes resulted in the first proposal for forest conservation. In 1864, the Imperial Forest Department was created and in 1865, the first Indian Forest Act was passed. At the same time 'scientific forestry' based on European silvicultural principles and centred around the production of sustained timber yields (often through the creation of mono-cultures) was introduced.

The reservation of certain forests for commercial purposes followed soon afterwards with the introduction of the Indian Forest Act of 1878. This divided India's forests into four categories: (1) Reserved Forests; (2) Protected Forests; (3) Private Forests; and (4) Village Forests. The Act also established the colonial state's monopoly right over forest lands by converting villagers' customary rights of forest use into 'privileges,' granted by the Forest Department[2]—a move that Guha argues failed to recognise that many peasant communities were unfamiliar with the concept of individual ownership (Guha 1989). Reserved Forests (unless specifically 'reserved with rights'), were thenceforth not to be used by local villagers except for the collection of certain minor forest produce[3] and for watering (and sometimes grazing) cattle. In Protected Forests,

[2] Many accounts refer to a forest 'golden age' prior to British colonial rule, when local people enjoyed unrestricted access to and use of forest land. Even if their *de jure* ownership rested with various local rulers, many forests were managed *de facto* as common property resources (Tiwari 1983; Prabhu 1983; Kulkarni 1983; Shiva 1988, Guha 1983 and 1989).

[3] Typically, villagers were allowed to collect edible fruits, flowers and roots for domestic use.

villagers were granted the 'privileges' of collecting wood for domestic needs and grazing their cattle.

Although Village Forests were set aside for subsistence use by local villagers, many communities were faced with severe limitations in the woodland areas available to them. In addition to this, they had to cope with a series of new rules regarding their access to forests, imposed by a highly bureaucratic Forest Department that was willing to punish 'forest crimes' with some force.

In areas where large scale forest reservation took place, additional pressure was placed upon forests that were 'open' to local communities by the need to satisfy increases in the colonial state's demand for timber products. As a result, many Protected and Reserved Forests quickly became degraded. To make matters worse, many people lost interest in managing and protecting Village Forests as they were afraid that this would encourage the state to reserve them. Some communities felt so alienated from Reserved Forests that they became violent towards them. In Uttarakhand, for example, there were a number of instances when villagers deliberately set fire to newly reserved forests in 1916 (Guha 1983 and 1989). On a few occasions, the intensity of villagers' opposition to the reservation policy caused the state to de-Reserve certain forests.

Post-Colonial Forest Policy

Instead of addressing these problems through the introduction of forest policies that showed more sensitivity to the needs of forest-dependent villagers, the post-colonial Forest Department maintained a surprising degree of continuity with its colonial predecessor. Forest reservation and 'scientific forestry' continued in the 'national interest' to satisfy India's large and growing industrial, commercial, communications and defence requirements. But to meet these demands, forest conservation practices gave way to timber exploitation on a vast scale (Guha 1983). This has, of course, had severe implications not only for forest stability, but for the livelihoods of forest-dependent populations, whose role in the management of forests (with the exception of Village Forests) remained minimal.

As was the case during the colonial period, local peoples' loss of control over forest resources often manifested itself in what Guha (1989) describes as a pervasive alienation from and loss of interest in forests. Illegal felling and forest exploitation by Forest Department employees (particularly, contract cutters) further exacerbated many villagers' sense of detachment from forests. It also heightened their unwillingness to try to re-establish traditional forms of community forest protection or management, since they felt sure they would not reap any benefits. Instead, many villagers thought they would be foolish not to follow the contractors' example and help themselves to the state's property.[4] This response further intensified the problem of deforestation and increased the antagonism between the Forest Department and local communities (Guha 1983; Joshi 1983; Palit 1993).

In some areas, forest communities became so angry about the commercial exploitation of forest lands that they resisted the imposition of Forest Department activities. In Uttarakhand, the Chipko movement (which grew out of a history of local peasant opposition to commercial forestry practices) was extremely effective in bringing clear-felling to a halt (Shiva 1988; Guha 1989). In Singhbhum District, Bihar, violent opposition by local tribal (*ādivāsī*) populations to clear-felling for the establishment of teak plantations reached such an intensity in the late 1970s and early 1980s that forest officers temporarily had to withdraw (Corbridge 1991). On many more occasions, however, such opposition to official forest policies called forth an increasingly repressive response by the state. This included greater levels of vigilance and policing to 'protect' forests from local people and, in some cases, the use of arms to put down 'unrest' (Anderson and Huber 1989; Corbridge 1991; Palit 1993).

The similarity between colonial and post-colonial forest policies apparent in the above examples is quite striking. Indeed, the main difference between the two sets of policies lay not in their structure or objectives,[5] but in the greater willingness and ability of the post-colonial state to enforce forest policies that were often more modernising and detrimental to the needs of forest-dependent populations than those of their colonial predecessors (Jewitt 1995). This is nowhere more apparent than in the proposed Indian Forest Act, 1980, which—while retaining 81 out of 84 of the provisions of the 1878 Indian Forest Act—proposed further restrictions on forest users and more severe penalties for forest offences. It also sought to increase the power of forest officers to implement these restrictions

---

[4] I heard this account many times, both from villagers and from forest officials, during the course of my fieldwork in the Jharkhand region.

[5] The Indian Forest Act, 1952 is based on the 1894 Resolution 22F on Forest Policy in India.

and to control illegal felling, despite the consistent misuse of such powers in the past (Guha 1983).

The 1980 Bill 'without any change in basic attitude' (Ghate 1992: 53) became the Forest Conservation Act, 1980. Due to the heavy criticism of the Act by various intellectuals, academics and organisations representing forest-dependent communities, a new policy document (emphasising the need to prevent further forest decline and to promote a more people-oriented set of forest policies) was prepared in 1983 and revised in 1987. Apart from acknowledging the power of local grassroots movements, these changes also reflected both a new climate of environmental awareness and pressures from the World Bank and other donor agencies to promote more environmentally sustainable forms of development.

Unfortunately, the 'top down' approaches used in many of the so-called people-oriented forestry (particularly social forestry) schemes seemed to cause more problems than they solved. Many programmes had very limited provisions for the involvement of local people: a situation that resulted in the failure of many schemes to involve women who are the main collectors of fuelwood in many areas (Shepherd 1985; Noronha and Spears 1988). It also created a situation where numerous landless people were forced, by the appropriation of village commons or 'wastes' by the state for afforestation purposes, into losing their traditional access to village common property resources (Noronha 1981; Shepherd 1985; Foley and Barnard 1985; Blaikie et al. 1986).

Villagers' Forest Management and Protection Strategies

As a result of these and other problems, large numbers of forest-dependent villagers became disillusioned with how little they gained from social forestry schemes. Many were also wary—after a history of conflict with the state over access to forest resources—of any promises by the Forest Department to improve the situation. As a result, a number of forest-dependent communities decided to take forest protection and management into their own hands.

In Bihar and Orissa, especially, the widespread neglect of local forests by the Forest Department (coupled with instances of illegal felling by forest officials) stimulated a number of communities into reviving (or re-inventing) informal village institutions for the purpose of village-level decision-making and forest protection (Kant et al.

1992; Sarin 1993; Mehrotra and Kishore 1990). This has been particularly common in *ādivāsī* areas where the socio-cultural links with local forests are particularly strong.

The remainder of this paper will explore the issue of autonomous forest protection with reference to two *ādivāsī*-dominated villages in the Jharkhand region of Bihar. One of the villages, Jamtoli, has been protecting its forest area successfully since the early 1950s. The other, Ambatoli, although registering concern about forest decline and aware of the need for forest protection, has been unable (so far) to sustain protection on a village-wide basis. Before I provide a more comprehensive introduction to these two villages, however, it is necessary to provide some background information on why forest protection became necessary in this area of the Jharkhand.[6]

Forest Management in the Jharkhand
During the colonial period, control over almost all of the non-reserved forests of this area was placed in the hands of local landowners or zamindars, who undertook little or no forest management. All villagers had customary concessions and rights to forest products (such as fuelwood and minor forest produce); the details of which were recorded in the Kattiyan Part II.[7] The amounts allocated to each household were determined (on the basis of need) by the zamindar or a village-level representative—usually the village religious leader (*mahto* or *pahan*). Some products were free and some

---

[6] Much of the information on local forest policy and forest management by the Bihar Forest Department comes from interviews with Sanjay Kumar, the former Divisional Forest Officer of Ranchi East Division and Anand Jha, the Forester for Bero Block. My accounts of local forest use, changing *ādivāsī*/forest interactions and Forest Department/local-villager relations are drawn mainly from participant observation techniques, informal interviews and group discussions with the villagers of Ambatoli and Jamtoli. This information was supported by oral histories obtained from six other villages in Ranchi District plus more formal interviews with forest officers in Bero Block and Ranchi.

[7] The Kattiyan Part II is a village-level record of rights that contains details of local people's fuelwood, timber, minor forest produce and grazing allowances. The types of minor forest produce collected by villagers in this region include fruit, seeds, tubers, edible leaves, mushrooms, medicinal herbs, liquor-making ingredients and sāl (*Shorea robusta*) leaves for leaf plates and bowls. Villagers also use the forest for religious purposes as *Sarna*, the main religion for *ādivāsīs* in this area is an animist faith in which forests play a central role.

had a small price. Any disputes over forest produce, illegal felling and so on tended to be dealt with through the traditional *parha* system which linked together up to twenty one villages. Led by hereditary *parharajas* (with assistance from village leaders and the local zamindar), these *parhas* dealt with most forms of village-level administration, decision-making, conflict resolution and resource management during this period (Roy 1984).

In Ambatoli and Jamtoli, a number of villagers now look back upon this period as a kind of golden age when the forests were well-stocked with large trees, restrictions on forest use were less severe and the villagers were provided with enough wood for all their construction and fuel requirements. Even the large scale extraction of timber for industrial and infrastructural use apparently did not cause any real problems, as the jungle was so dense at this time. From an administrative point of view, too, the lack of British interference with the *parha* system and their 'respect for local customs' is remembered with a certain nostalgia by some of the older villagers.

After independence, a process of land reforms was implemented throughout India. The *zamindārī* system was abolished in Bihar with the introduction of the Bihar Land Reforms Act in 1950. This Act vested in the state the ownership of all land that was not privately owned (i.e., tilled) by *zamindārs* or their tenants. In addition, all forests that had been designated as 'Private Protected' forests prior to 1950 were re-notified as 'Protected' forests and brought under state control. Before the Act was implemented, many local forests were plundered by the *zamindārs*, who were determined to make as much profit as they could before they lost their access to these resources.

As a result, many Protected Forests were in a degraded state when the Forest Department took them over, so efforts were made to improve their condition through coppicing and re-planting. In addition, villagers were expected to protect forests in exchange for the continuation of their rights to dry branches for fuelwood and minor forest produce. These rights were listed, as during the colonial period, in the Kattiyan Part II.

The 'scientific management' of each forest in this area was carried out on the basis of ten to twenty year working plans. Because most Protected Forests (and some of the smaller Reserved Forests) were heavily 'right burdened', their management plans were 'quasi commercial' in nature. This meant, in theory, that local needs would be met first from annual coupe cutting operations and any surplus would be sold at auction or to villagers at concessionary rates. In practice, many of the contractors employed by the Forest Department to undertake coupe cutting operations refused to recognise villagers' rights to forest produce and neglected to hand over their share of the coupe. They also tended to fell more of the forest than they were supposed to (often employing villagers to help them) in order to sell off the surplus wood to charcoal-makers for their own profit.

To compound matters, villagers who continued to get wood illegally from state forests stopped taking care to cut trees in a way that stimulated coppice growth, as they were afraid of being caught by the forest guard. At the same time, fuel shortages combined with the realisation that profits could be made from forest exploitation, encouraged the spread of fuelwood selling. Increasingly, villagers started to ignore erstwhile unspoken restrictions about the cutting of fruit and non-coppicing trees in favour of making a quick profit. This had severe implications for long term forest regeneration.

Interestingly, this shift in attitudes towards forests coincided with the breakdown of many traditional *parha* systems of administration following the introduction, in 1949, of the *grām panchāyat* system of local government. The *parha* system had formerly dealt with conflicts over access to forest resources and had acted as an intermediary between local villagers and the Forest Department, and its decline meant the loss of an important safety valve in a situation of growing tensions.[8] Cases of illegal felling by villagers were taken up at the Block level, instead of being resolved locally by the *parha* authorities. Between the mid 1970s and early 1980s, the antagonism between villagers and the Forest Department came to a head in many areas of the Jharkhand. Small 'offences' brought large penalties, such as the cutting of a sapling resulting in imprisonment.

Fieldwork in Jamtoli and Ambatoli
It will be apparent that many of the generalisations offered in this paper depend upon more specific observations from my doctoral fieldwork in Ranchi district, Bihar.[9] This fieldwork was carried out in

---

[8] Many illiterate villagers felt unable to cope with formal interactions with the Forest Department. Assistance from the *parha* alleviated villagers' concerns that the state would exploit their illiteracy and lack of familiarity with legal documents, in order to claim unreasonable fines for forest 'crimes'.

[9] In collecting this information, I became deeply indebted to the villagers of Ambatoli and Jamtoli who taught me about forest history, use and

two main phases during 1993 and updated during a brief visit to the research area in April 1995. In the first half of 1993, I rented a hut from an *ādivāsī* family in Ambatoli, a large village (1,547.16 hectares in total) fringed to the east by a degraded Protected Forest of 555.39 hectares.[10] This is the largest such forest in Ranchi District, and is typical of forests in the region in that it is dominated by regenerating *sāl* trees.[11] The village is settled predominantly by members of the Oraon tribe and has a total population of around 1750 people. Ambatoli, like most villages in this area, is not served with electricity.

From October to December, 1993, I lived mainly in Jamtoli, a somewhat smaller (857.14 hectares) and hillier village which is seven kilometres away from Ambatoli as the crow flies, but which takes forty minutes to reach by motor scooter. Jamtoli has a population of around 1330 people, and, like Ambatoli, is fringed by a fairly extensive area (246.43 hectares) of sāl dominated forest.

Unusually for this area, the forest surrounding Jamtoli is a Reserved Forest.[12] The reason for this is that Jamtoli was one of the area's few non-*zamindārī* villages during the British colonial period and its forest was an obvious target for reservation as it belonged directly to the state.[13] Nevertheless, the fact that Jamtoli forest was

---

management in this area. I am especially grateful to Pyari Lakra and Subani Kujur who assisted me in the field and to Pothwa Bhagat and Simon Oraon who spared much time for me and welcomed me into their homes.

[10] Ambatoli forest was re-notified as a Protected Forest in 1953. Before this, it was a Private Protected Forest, owned and managed by a *zamindār*.

[11] According to the villagers of Ambatoli and Jamtoli, tree species such as asan *(Terminalia tomentosa)*, bar *(Ficus bengalensis)*, dahu *(Artocarpus lakoocha)*, dumar *(Ficus glomerata)*, gamhar *(Gmelina arboria)*, jamun *(Prunus cornuta)*, karonda *(Carissa carandas)*, karam *(Adina cordifolia)*, karanj *(Pongamia pinnata)*, kend *(Diospyros melanoxylon)*, kusum *(Schleichera oleosa)*, mahuā *(Bassiu latifolia)*, mango *(Mangifera indica)*, palasa *(Butea monosperma)*, pipal *(Ficus religiosa)* and piyar *(Buchanania latifolia)* used to be abundant in the forests of Ranchi District. During the 1950s, most of the large trees in these forests were felled by zamindars and contract cutters. Sāl, as a result of its rapid regeneration through coppicing, became the dominant species.

[12] Jamtoli forest was notified as a Reserved Forest in 1944.

[13] Forest reservation was a long and complicated task unless the forest in question belonged directly to the state. Indeed, it was partly for this reason that the ex-*zamindars'* Private Protected Forests were re-notified as right-

heavily right-burdened meant that its management regime (and availability for use by local people) was very similar to that of Ambatoli forests.[14]

Jamtoli

Jamtoli is home to Simon Oraon, one of the area's few active *parharajas*. Jamtoli is also a rather unique village as Simon has tried extremely hard to maintain the role of his *parha* as a local administrative and developmental, as well as a social institution. Indeed, it was primarily around the issue of forest protection that Simon started to reorganise his *parha* following the introduction of the *grām panchāyat* system.

In Jamtoli there was a long tradition of local forest protection prior to the establishment, by Simon, of a more organised and formal forest protection committee. The change to a more formal system occurred soon after independence, when commercial timber exploitation and a steadily expanding local population started to put pressure on the village's forest resources. This was compounded by excessive (and illegal) forest felling by contractors which made it especially difficult for villagers to obtain (legally) timber large enough for house construction and plough making. In addition, a change in many villagers' attitudes towards forests that had suddenly come under Forest Department management, encouraged them to exploit these resources for their own profit.[15]

The establishment of a forest protection committee in Jamtoli was stimulated by an incident that occurred in the early 1950s. A group of contractors came to Jamtoli forest with instructions from the Forest Department to undertake routine felling operations. Seeing that the contractors were felling more than the allocated area and foreseeing the long term difficulties that such illegal forest exploitation would cause local villagers if it continued, Simon Oraon gathered together

---

burdened Protected Forests rather than as right-burdened Reserved Forests after the implementation of the Bihar Land Reforms Act, 1950.

[14] The main criterion for the reservation of right-burdened forests was that they should be sufficient in timber both for local use and commercial production. As right holders' requirements were, in theory, supposed to be met first, many small right-burdened Reserved Forests were managed *de facto* on a quasi-commercial basis which closely resembled that found in Protected Forests.

[15] Villagers of both Ambatoli and Jamtoli offered this interpretation freely, but it is also supported by census data for Ranchi District.

many of the inhabitants of Jamtoli's three *tolas* (hamlets) to challenge the contractors. Carrying bows and arrows, the villagers succeeded in chasing away the contractors and confiscating the cut timber.

This outcome encouraged Simon to use his influence as *parharaja* to persuade local people of the need for long term forest protection. Immediately afterwards, at several village meetings he managed to convince the people of Jamtoli that their lives were so bound up with the forest, they would not be able to survive unless they protected it. At first, many villagers were opposed to the idea of protecting a state forest from which the Forest Department (or forest contractors) would reap all of the benefits. Nevertheless, they could see the sense in what Simon was saying and met to decide upon the division of Jamtoli forest between the three *tolas* (Jamtoli, Bertoli and Kaxitoli) and the way in which forest protection would be administered. Within a few weeks, a committee consisting of one male member per household was established in each of the three hamlets.

The Forest Department, meanwhile, was rather harder to convince about the merits of Simon's village-based forest protection system and reacted to the incident by taking out a case against the Jamtoli villagers. After about ten years, however, the success of Simon's forest protection scheme impressed local forest officers so much that they dropped their case against the people of Jamtoli and started to show an interest in their initiative.[16]

By the late 1960s, however, the rate of regeneration in Jamtoli's and Bertoli's forest area was much slower than that of Kaxitoli. The main reasons for this were that the Jamtoli and Bertoli forest areas lie on rather infertile, rocky land and their greater accessibility to outsiders made them harder to guard. As a result, much stress was placed on the forest resources actually available to Jamtoli and Bertoli villagers and their protection systems started to falter. Kaxitoli (the hamlet in which Simon Oraon lives), meanwhile, maintained its guard over the forest. But Simon refused to allow the villagers of Jamtoli and Bertoli to have access to Kaxitoli's timber until they re-established their own committees. Consequently, village-wide forest protection soon returned, bringing with it rapid coppice regeneration.

Since the formation of a formal system of forest protection in Jamtoli, wood from the protected area has been distributed to the

---

[16] Indeed, when the villagers objected to an auction of a coupe for Jamtoli forest in 1978, the Forest Department agreed to find another forest from which the timber could be taken.

villagers of each *tola* during an annual coupe in which the whole community participates. Usually, the trees to be cut are selected in advance by the committee, to ensure that the required number of good timber trees are cut for house building purposes. Crooked and otherwise deformed trees, or 'single crop' species such as *asan* (*Terminalia tomentosa*) that are used only for wood, are felled for fuel purposes. Fruit trees are almost never cut unless there is something wrong with them. Other trees are chosen mainly on basis of their ability to regenerate rapidly through coppicing.

During the coupe, villagers are allowed to take a specified (usually three or four) number of bullock carts of wood per family for fuel. This has to last them all year and if they run short of fuelwood, they have to cut their own trees or search for dry branches or 'weed' bushes [such as putus (*Lantana camera*)] in the forest. Villagers in need of additional timber for household or agricultural purposes must ask the committee's permission for this. The committee then decides whether the need is justified. If so, a specific tree is set aside for this purpose and is felled during the coupe, or, if the requirement is urgent, at other times of the year. Unauthorised cutting or grazing in the forest is punished by way of fines.

On some occasions re-planting is undertaken by villagers after the annual coupe. This has been particularly popular in recent years as state finances have been available for tree planting. The trees chosen by the committee have tended to be fruit trees because sāl and asan (which are the main timber trees used by the villagers) regenerate through coppice growth. Particularly popular are *Mangifera indica, Psidium guajava, Bassia latifolia, Prunus cornuta, Aegle marmelos, Ziziphus mauritiana* (for fruit and as a host tree for lac) and *Artocarpus heterophyllus*. These trees are donated by the Forest Department and planted by committee members. In order to ensure that animals do not graze or damage the young saplings, fast growing Ipomoea plants and thorny putus (*Lantana camera*) bushes are used as a living fence. This and other maintenance work is carried out by committee members.

Ambatoli

Ambatoli belongs to a separate *parha* from Jamtoli and its exposure to strong and charismatic leaders such as Simon Oraon is more limited. It is also a larger, more spatially dispersed village consisting of seven *tolas* and its village-level administrative and decision-making systems are much less well developed. Although the two villages are actually linked by a continuous stretch of so called forest land, the jungle surrounding Ambatoli, although extensive, is extremely degraded and now contains only a handful of large trees. According to existing forest records and local oral histories, however, the condition of Ambatoli and Jamtoli forests were very similar during the early 1950s when the bulk of the ex-*zamindāri* Private Protected Forests were re-notified as state-owned Protected Forests.[17]

During the 1950s and 1960s, the contractor system of forest felling (combined with population increases) caused the villagers of Ambatoli—like those of Jamtoli and many other villages in the Jharkhand—to encounter difficulties in obtaining timber from nearby forests. Ambatoli, like the majority of villages in this area that I visited during the course of my fieldwork (with the exception of Jamtoli), had no strong leader to mobilise support against forest exploitation. As a result, most villagers accepted their share of the coupe from the contractors when they got it, and, when they did not, they started to cut the forest by themselves.

One of the major factors responsible for changes in local attitudes towards the forests was the employment of local villagers by the contractors to help with coupe cutting. Increasingly, local people came to see 'their' forests as government forests that they would be fools not to try to profit from. As a result, cutting was soon carried out on a daily basis. Nowadays, villagers (women in particular) often cut up to fifteen young saplings during each trip. Deliberate coppicing has become rare and species selectivity is often minimal, with the result that young, non-coppicing fruit trees (provided they are of the right size), are often cut along with sāl and asan. Even when regeneration does occur, the practice of grazing cattle in the jungle frequently results in the trampling or browsing of new growth.

On several occasions during the 1980s, the Forest Department did try to ameliorate these problems by undertaking re-planting within the forest as part of a local social forestry scheme. Some villagers were paid Rs 15 per day by the Forest Department to plant trees (mainly

[17] Jamtoli, being a non-*zamindāri* village, was little affected by the exploitation that followed the Bihar Land Reforms Act of 1950, but forest records from the early 1950s suggest that after six years of commercial management, the density of Jamtoli forest was very similar to that of Ambatoli forest during the same period. The main difference between the two forests would have been a slightly higher proportion of large trees in Jamtoli forest resulting from the Forest Department's improvement felling.

eucalyptus and acacia plus a few fruit trees) in particularly degraded parts of Ambatoli forest. When these trees mature, villagers will be allowed to use their leaves and branches for fuel purposes, but they will not be able to cut them down until the Forest Department authorises them to do so. When this happens, the timber from these trees will be distributed amongst the *tolas*.

In spite of these efforts, villagers estimate that Ambatoli forest has declined by fifty percent since the mid 1980s. Many of the wild animals (such as deer, wild pigs and even tigers) that used to inhabit the forest have disappeared along with their former habitats. It is now very difficult to obtain trees large enough for house construction or plough-making, so local people are often forced to buy wood for these purposes. Villagers also complain that the loss of forest land is responsible for the difficulties that they are having in finding suitable areas of underground water for well construction.

One of the most obvious reasons for recent increases in the rate of forest loss is the growing incidence of fuelwood selling. For some of the poorer villagers, fuel sales provide the only real source of cash income, but for others, the activity is seen as an attractive alternative to agricultural labour.[18] To compound matters, the 'forest guard' refuses to clamp down on this practice as this would deprive him of the bribes (half the market value of the wood) he gets whenever he catches somebody cutting wood for sale.[19]

Nevertheless, many villagers have come to believe that they can and should protect Ambatoli forest 'for the sake of their grand children'. Unfortunately, the establishment of sustained unity between Ambatoli's seven *tolas* has been a major problem for forest protection at the village level. An additional problem is that although villagers are willing to protect Ambatoli forest from outsiders, they are less keen to restrict their own use of the forest as a source of fuel wood, timber, minor forest produce and free cattle grazing.

[18] Shoulder- and head-loads of fuelwood fetch around Rs 18-20 and Rs 14-16 respectively at the local weekly markets. The average daily wage for a male agricultural labourer with his own bullocks and equipment is Rs 15. Women's wages tend to be significantly less than this. Rice transplanting work, for example, is paid at a rate of less than Rs 10 per day in Ambatoli.

[19] The 'forest guard' who takes these bribes was actually replaced by different guard over five years ago. Nevertheless, the old guard still comes to the village and threatens to institute court cases against villagers who sell fuelwood, unless they give him a share of their income.

From the accounts given above, it can be seen that the villagers of Ambatoli and Jamtoli have had widely differing degrees of success in sustaining autonomous forest protection. In terms of the potential for this type of forest protection to ameliorate India's deforestation problem, however, the important issue is the extent to which the problems faced by voluntary organisations can be dealt with internally and whether (if at all) formal or informal assistance from external organisations such as the Forest Department or NGOs can help.

The possibility that the Ambatoli villagers can fully overcome their internal conflicts on their own initiative seems quite limited. The village is large, fragmented and has no functioning institution for decision-making. In addition, its *grām panchāyat* headman or *mukhia* lives in a neighbouring village (Patratoli) and takes little interest in forest protection: Patratoli has no forest of its own. Indeed, many people in Patratoli are very opposed to the idea of forest protection in Ambatoli as they do not want their access to Ambatoli forest to be stopped. Yet in the absence of protection, conflict over access to the forest and the amounts of fuelwood that villagers cut is unavoidable.

An alternative stimulus to the establishment of village-wide forest protection in Ambatoli would be interest by the Forest Department. A good start could be made by persuading the bribe-taking ex-forest guard to leave. If the Forest Department could then go on to address Ambatoli's lack of unity and conflicts over selling fuel (not to mention those resulting from the villagers' enthusiastic drinking habits), it might just be able to give the village the 'push' that it needs to get sustained village-level forest protection off the ground.

In contrast to Ambatoli, Jamtoli is much more unified, has a far stronger tradition of inter-*tola* co-operation and, to quote some of its residents, ' it has only a few drinking households'. The main reason for the success of forest protection in this village is undoubtedly the influence of Simon Oraon who, as *parharaja* for forty-six years, has been in a position to command respect and make his ideas known. He has also earned himself a reputation for honesty and a willingness to help others which has gained him the support of the villagers of Jamtoli and enabled him to persuade many other villages to start protecting their forest. This, in turn has won him the support of local forest officers who—despite the fact that he has effectively seized control over a Reserved Forest and brought a halt to its commercial timber production—now come to him for advice on how to settle forest-related disputes.

'Official' Forest Management and Protection Committees

Initially, much of the Indian state's emphasis on the involvement of local people in forest protection was linked to an attempt to make villagers aware of their 'duty' to protect the forest: a duty that was expected in exchange for their access to forest produce. The National Forest Policy, 1988, for example, states that 'the holders of customary rights and concessions in forest areas should be motivated to identify themselves with protection and development of forests from which they derive benefits' (quoted in Kant et al. 1992: 2-3).

During the late 1980s and early 1990s, this attitude gave way to a growing interest in the possibility of developing 'partnerships between local institutions and [Forest Departments] for the sustainable management of forest areas on the basis of trust and mutually defined rights and responsibilities of both parties' (Sarin 1993: 2). This new emphasis on joint forest management has marked a significant shift in attitudes towards rural people in forest areas. For the first time, they were seen as part of the solution to deforestation, rather than as the main problem.

These changes were first formalised at the State level in August 1988 and July 1989, when the Governments of Orissa and West Bengal issued orders to involve local people in forest management and protection. In West Bengal, provisions were made for 25 per cent of the sale value of timber grown in protected areas to be given back to the committee after harvesting. The idea behind this was to provide local communities with a powerful incentive to undertake long term forest management and protection. In June 1990, this innovation was taken up by the Government of India in a resolution which stated that if local communities 'successfully protect the forest, they may be given a portion of the proceeds from the sale of the trees when they mature' (Government of India 1990).

Since the West Bengal and Orissa resolutions on community-based forest protection were passed, over 320,000 hectares of forest land have been protected. In addition, fourteen other states (Gujarat, Rajasthan, Haryana, Jammu and Kashmir, Madhya Pradesh, Maharashtra, Andhra Pradesh, Bihar, Tripura, Punjab, Karnataka, Tamil Nadu, Meghalaya and Himachal Pradesh) have developed their own joint forest management initiatives (Sarin 1993).

The Bihar model, called the 'Development of Forests through Peoples' Participation Programme' was adopted in August 1990 and claims to be revolutionary in its provisions for returning around 80 percent of the profits raised from forest protection back to forest protection committees.[20] The programme applies, so far, only to Bihar's 'degraded' Protected Forests, of which there are 14,000 square acres.[21] The committees formed under the programme are known as 'village forest protection and management committees' (VFPMCs) and the aim is to create one committee for each area of degraded Protected Forest. The revenue village is the unit within which the committee is formed and if a forest serves more than one village, it is to be divided up into separate areas, each of which serves a different village.

The VFPMCs are made up of one member from each household. In larger villages where this system would present administrative problems, an 'executive committee' is established. This is made up of between fifteen and eighteen people including the elected and defeated Mukhia, the Sarpanch, the village religious leader, a local school teacher, four elected Scheduled Caste and/or Tribe representatives and between three and five women. The Forester holds the position of Member Secretary to the Executive Board and acts as the main problem solver and co-ordinator between the villagers and the Forest Department. The forest guard is a specially invited member, but is expected to attend the committee's monthly meetings.

The main duties of the VFPMC are to prevent further forest decline within the protected area, to report and punish illegal tree felling and to formulate detailed management plans for the forest. These plans are supposed to address local needs and to promote rapid forest regeneration. Before being implemented, they are submitted to the Forest Department for approval and amendment, if necessary. The Forest Department then provides the committee with the materials and financial help necessary for their implementation. There is also a provision within the programme for other development needs such as roads, wells and small dams, although the Forest Department's funds for these are small.

In return for the protection and management of the forest. villagers are allowed to take fuelwood and minor forest produce for

[20] Most of my information on the Bihar Joint Forest Management Programme comes from interviews with Sanjay Kumar and Anand Jha and discussions with villagers (particularly the inhabitants of Ambatoli and Jamtoli) in Ranchi District during 1993 and 1995.

[21] 'Degraded' is defined as having a vegetation density less than 0.4 as opposed to a closed canopy which has a vegetation density of 1.0.

their own use. If they succeed in protecting the forest until the trees within it mature, they will each receive a share of the final harvest (in addition to periodic coupes and thinnings) according to their customary rights for large timber as set out in the Kattiyan part II. Any surplus timber can then be sold by the committee, either to local villagers or on the open market. The resulting income (minus a royalty which is kept by the Forest Department) is then divided into three parts: one part for the future development of the forest, one part for the development of the village, and the remainder for the VFPMC's executive fund. [22]

To date, only a hundred or so VFPMCs have been formally recognised by the Bihar Forest Department. There are many more, however, that are actively protecting their forests but have no official standing as yet. One such case is Jamtoli which is in a particularly tricky position because Reserved Forests do not come under the jurisdiction of the Bihar Joint Forest Management Programme.

As the villagers of Jamtoli have been so active in forest protection in the past, however, local forest officers have encouraged them to form a VFPMC in the hopes that the Bihar Joint Forest Management Programme will be extended to include Reserved and non-degraded Protected forests at a later date.[23] In addition, some of the Forest Department's afforestation funds have been used to pay villagers Rs 25 per day to plant more than 100,000 trees. These were put mainly on degraded land around Bertoli and Jamtoli, but some were also planted within the Protected forest itself.

To consolidate its afforestation efforts and forest protection activities, Jamtoli's VFPMC has allocated a guard for each *tola* who patrols the forest and maintains the young growing stock in a newly established village tree nursery. The official forest guard, who is

[22] In Ranchi, the Forest Department expects to claim 20 per cent of the trees left at the end of the final rotation. The majority of these will be left to form a coppice-with-standards system that will provide soil protection in the short term and good quality timber in the long term.

[23] To the best of my knowledge, the people of Jamtoli are not aware that there may be problems regarding the formal recognition of their VFPMC and that this may have implications for their rights to the trees that they protect. When I raised this issue with forest officials in Ranchi, however, they were confident that the Bihar Joint Forest Management Programme would be extended to include Reserved Forests and non-degraded Protected Forests in the near future.

described as 'an honest man' by the villagers of Jamtoli, also helps to keep outsiders out of the forest. In addition, villagers have established a rota system according to which four or five people (women are not excluded) go into the forest each day to check for and discourage illegal felling. To ensure that cattle cannot enter the forest and damage regenerating trees, the villagers have dug a trench around the protected area. In addition, the guards ensure that cattle grazing is strictly controlled.

The trees planted have all been chosen by the VFPMC and consist mainly of species such as *Bassia latifolia, Tamarindus indica, Prunus cornuta, Artocarpus heterophyllus* and *Pongamia pinnata* which can provide timber as well as fruit or seeds for chutney or oil. A few fast-growing timber trees such as eucalyptus and *Gmelina arboria* have also been planted to cut down the lead time before villagers see some of the scheme's financial benefits.

In Ambatoli where the formal recognition of a VFPMC would present no problems, progress has been slow.[24] In 1993, several of the village leaders attended meetings about the Bihar Joint Forest Management Programme and many villagers said that they were looking forward to the formation of a VFPMC. This view was encouraged by local leaders such as Simon Oraon and Vishvanath Bhagat, the local representative of the Jharkhand Mukti Morcha (JMM) party. Both are strong believers in the scheme and have helped a number of other villages to establish village protection and management committees.

Between the end of 1993 and April 1995, however, little effort was put either into forest protection or joint forest management. One reason for this is that Vishvanath Bhagat, who was supposed to be helping the Ambatoli villagers to establish a VFPMC, was concentrating hard on his campaign for the Bihar State elections (he was elected as a Member of the Legislative Assembly) and had no time to visit Ambatoli. By April 1995 the villagers seemed to have lost interest in the scheme and with (they say) no visits from the Forest Department to motivate them about the need for forest pro-tection, continued to exploit the forest as before. To make matters worse, Ambatoli's Mukhia (who will be part of Ambatoli's com-mittee when it is created) refused to show any interest in the scheme.

---

[24] When I returned to Ambatoli in April 1995 to assess the progress of joint forest management there and to gain a sense of villagers' attitudes towards it, I got the sense that little had changed since I left in December 1993.

When I returned to Ambatoli in April 1996, however, several individuals (Bineswar Thakur, Jageshwar Ram Manjhi and Indru Sawansi) had established forest protection systems within their own *tolas* and were trying to convince non-protecting *tolas* about the need for village-wide forest protection. Six months later, a village-wide forest protection committee was established and was meeting regularly when I visited Ambatoli in December 1996. Given Ambatoli's past experience of intra-village conflict and the lack of interest shown by the Mukhia, however, the initiative is likely to be short-lived unless the rights of different villages in Ambatoli forest are clarified and the committee itself is awarded some formal standing.

Conclusion

In Ambatoli's case, the Bihar Joint Forest Management Programme may be exactly what the villagers need to find the unity that they need for sustained village-wide forest protection, something that most people want to undertake but are unlikely to achieve without assistance. The problems associated with the Mukhia's lack of interest in the scheme, for example, could be ameliorated if the Forest Department tried to explain to him that his village would gain and not lose from the scheme. The fact that this message was put across by 'outsiders' rather than by villagers (amongst whom long standing suspicion and jealousy often exists), could produce more interest in the programme. In addition, the scheme's provision for villagers to plant trees on village lands as well as to stimulate regeneration in existing state forests, means that villages without their own forests (like the Mukhia's village) can create and manage them as they like.

In more unified villages, the Bihar Joint Forest Management Programme's 'care and share' principal is acting as such a good incentive to participate that both eligible and non-eligible VFPMCs are virtually queuing up to be formally recognised. The programme has also been successful (to date) in avoiding a number of the problems associated with some of the early joint forest management programmes (Kant et al. 1992; Sarin 1993).

If joint forest management is to be the model for the future, however, the likely success of state-formed as opposed to autonomous forest protection committees must be considered. From the examples discussed above, it seems as though the main places in which the state can make a difference is in the case of very heterogeneous, or non-unified villages such as Ambatoli: the crucial factor being a history or an awareness of the need for forest protection which would result in the formation of autonomous forest protection committees, if only villagers had an extra stimulus to enable them to act and make decisions collectively.

In such cases, initiatives like the Bihar Joint Forest Management Programme could be an ideal solution, as they allow villagers to actually manage local forests with little danger of the state taking the benefits. At the same time, if Forest Department staff are prepared to spend time looking into the ways in which different village groups use and benefit from the forest, they may be in an excellent position to make sure that the requirements of poor or underprivileged groups are met. The presence of 'outsiders' on the executive committee may also stimulate the solution of problems that could not be tackled internally, and should help to ensure that executive committees are not taken over by vested interest groups.

Nevertheless, these benefits do not guarantee that joint forest management will work over a long period of time. Many of the problems associated with these schemes relate to the fact that even though they may address a strongly felt local need, they are, like social forestry and many other rural development projects, essentially 'imposed' by the state. Palit, for example, when writing about joint forest management, stresses the need for 'creating awareness among the rural poor and organising them for collective action' (1993: 23). But awareness of the need for forest protection cannot be created out of thin air and the populist ideal of trying to return to some previous 'golden age' is not likely to be shared by most local communities. Instead, they must feel the need to and want to protect local forests before joint forest management is likely to be undertaken seriously by them.

Where villagers are not committed to forest protection, the long lead time associated with it is likely to add additional stress to existing community tensions. Even in 'incentive based' initiatives such as the Bihar Joint Forest Management Programme, villagers must still remain united long enough for the benefits of forest protection to reach them. More crucially, they also have to meet their subsistence needs in the meantime, from what are often extremely degraded forests. If provisions are not made for this, tension over access to scarce (but rapidly regenerating) forest produce may well result in the sudden felling of the protected area.

Overall, the greatest potential for joint forest management seems to be in villages where local people are both aware of and willing to tackle the problem of forest decline. In such cases, the state (ideally accompanied by NGOs) could play a facilitative role and, in ways sensitive to individual village circumstances, help local communities to overcome the obstacles that had prevented them from forming more autonomous forest protection and management systems.

In cases where there is little concern or awareness about forest decline, however, the state's attempt to create community-based forest protection systems will, of necessity, be significantly more 'top down' and imposed in nature. The danger here is that the resulting committees would be more likely to fall prey to vested interests and many of the other problems associated with 'top down' rural development projects. Although efforts would undoubtedly be made to try to prevent or ameliorate these difficulties, the problem remains that if local communities see no need for forest management or have no concern about forest decline, it is unlikely that the state will be able to create it.

If attempts to do this are made, and a large number of the resulting committees fail, decisions may be taken to abandon what could be—if properly applied—a potentially very successful, worthwhile and necessary project. To avoid this problem, it might be more sensible for the Indian state to concentrate its resources on the facilitation of new committees and the stabilisation of existing autonomous ones in areas where the need for forest protection is keenly felt by local communities. Then, the 'demonstration effect' of their success (plus the declining resources available to non-protecting communities) may result in a growing interest in forest protection. Along with this, the potential for the spread of community-based autonomous and joint forest management throughout India—and possibly elsewhere too—could increase.

Bibliography

Acheson, J. M. (1989) 'Where Have All the Exploiters Gone? Co-Management of the Maine Lobster Industry,' pp. 199-217 in F. Berkes (ed.) *Common Property Resources. Ecology and Community-Based Sustainable Development*, London: Belhaven Press.

Achyutha Menon, C. (1943) *Kali Worship in Kerala* [Malayalam] Madras: University of Madras.

Agarwal, B. (1992) 'The Gender and Environment Debate: Lessons from India,' *Feminist Studies* 18: 119-58.

Aiyappan, A. (1937 [1965]) *Social Revolution in a Kerala Village: A Study in Culture*, London: Asia Publishing House.

Aiyappan, A. and K. Mahadevan (1990) *Ecology, Economy, Matriliny and Fertility of Kurichiyas*, Delhi: B. R. Publishing Corpn.

Ali, Salim (1985) *The Fall of a Sparrow,* Delhi: Oxford University Press.

Anderson, R. S. and W. Huber (1988) *The Hour of the Fox: Tropical Forests, the World Bank and Indigenous People of Central India*, Seattle: University of Washington Press.

Archer, W. G. (1974) *The Hill of Flutes*, Pittsburgh: University of Pennsylvania Press.

Arnold, J. E. N. (1990) *Social Forestry and Communal Management in India*, ODI Social Forestry Network, Paper 11 b.

Arnold, J. E. N. and J. G. Campbell (1985) 'Collective Management of Hill Forests in Nepal: the Community Forestry Development Project,' pp. 425-454 in *Proceedings of the Conference on Common Property Resource Management* (Prepared by: Panel on Common Property Resource Management, Board on Science and Technology for International Development, Office of International Affairs and National Research Council), Washington, D. C.: National Academy Press.

Ashley, Wayne (1979): 'The Teyyam Kettu of Northern Kerala,' *Drama Review* 23, 2: 99-112.

Bahuguna, V. K. (1994) 'Collective Forest Management in India,' *Ambio,* 23, 4-5: 269-73.

Bandyopadhyay (Banerji), Bibutibhusan (1938) *Aranyak*, Calcutta: Mitra & Ghosh.

Basham, A. L. (1971) (paperback ed. Fontana Books, 1971) *The Wonder that was India*, 3rd ed., London: Sidgwick and Jackson.

Bayly, C. A. (1975) *The Local Roots of Indian Politics, Allahabad, 1880-1920*, Oxford: Clarendon Press.

Bebbington, A. J. (1992) 'Searching for an "Indigenous" Agricultural Development: Indian Organisations and NGOs in the Central Andes of Ecuador,' Centre of Latin American Studies, University of Cambridge, Working Paper No. 45.

Benton, T. (1994) 'Biology and Social Theory in the Environment Debate,' pp. 28-50, in M. Redclift and T. Benton (eds) *Social Theory and the Global Environment*, London: Routledge.

Berkes, F. (1989) 'Co-operation from the Perspective of Human Ecology,' pp. 70-88 in F. Berkes (ed.) *Common Property Resources, Ecology and Community-Based Sustainable Development*, London: Belhaven Press.

Berreman, G. D. (1993) 'Prologue: Behind Many Masks: Ethnography and Impression Management,' pp. xvii-lvii in his *Hindus of the Himalayas: Ethnography and Change*, Delhi: Oxford University Press.

Biardeau, Madeleine (1981) *L'Hindouisme: Anthropologie d'une civilisation*, coll. Paris: Champs, Flammarion.

Blaikie, P. M., J. C. Harriss and A. N. Pain (1986) 'The Management and Use of Common Property Resources in Tamil Nadu, India,' pp. 480-504 in *Proceedings of the Conference on Common Property Resource Management* (Prepared by: Panel on Common Property Resource Management, Board on Science and Technology for International Development, Office of International Affairs and National Research Council), Washington, D. C.: National Academy Press.

Blauert, J. (1988) 'Autochthonous Development and Environmental Knowledge in Oaxaca, Mexico,' pp. 33-54 in P. Blaikie and T. Unwin (eds) *Environmental Crises in Developing Countries*, Monograph No. 5, Developing Areas Research Group, Institute of British Geographers.

Bombay Natural History Society (BNHS) (1988) *Ecology of Semi-tropical, Monsoonal Wetland in India, The Keoladeo National Park, Bharatpur, Rajasthan*, Final Report, September.

Bose, P. K. (1991) 'Shifting Cultivation in South India,' pp 131-47 in S. Bose (ed.) *Shifting Cultivation in India*, Calcutta: Anthropological Survey of India.

Bose, S. (ed.) (1991) *Shifting Cultivation in India*, Calcutta: Anthropological Survey of India.

Brown, Katrina (1995) 'Plain Tales from the Grasslands: The Utilisation of Natural Resources in Royal Bardia National Park, Nepal,' paper presented at the International Association for the Study of Common Property Conference, Bodø, Norway.

Bruun, O. and Kalland, A. (1995) *Asian Perceptions of Nature: A Critical Approach*, London: Curzon Press.

Buchanan, Francis (1870 [1807]) *A Journey from Madras through the Countries of Mysore, Canara, and Malabar*, Madras: Higginbotham and Co.

Cattopadhyay, Bankim Candra (1866) *Kapalkundala, Bankim Racanavali*, vol. 1, Calcutta: Sahitya Samsad.

——(1882) *Anandamath, Bankim Racanavali*, vol. 1, Sahitya Samsad, Calcutta, pp. 715-88, trans. from *Le monastère de la félicité*, Paris: Publications Orientalistes de France, trans. France Bhattacharya.

Chakravarty-Kaul, M. (1996) *Common Lands and Customary Law: Institutional Change in North India over the Past Two Centuries*, Delhi: Oxford University Press.

Chambers, R. and M. Leach (1990) 'Trees as Savings and Security for the Rural Poor,' *Unasylva* 41: 161.

Chatterji (see Cattopadhyay).

Chattopadhyay, Srikumar (1984) *Deforestation in Parts of the Western Ghats Region (Kerala), India*, Trivandrum: Centre for Earth Science Studies.

Clark, I. (1991) *Democratising Development: The Role of Voluntary Organisations*, London: Earthscan.

Clothey, F. W. (1977) *The Many Faces of Murukan: The History and Meaning of a South Indian God*, The Hague, Paris & London: Mouton.

Corbridge, S. E. (1991) 'Ousting Singbonga: the Struggle for India's Jharkhand,' pp. 153-82 in C. Dixon and M. J. Heffernan (eds) *Colonialism and Development in the Contemporary World*, London: Mansell.

Cruz, Ma. Concepcion J. (1989) 'Water as Common Property: The Case of Irrigation Water Rights in the Philippines,' pp. 219-35 in F. Berkes (ed.) *Common Property Resources. Ecology and Community-Based Sustainable Development*, London: Belhaven Press.

Curgenven, A. J. (Trans.), (1911) *The Hukumnama of Lingarajendra Wodeyar, Raja of Coorg*, Mercara: Coorg District Press.

D'Abreo, D. (1982) *People and Forests. The Forest Bill and a New Forest Policy,* New Delhi: Indian Social Institute.

Damodaran Pillai, P. (1955) 'Sylvan Civilisation in Kerala,' pp 155-61 in P. K. Narayanan Pillai (ed.) *Kerala Studies: Professor A. Gopala Menon Commemoration Volume,* Trivandrum: Alliance Printing Works.

Daniels, R., M. Gadgil and M. Joshi (1993) unpublished paper, 'Impact of human extraction on tropical humid forests of Western Ghats in Uttara Kannada. South India,' Centre for Ecological Sciences, Indian Institute or Science, Bangalore.

Devi, Mahasveta (1977) *Aranyer Adhikar,* Calcutta: Karuna Prakasani, 2nd ed.

Dogra, B. (1983) *People and Forests (a Report on the Himalayas),* New Delhi: Indian Social Institute.

Douglas, M. (1970) 'Environments at Risk,' *Times Literary Supplement,* 30 October, pp. 1273-75.

Dove, M. (1995) 'Forest Discourses in South and South East Asia: Local, National and Trans-National Perspectives,' paper presented at an SSRC conference on *Environmental Discourses in South and Southeast Asia,* December, Hawaii.

Dumont, Louis (1970 [1966]) *Homo Hierarchicus: The Caste System and its Implications,* trans., Mark Sainsbury et al., Chicago: University of Chicago Press.

Eckholm, E. (1975) 'The other energy crisis: firewood,' *Worldwatch Paper 1,* Washington: Worldwatch Institute.

Eder, K. (1996) *The Social Construction of Nature,* London: Sage Publications.

Elizarenkova, T. (1994) 'Forests in the Rgveda,' Paper presented to the Panel on Forests at the 12th Modern European South Asian Studies Conference, Toulouse, September.

Ellen, R. (1993) *The Cultural Relations of Classification: An Analysis of Nuaulu Animal Categories from Central Seram,* Cambridge: Cambridge University Press.

Elwin, H. V. H. (1936) *Leaves from the Jungle: Life in a Gond Village,* London: John Murray.

——(1939) *The Baiga,* London: John Murray.

——(1949, reprint, 1991) *Myths of Middle India,* Delhi: Oxford University Press.

——(1964) *The Tribal World of Verrier Elwin. An Autobiography,* London: Oxford University Press.

Escobar, A. (1992) 'Reflections on "Development",' *Futures* 24: 411-36.

——(1996) 'Constructing Nature: Elements for a Poststructural Political Ecology,' in R. Peet and M. Watts (eds.) *Liberation Ecologies: Environment, Development, Social Movements,* New York and London: Routledge.

Esteva, G. (1987) 'Regenerating People's Space,' *Alternatives* XII: 125-52.

Ewans, Martin (1989) *Bharatpur: Bird Paradise,* New Delhi: Lustre Press.

Fairhead, J. and M. Leach (1996) 'Enriching the Landscape: Social History and the Management of Transition Ecology in the Forest-Savanna Mosaic of the Republic of Guinea,' *Africa,* 66, 1: 14-36.

Falconer, J. (1987) *Forestry Extension: A Review of the Key Issues,* ODI Social Forestry Network, Paper 4e.

FAO (1978) *Forestry for Local Community Development,* Forestry Paper 7, Rome: FAO.

——(1985) *Tree Growing by Rural People,* Forestry Paper 64, Rome: FAO.

——(1986) *Forestry Extension Organisation,* Forestry Paper 66, Rome: FAO.

——(1991) *Community Forestry: Ten Years in Review,* by J. E. M. Arnold, Rome: FAO.

Farrington, J. and D. Lewis (eds) (1993) *Non-Governmental Organisations and the State in Asia,* London: Routledge.

Feeny, David, et al. (1990) 'The Tragedy of the Commons: Twenty-two Years Later,' *Human Ecology* 18, 1: 1-19.

Fernandes, W. and S. Kulkarni (eds) (1983) *Towards a New Forest Policy. Peoples' Rights and Environmental Needs,* New Delhi: Indian Social Institute.

Foley, G. and G. Barnard (1985) *Farm and Community Forestry,* ODI Social Forestry Network, Paper 1 b.

Freeman, J. R. (1991) 'Purity and Violence: Sacred Power in the Teyyam Worship of Malabar,' PhD Dissertation, Department of Anthropology, University of Pennsylvania.

Gadgil, M. (1983) 'Forestry with a Social Purpose,' pp. 111-34 in W. Fernandes and S. Kulkarni (eds) *Towards a New Forest Policy. Peoples' Rights and Environmental Needs,* New Delhi: Indian Social Institute.

——(1989) 'Husbanding India's Natural Resources: The Tradition and the Prospects,' pp. 323-32 in Carla Borden (ed.) *Contemporary Indian Tradition: Voices on Culture, Nature and the Challenge of Change,* Washington and London: Smithsonian Institution Press.

——(1991) 'Deforestation: Problems and Prospects,' pp 13-85 in A. S. Rawat (ed.) *History of Forestry in India,* New Delhi: Indus Publishing Co.

Gadgil, M. and M.D.S. Chandran ('992) 'Sacred Groves,' in G. Sen (ed.) *Indigenous Vision: Peoples of India Attitudes to the Environment.* New Delhi: Sage Publications and India International Centre.

Gadgil, M. and R. Guha (1992) *This Fissured Land. An Ecological History of India,* Delhi: Oxford University Press.

Gadgil, M. and K.C. Malhotra (1989) 'Adaptive Significance of the Indian Caste System: An Ecological Perspective,' *Annals of Human Biology* 10: 465-8.

Gadgil, M. and V. D. Vartak (1976) 'The Sacred Groves of Western Ghats in India,' *Economic Botany,* 30.

——(1981a) 'Sacred Groves of Maharashtra: An Inventory,' pp. 279-94 in S. K. Jain (ed.) *Glimpses of Indian Ethno-Botany,* New Delhi: Oxford and IBH.

——(1981b) 'Studies on Sacred Groves along the Western Ghats from Maharashtra and Goa: Role of Beliefs and Folklores,' in S. K. Jain (ed.) *Glimpses of Indian Ethno-Botany,* New Delhi: Oxford and IBH.

Galey, J-C (1990) 'Reconsidering Kingship in India: An Ethnological Perspective,' pp. 123-87 in J-C. Galey (ed.) *Kingship and the Kings,* London: Harwood Academic Publishers.

Ganesh, K. N. (1991) 'Ownership and Control of Land in Medieval Kerala: *Janman-Kanam* Relations during the Sixteenth to Eighteenth Centuries,' *Indian Economic and Social History Review,* 28, 3: 299-328.

Gangopadyay, S. (1968) *Aranyer Din Ratri,* Calcutta: Ananda Publishers.

Geertz, C. (1973) *The Interpretation of Cultures: Selected Essays,* New York: Basic Books.

Ghate, R. S (1992) *Forest Policy and Tribal Development. A Study of Maharashtra,* New Delhi: Concept Publishing Ltd.

Giddens, A. (1979) *Central Problems in Social Theory: Action, Structure and Contradiction in Social Analysis*, London and Basingstoke: Macmillan Press.

———(1984) *The Constitution of Society: Outline of the Theory of Structuration*, Cambridge: Polity Press.

Giriappa, S. (1993) *Rural Development in Action: A Case Study of Coastal Areas [in Karnataka]*, Delhi: Daya Publishing House.

GOI (Government of India) (1989) *Report of the Steering Group on Environment, Forests and Wasteland Development for the Formulation of the Eighth Five Year Plan (1990-1995)*, Faridabad: Government of India Press.

———(1990) Resolution (1st June) on 'Involvement of Village Communities and Voluntary Agencies for Regeneration of Degraded Forest Land.'

———(1992) *Eighth Five Year Plan, 1992-97*, Vol. II, Faridabad: Government of India Press.

Gough, E. K. (1961) 'Nayar: Central Kerala; Nayar: North Kerala,' pp. 298-442 in D. Schneider and E. K. Gough (eds) *Matrilineal Kinship*, Berkeley: University of California Press.

Government of India: Ministry of Agriculture and Irrigation (1976) *Report of the National Commission on Agriculture Part IX: Forestry*, New Delhi: Government of India.

Government of Karnataka (1985) *Uttara Kannada* (District Gazetteer), Bangalore.

Government of Orissa (1990) Resolution (11th December 1990) on 'Protection of Reserved Forests and Protected Forests and Enjoyment of Certain Usufructs by the Community.'

Greenough, Paul (1992) 'Naturae Ferae: Wild Animals and Mortal Risks in South Asia Environmental History,' (unpublished).

Grindle, M. and J. Thomas (1991) *Public Choices and Policy Change: The Political Economy of Reform in Developing Countries*, Baltimore: John Hopkins University Press.

Guha, R. (1983) 'Forestry in British and Post British India. A Historical Analysis,' *Economic and Political Weekly*, 18: 1882-97 and 1940-47.

———(1989) *The Unquiet Woods. Ecological Change and Peasant Resistance in the Himalaya*. Delhi: Oxford University Press.

Gupta, A. K. (1986) 'Socioecology of Stress: Why do Common Property Resource Management Projects Fail?,' pp. 305-21 in *Proceedings of the Conference on Common Property Resource*

Management. (Prepared by: Panel on Common Property Resource Management, Board on Science and Technology for International Development, Office of International Affairs and National Research Council), Washington, D. C.: National Academy Press.

Hardin, G. (1968) 'The Tragedy of the Commons,' *Science* 162: 1243-48.

Hart, George L. (1975) *The Poems of Ancient Tamil: Their Milieu and their Sanskrit Counterparts,* Berkeley: University of California Press.

Haynes, Edward S. (1992) 'The Natural and the Raj: Customary State Systems and Environmental Management in Preintegration Rajasthan and Gujarat,' paper presented at the International Seminar on Environmental History of South and South East Asia, NISTADS, PUSA Campus, New Delhi (18-21 February).

Herring, Ronald (1995) 'State Property in Nature: Beginning Considerations,' paper presented at the conference on Rural and Urban Environments in South Asia organised by the Nordic Association for South Asian Studies, Oslo (18-22 May).

Hockings, Paul (1980) *Ancient Hindu Refugees: Badaga Social History, 1550-1975,* New Delhi: Vikas Publishing House.

Holloway, R. (ed.) (1989) *Doing Development: Government, NGOs and the Rural Poor in Asia,* London: Earthscan.

Hulme, D. and M. Edwards (eds) (1992) *Making a Difference? NGOs and Development in a Changing World,* London: Earthscan.

Indian Council of Forestry Research and Education, 1992, *Annual Report 1991-1992,* Dehra Dun.

Indurkar, P. (1992) *Forestry. Environment and Economic Development,* New Delhi: Ashish Publishing House.

Innes, C. A. (1908) *Madras District Gazetteers: Malabar and Anjengo,* F. B. Evans (ed.), Madras: Government Press.

Irschick, Eugene (1994) *Dialogue and History: Constructing South India, 1795-1895,* Berkeley: University of California Press.

Jackson, C. (1994) 'Environmental Reproduction and Gender Relations,' *Development* 1: 72-75.

Jackson, P. (1989) *Maps of Meaning: An Introduction to Cultural Geography,* London: Unwin Hyman.

Jain, Pushp K. (1995) 'Keoladeo Sanctuary,' *India Perspectives* 1: 2-7.

Jeffery, R. and N. Sundar (Forthcoming) 'A Shift from Minor to Major: Non-Timber Forest Products and Joint Forest Management in India,' in P. Greenough and A. Tsing (eds) *Environmental Discourses in South and Southeast Asia.*

Jewitt, S. L. (1995) 'Europe's "Others"? Forestry Policy and Practices in Colonial and Post-Colonial India,' *Environment and Planning D: Society and Space* 13: 67-90.

Joshi, G. (1983) 'Forest Policy and Tribal Development: Problems of Implementation, Ecology and Exploitation,' pp. 25-47 in W. Fernandes and S. Kulkarni (eds) *Towards a New Forest Policy. Peoples' Rights and Environmental Needs*, New Delhi: Indian Social Institute.

Kalam, M. A. (1994) 'Forest Abodes for Deities: Sacred Groves in Coorg (South India),' paper presented at the 13th European Conference of Modern South Asian Studies, Toulouse, France, 31 August to 3 September.

Kalpavriksh (Rajasthan) (1986) 'Bharatpur Firing,' pp. 44-47 in A. R. Desai (ed.) *Violation of Democratic Rights in India*, vol. 1, Bombay: Popular Prakashan.

Kangle, R. P. (1963) *The Kauṭilīya Arthasastra, Part II: An English Translation with Critical and Explanatory Notes*, University of Bombay Studies: Sanskrit, Prakrit, and Pali, No. 12. Bombay: University of Bombay.

Kant, S. N. S. Singh and K. S. Singh (1991) *Community Based Forest Management Systems (Case Studies from Orissa)*, Bhopal: Indian Institute of Forest Management, New Delhi: Swedish International Development Authority and New Delhi: ISO/Swedforest.

Kanvalli, S. (1993) *Quest for Justice*, 2nd ed. Dharwad: Samaj Parivartana Samudaya, et al.

Kelkar, G. and D. Nathan (1991) *Gender and Tribe: Women, Land and Forests in Jharkhand*, New Delhi: Kali for Women.

KFD (Karnataka Forest Department) (1991) 'Western Ghats Forestry and Environmental Project, Karnataka, India: Final Project Document (April),' cyclostyled.

Khator, R. (1991) *Environment, Development and Politics in India*, London: University Press of America.

Korton, D. C. (1986) 'Introduction: Community-Based Resource Management,' pp. 1-15 in D. C. Korton (ed.) *Community Management: Asian Experience and Perspectives*, West Hartford, Conn.: Kumarian Press.

——(ed.) (1986) *Community Management: Asian Experience and Perspectives*, West Hartford, Conn.: Kumarian Press.

Kothari, A., N. Singh and S. Suri (1996) *People and Protected Areas: Towards Participatory Conservation in India.* New Delhi: Sage Publications.

Krengel, M. (1989) *Sozialstrukturen im Kumaon: Bergbauern im Himalaya,* Stuttgart: Steiner Verlag Wiesbaden.

Kulkarni, S. (1983) 'The Forest Policy and Forest Bill. A Critique and Suggestions for Change,' pp. 84-102 in W. Fernandes and S. Kulkarni (eds) *Towards a New Forest Policy. Peoples' Rights and Environmental Needs,* New Delhi: Indian Social Institute.

——(1992) 'Encroachment on Forests. Government Versus People,' *Economic and Political Weekly* 27, 3: 55-59.

——(1994) 'Proposed Forest Act: An Assessment,' *Economic and Political Weekly,* 29, 29: 1909-12.

Kumar, K. (1992) *Keoladeo National Park: Fauna with German, French, English, Latin, Hindi Names, Flora with Latin, Common Names, Bharatpur,* Ghana Keoladeo Natural History Society.

Kunhikrishnan, K. V. (1987) 'The British Indian Forestry Experience,' PhD Dissertation, Department of History, University of Calicut.

Kuññan Pilla, S. (ed.) (1956) '*Nāyāṭṭuvidhi*' [Malayalam]. *Bhāṣā traimā-sikam (Malayalam Quarterly).* 6, 3 and 4: 207-14.

Kurup, K. K. N. (1973) *The Cult of Teyyam and Hero Worship in Kerala,* Indian Folklore Series, No. 21, Calcutta: Indian Publications.

——(1977) *Aryan and Dravidian Elements in Malabar Folklore.* Trivandrum: Kerala Historical Society.

——(1984) 'Introduction,' pp. xi-xlvii in K. K. N. Kurup (ed.) *Kavalappara Papers,* Calicut University Historical Series, No. 2. Calicut: Calicut University.

——(1988) 'Peasant Migration and Social Change in the Highlands,' pp. 151-59 in K. K. N. Kurup (ed.) *Modern Kerala (Studies in Social and Agrarian Relations),* Delhi: Mittal Publications.

Linkenbach, A. (1994) 'Ecological movements and the critique of development: agents and interpreters,' *Thesis Eleven* 39 (Special Issue: India and Modernity): 63-85.

——in press, 'Social struggle and conflict of interests in the Garhwal forest,' in I. Stellrecht (ed.), *Perspectives on history and change in the Karakorum, Hindukush, and Himalaya,* Reinbek: I. Wezler.

——unpublished manuscript, 'Forest protection and concepts of development in the Garhwal Himalayas—People's perspectives.'

Logan, William (1887) *Malabar Manual, Volumes I and II* Madras: Government Press.

Low, S. M. (1994) 'Place Attachment in Cultural Anthropology,' *National Geographical Journal of India* 40, 1-4: 47-61.

Maan, Michael (1992) 'Ecological change in north India: Deforestation and agrarian distress in the Doab 1800-1850,' paper presented at the International Seminar on Environmental History of South and South East Asia (18-21 February), NISTADS, PUSA Campus, New Delhi.

Malamoud, C. (1976) 'Village et forêt dans l'idéologie de l'Inde brahmanique,' *Archives Européennes de sociologie* 17: 3-20.

——(1996) *Cooking the World: Ritual and Thought in Ancient India,* Delhi: Oxford University Press.

Mathur, P. R. G. (1977) *Tribal Situation in Kerala,* Trivandrum: Kerala Historical Society.

McCarry, J. (1995) 'Bombay: India's Capital of Hope,' *National Geographic* 187, 3: 42-67.

Mehrotra, S. and C. Kishore (1990) *A Study of Voluntary Forest Protection in Chotanagpur, Bihar,* Unpublished report, Host organisation: ISO/Swedforest, Bhopal: Indian Institute of Forest Management.

Meinig, D.W. (1979) 'Introduction,' pp. 1-7 in D. M. Meinig (ed.) *The Interpretation of Ordinary Landscapes: Geographical Essays,* New York and Oxford: Oxford University Press.

Menon, D. (1994) *Caste, Nationalism and Communism in South India: Malabar, 1900-1948,* Cambridge South Asian Studies, No. 55, Cambridge: Cambridge University Press.

Miller, D. L. (1989) 'The Evolution of Mexico's Caribbean Spiny Lobster Fishery,' pp. 185-98 in F. Berkes (ed.) *Common Property Resources. Ecology and Community-Based Sustainable Development,* London: Belhaven Press.

Misra, R. (1976) *Mullukurumbas of Kappala* Indian Museum Calcutta, Memoir No. 30, Calcutta: Anthropological Survey of India.

Moench, Marcus (1991) 'Politics of Deforestation: Case Study of Cardamom Hills of Kerala,' *Economic and Political Weekly,* 26, 4: PE47-60.

Nambūtirippāṭu, K V (ed.) (1976) *The Malayalam Lexicon,* Vol. 111, Trivandrum: University of Kerala.

Nesmith, C. (1991) 'Women and Trees: Social Forestry in West Bengali India,' PhD Dissertation, University of Cambridge.

Nipunage, D. S. et al., (1988) 'Cultural Heritage of Sacred Groves,' in *Proceedings of the Ninth Annual Conference*; Poona: South Indian History Congress.

Nordin, Torgny (1995) 'Snötranan går en osäker framtid till mötes,'(in Swedish), *Vår Fågelvärld* 4: 18-21.

Noronha, R. (1981) 'Why is it so Difficult to Grow Fuelwood?' *Unasylva* 33: 131.

Noronha, R. and J. S. Spears (1988) 'Sociological Variables in Forest Project Design,' pp. 227-66 in M. Cernea (ed.) *Putting People First*, Oxford: Oxford University Press.

Oriental Bird Club Bulletin (1995) 'Pesticides threaten Corbett's Lesser Fish-Eagles,' *Oriental Bird Club Bulletin* 22: 17.

Padhi, G. S. (1982) *Forestry in India: A Critical Study*, Debra Dun: International Book Distributors.

Palit, S. (1993) *The Future of Indian Forest Management: Into the Twenty First Century*, National Support Group for Joint Forest Management, Society for Promotion of Wastelands Development, New Delhi, and Ford Foundation, Joint Forest Management Working Paper 14.

Pandya, M. (1992) 'Bharatpur Bird Sanctuary: Wheels within Wheels in an Ecosystem,' *Newsletter for Birdwatchers* 32, 1 & 2: 14-17.

Pant, G. B. (no date) (Reprint of 1922 edn.) *Forest problems in Kumaon: Forest Problems and National Uprisings in the Himalayan region* (with a commentary by A. S. Rawat), Nainital: Gyanodaya Prakashsan.

Panur, K. (1963) *Kēraḷattile Āphrikka* [Malayalam] Kottayam: National Book Stall.

Pathak, A. (1994) *Contested Domains: The State, Peasants and Forest in Contemporary India*, New Delhi: Sage.

Poffenberger, M. (1990) *Joint Forest Management for Forest Lands. Experiences from South Asia*, A Ford Foundation Statement, New Delhi: Ford Foundation.

Poffenberger, M. and B. McGean (1996) *Village Voices, Forest Choices*, Delhi: Oxford University Press.

Pottekkatt, S. K. (1980) *Vishakanyaka*, trans. V Abdulla, Trichur: Kerala Sahitya Akademi.

Pouchepadass, Jacques (1990) 'The Ecological History of the Central Western Ghats in the Modern Period: A Preliminary Survey,'

Pondy Papers in Social Sciences, No. 6, Pondicherry: French Institute of Pondicherry.

—— (1994) 'British Attitudes towards Shifting Cultivation in Colonial South India: A Case Study of South Canara District, 1800-1920,' pp. 123-51 in D. Arnold and R. Guha (eds) *Nature, Culture, Imperialism: Essays on the Environmental History of South Asia,* Delhi: Oxford University Press.

Prabhu, P. (1983) 'Social Forestry: an Adivasi Viewpoint,' pp. 134-44 in W. Fernandes and S. Kulkarni (eds) *Towards a New Forest Policy. Peoples' Rights and Environmental Needs,* New Delhi: Indian Social Institute, New Delhi.

Rackham, Oliver (1990) *The History of the Countryside. The full fascinating story of Britain's landscape,* London: J. M. Dent and Sons.

Ramaswamy, S. and G. Prasad (1990) 'An Experiment in Working Together,' Bangalore, FEVORD-K, privately printed.

Rangarajan, M. (1994a) 'Tiger's choice,' *Down to Earth* (September 30): 46.

——(1994b) 'Imperial Agendas and India's Forests,' *Indian Economic and Social History Review* 31.

Rangan, H. (1993) 'Romancing the Environment: Popular Environmental Action in the Garhwal Himalayas,' pp. 155-81 in J. Friedman and H. Rangan (eds), *In Defense of Livelihood: Comparative Studies on Environmental Action,* West Hartford, Connecticut.: Kumarian Press,.

Rawat, A. S. (1989) 'History of Garhwal 1358-1947: An Erstwhile Kingdom in the Himalayas,' New Delhi: Indus Publishing Co.

——(1991) 'History of forest management, conflicts and their impact in the Central Himalaya,' pp. 280-325 in A. S. Rawat (ed.) *History of forestry in India,* New Delhi: Indus Publishing Company,.

Rodman, M. C. (1992) 'Empowering Place: Multilocality and Multivocality,' *American Anthropologist* 94, 3: 640-56.

Roy, S. C. (1970) *The Mundas and Their Country,* London: Asia Publishing House.

——(1984) *The Oraons of Chota Nagpur: their History, Economic Life and Social Organisation,* Ranchi: Man in India Office .

——(1985) *Oraons Religion and Customs,* Delhi: Gian Publishing House.

Ruddle, K. (1989) 'Solving the Common-Property Dilemma: Village Fisheries Rights in Japanese Coastal Waters,' pp. 168-84 in F.

Berkes (ed.) *Common Property Resources, Ecology and Community-Based Sustainable Development,* London: Belhaven Press.

Saberwal, Vasant (1995) 'Conserving Biological Diversity Outside India's Protected Area Network,' Yale School of Forestry and Environmental Studies, unpublished mimeo.

Sachs, W. (ed.) (1992) *The Development Dictionary,* London: Zed Books Ltd.

Sachs, W. S. (1991) 'Ritual and Performance in the *Pandavalila* of Garhwal,' pp. 274-295 in A. Sharma (ed.), *Essays on the Mahabharata,* Leiden: E. J. Brill.

Sankhala, K. (1990) *Gardens of God. The Waterbird Sanctuary of Bharatpur,* New Delhi: Vikas Publishing.

Sanzgiri, M. N. (1993) 'Wildlife and Prey-Predator Relationship in Borivali Forest,' *Tigerpaper* XX, 3: 37-40.

Sarin, M. (1993) *From Conflict to Collaboration: Local Institutions in Joint Forest Management,* National Support Group for Joint Forest Management, Society for Promotion of Wastelands Development, New Delhi, and Ford Foundation, Joint Forest Management Working Paper 14.

——(1992) 'Only males need apply,' *Down to Earth* (November 15).

Sastri, K. Sambasiva (1972-73 [1930-1945]) *Kauṭalīyam: Bhāṣāvyā- khyānasahitam.* Vol. 1-3 [Malayalam and Sanskrit], Trivandrum: University of Kerala.

Savyasaachi (1994). 'The Tiger and The Honey-bee,' *Seminar* 423.

Sen, Manjula (1993) 'A Dream Realised,' *The Times of India* (Review Section), 28 March: 3.

Shepherd, G. (1985) *Social Forestry in 1985: Lessons to be Learned and Topics to be Addressed,* ODI Social Forestry Network, Paper 1 a.

——(1993) 'Managing the Forest Boundary: Policies and their Effects in Two Projects in the Tropical Moist Forests of Cameroon and Madagascar,' ODI Internal Report.

Shiva, V. (1988) *Staying Alive: Women, Ecology and Survival in India,* New Delhi: Kali for Women.

——(1991) *Ecology and the Politics of Survival: Conflicts Over Natural Resources in India.* New Delhi: Sage Publications and the United Nations University Press.

Shiva, V., H. C. Saratchandra and J. Bandyopadhyay (1983) 'The Challenge of Social Forestry,' pp. 48-75 in W. Fernandes and S.

Kulkarni (eds) *Towards a New Forest Policy. Peoples' Rights and Environmental Needs,* New Delhi: Indian Social Institute.

——(1986) 'Social Forestry for Whom?' pp. 238-46 in D. C. Korton (ed.) *Community Management: Asian Experience and Perspectives,* West Hartford, Conn.: Kumarian Press.

Shulman, D. (1980) *Tamil Temple Myths,* Princeton: Princeton University Press.

Singh, K. and Ballabh, V. (1996) *Co-operative Management of Natural Resources,* New Delhi: Sage Publications.

Singh, S. (1966) *The Dust-Storm and the Hanging Mist: A Study of Birsa Munda and his Movement in Chhotanagpur (1874-1901),* Calcutta: Firma K. L. Mukhopadhyay.

Sinha, S. C., Jyoti Sen and Sudhir Panchbhai (1969) 'The Concept of Diku among the Tribes of Chotanagpur,' *Man in India,* 49, 2: 121-38.

Sinha, S. and R. Herring (1993) 'Common Property, Collective Action and Ecology,' *Economic and Political Weekly,* 28, 27 and 28: 1425-32.

Sinha, S. P. (1961) *Life and Times of Birsa Bhagwan,* Ranchi: Bihar Tribal Research Institute.

Sivaramakrishnan, K. (1995) 'Colonialism and Forestry in India: Imagining the Past in Present Politics,' *Comparative Studies in Society and History* 37, 1, 3-40.

Sontheimer, G-D. (1987) 'The *vana* and the *ksetra*: The Tribal Background of Some Famous Cults,' pp. 117-164 in G. C. Tripathi and H. Kulke (eds) *Eschmann Memorial Lectures Vol. I, 1978-1986,* Bhubaneshwar: Eschmann Memorial Fund,.

Sprockhoff, J. F. (1981 and 1984), '*Aranyaka* und *vanaprastha* in der vedischen Literatur: neue Erwägungen zu einer alten Legende und ihren Problemen,' *Wiener Zeitschrift für die Kunde Südasiens und Archiv für indische Philosophie* 25: 19-90 and 28: 5-43.

SPS (Samaj Parivartana Samudaya) et al. (1991) *Janaaraya; People's Participation in the Management of Natural Resources,* SPS et al. (printed in Belgaum).

SPWD (Society for Promotion of Wastelands Development) (1993) *Joint Forest Management Update, 1993,* New Delhi: SPWD.

Sreedhara Menon, A. (ed.) (1972) *Kerala District Gazetteers: Cannanore,* Trivandrum: Government Press.

Statesman, The (1991) 'Return buffaloes to Bharatpur: BNHS,' (August 28).

Stebbing, E. P. (1926) *The Forests of India*, London: John Lane the Bodley Head Ltd.

Stevenson, G. G. (1991) *Common Property Economics. A General Theory and Land Use Applications,* Cambridge: Cambridge University Press.

Sturrock, J. (1894) *Madras District Manuals: South Canara*, Madras: Government Press.

Sundar, N., A. Misra and N. Peter (1996) 'Defending the Dalki Forest: "Joint" Forest Management in Lapanga,' *Economic and Political Weekly* 31: 3021-25.

Tandon, R. (1989) *NGO-Government Relations: A Source of Life or a Kiss of Death,* New Delhi: Society for Participatory Research in Asia.

Thapa, V. J. and R. Brijnath (1995) 'The Perils of Protection,' *India Today*, June 15: 96-99.

Tharakan, P. K. Michael (1984) *Intra-Regional Differences in Agrarian Systems and Internal Migration: A Case Study of the Migration of Farmers from Travancore to Malabar, 1930-1950,* Working Paper No. 194, Trivandrum: Centre for Development Studies.

Times of India, The (1993) 'It's time to take stock of Project Tiger,' 31 March.

Tiwari, K. M. (1983) *Social Forestry in India,* Dehra Dun: Natraj Press.

Trivedi, V. R. (1995) *Autonomy of Uttarakhand*, New Delhi: Mohit.

Upadhyay, K. P. (1988) *Forests and Food Security in the Densely Populated Upland Ecosystems of the Himalayas*, Rome: FAO Satellite Paper (draft).

Vartak, V. D. and Madhav Gadgil (1981) 'Studies in Sacred Groves along the Western Ghats form Maharashtra and Goa: Role of Beliefs and Folklores,' pp. 272-78 in S. K. Jain (ed.) *Glimpses of Ethnobotany* New Delhi: Oxford and IBH Publishing Co.

Viṣṇunambūtiri, M. V. (1982) *Nambūtiribhāṣāśabdakōśam* [Malayalam], Kottayam: National Book Stall.

Viṣṇunambūtiri, M. V. (1979) *Māntrikavidyayum Mantravāda-pāṭṭukayum* [Malayalam], Kottayam: National Book Stall.

Vidyarthi, L. P. (1964) *Cultural Contours of Tribal Bihar*, Calcutta: Punthi Pustak.

Wade, R. (1985) 'Common Property Resource Management in South Indian Villages,' pp. 231-53 in *Proceedings of the Conference on*

Common Property Resource Management (Prepared by: Panel on Common Property Resource Management, Board on Science and Technology for International Development, Office of International Affairs and National Research Council), Washington, D. C.: National Academy Press.

Weber, T. (1988) *Hugging the Trees: The Story of the Chipko Movement*, New Delhi: Viking.

Whitney, W. D. (1905) *Atharva-Veda Samhita, translated with a critical and Exegetical Commentary* 1st Half, 2nd Half. Cambridge, Mass.: Harvard Oriental Series, Vol. VII, VIII.

World Bank (1978) *Forestry: Sector Policy Paper*, Washington: World Bank.

——(1981) *Community Forestry: Notes and Questions from a Field Visit in South Bihar* (draft).

Ziddi, Suraj (1984) *Guide Book on Keoladev National Park, Bharatpur*, Agra: Sankalp Prakashan.

Zimmermann, Francis (1987) *The Jungle and the Aroma of Meats: An Ecological Theme in Hindu Medicine*, trans. Janet Lloyd, Berkeley: University of California Press.

Zoller, C-P. (1994) 'Saying good-bye the Himalayan way,' in Dilip Chitre et al. (eds) *Tender Ironies: A Tribute to Lothar Lutze*, New Delhi: Manohar Publishers.

——(1996) unpublished Habilitation thesis, *Die Panduan. Ein mündliches Mahabharata-Epos aus dem Garhwal-Himalaya.*

Notes on Contributors

Roger Jeffery is Professor of the Sociology of South Asia, Department of Sociology, University of Edinburgh, Scotland.

Alexander M. Dubiansky is a Professor at the Institute for Asian and African Studies, Moscow State University, Russia.

France Bhattacharya is Professor at the Institut national des Langues et Civilisations orientales–Centre d'Etudes de l'Inde et de l'Asie du sud, Paris, France.

M A Kalam is Reader in the Department of Anthropology, University of Madras, Chennai, India.

Rich Freeman is Professor in the Department of Anthropology, University of Pennsylvania, Philadelphia, USA.

Antje Linkenbach is at the Ethnology Seminar, South Asia Institute, University of Heidelberg, Germany.

Stig Toft Madsen is at the Department of International Development Studies at the University of Roskilde, Denmark.

David Potter is Professor of Social Sciences, Open University, Milton Keynes, England.

Sarah Jewitt is at the Department of Geography, School of Oriental and African Studies, London, England.